MESSAGES THAT WORK

A GUIDE TO COMMUNICATION DESIGN

MESSAGES THAT WORK

A GUIDE TO COMMUNICATION DESIGN

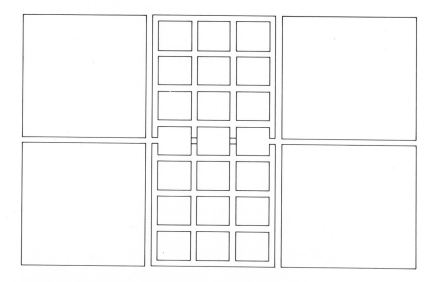

Patrick O. Marsh, Ph.D.

California State University, Sacramento
Department of Communication Studies

EDUCATIONAL TECHNOLOGY PUBLICATIONS
ENGLEWOOD CLIFFS, NEW JERSEY 07632

Library of Congress Cataloging in Publication Data

Marsh, Patrick O.
  Messages that work.

  Bibliography: p.
  Includes index.
  1. Communication. 2. Information theory. I. Title.
P90.M28 1983   001.51   83-1573
ISBN 0-87778-184-2

Printed in the United States of America.

Library of Congress Catalog Card Number:
83-1573.

International Standard Book Number:
0-87778-184-2.

First Printing: April, 1983.

Dedication

In memory of my Major Professor,

Orville Pence

In appreciation for the encouragement
extended by my colleague,

Raymond Koegel

In recognition of the applications of
this process by my former student,

Marco Poncé

v

Table of Contents

APPENDICES

List of Steps in Design Process

Table of Matrices

Introduction and Context

An encyclopedia written in Italian! Innocent as this fourteenth century artifact may appear, it symbolizes for me one of the most formative developments in the course of Western civilization. It placed a compendium of knowledge into the hands of the populus. By translating treasures of knowledge, previously available only to the elite (those who could read Latin), Dante's teacher, Latini, gave impetus to the humanistic movement that ultimately blossomed into the Renaissance. No institution of our times has escaped the impact of that re-birth of civilization.

What will the museum curators of four or five decades hence designate as the most telling symbols of our "information age"? A country in which the creation, production, and distribution of information account for over half of its GNP can surely be identified as being in an information age.

I would like to nominate some symbols for the curators' future consideration:

Perhaps a microfiche card: It symbolizes the corporate memory of civilization made readily accessible to the public. It is technology's answer to Latini's encyclopedia.

Perhaps a parabolic antenna used to up-and-down-link transmissions through satellites: It far surpasses the wildest dreams of Gutenberg, for it has broken the boundaries of print technology and can, at least potentially, deliver a given message to everyone on earth.

Maybe a Susan B. Anthony dollar—shrunken in its purchasing power, yet celebrating the extension of human rights: Both the economic and human rights considerations define significant dimensions of our culture which impact upon our creation and communication of information. As the classic Renaissance expanded human liberation, our neo-Renaissance is cradling an egalitarian movement limited only by economic constraints. Such a fundamental change in our social fabric will inevitably modify our communication practices.

Possibly a bipolar thermostat with only summer (80°) and winter (60°) settings: How does the energy crisis contribute to the shape of the information age? Electronic communication is steadily being regarded as a substitute for energy-consuming transportation. Futurists predict that we will shop, work, and become educated (or re-trained) through home communication centers, thus by-passing with our computers the freeways as airways have leapfrogged railroads.

Perhaps the symbol of the information age will be an employment application blank with pictographic translations for the print-illiterate and multi-lingual translations for our cultural subsets. The massive shift from typeface to icon demands modified means of designing our communication instruments. Given a heterogenous population, any given message will have to be translated into numerous formats to meet the rights and needs of an egalitarian culture.

Several other nominations are equally plausible: Organized-protest banners, a legal dictionary, taxpayer revolts, and numerous others. But one group that ought to be specified includes aspirin, Excedrin, and Valium bottles, a martini glass, and a roach clip. These are reminders of what I call the "information paradox." The prime function of information is to reduce stress-causing uncertainty. Yet, our technology has been so efficient in producing information that our circuits have become information-overloaded. Information overload also causes stress. The pain reliever, in whatever form, is thus as true a symbol of the information age as any.

If we were to create a montage including all of these symbols, its message would be: Our complex social institutions, in an effort to adapt to the advancing technology, require greater efficiency and effectiveness in managing and communicating information than our less confounded social structures have demanded. The emphasis on *egalitarianism* entails adapting our messages so that everyone has access to public information. The *legalism* that accompanies expanded civil and personal rights requires designing messages that insure accuracy as well as easy comprehension. The *stagflationary strain* on the economy precludes the extravagance of simple, intuitive approaches to message designing that are less predictable and more costly. Stagflationary pressures also promote tax revolts which threaten public institutions, thus placing greater demands upon the private sector to provide educational and information services.

This montage would further serve to remind us that exhausting supplies of traditional *energy resources*, changing *social models*, accelerating patterns of *employment mobility*, and the increasing incidence of *print illiteracy* are all forces that are shaping the ways we communicate. We must develop better methods of training and retraining, organizing social action, saving energy, and meeting the unique needs of information consumers. Improved means of communication is at the heart of each of these challenges, and at the heart of every communication is a *message*. The way we design our messages can make the difference.

Messages That Work is an attempt to meet those socially-imposed needs. As such, it has been designed to include a number of unique features:

- It provides a general design model which accounts for a variety of cognitive styles and applies to a wide range of message types.
- It employs several matrices derived from the model that enable the generation of thousands of variations of any given message.
- It is organized into steps which systematically eliminate all but the optimal possible variations.
- It identifies learning objectives and their correlated exercises to enable you to internalize the process and practice it with competence.
- It serves equally well as a textbook for students and a handbook for practicing professionals.
- It operationalizes the general theoretical model so that variables can be quantified.

- It posits a formal theoretical statement which will generate and guide empirical research in message theory.
- It identifies applications in practice, in research, and in the near future.

It should be clear that *Messages That Work* is not this decade's revised version of rhetorics from decades past. It is a fresh, new approach, which while retaining the strengths of previous approaches, goes beyond them to answer the requirements of the message's source, the cognitive needs of the receiver, the demands of contemporary society, and the opportunities provided by our proliferating technology. *Messages That Work* is a systemic and systematic attempt to improve the quality of human life by improving the *sine qua non* of every communicative act—the message.

The Theoretical Model

In order to understand the message-designing process developed in *Messages That Work*, you must understand at least the essentials of the model from which the process was derived. The degree of understanding required will vary with the objectives of different readers. You are, therefore, offered a choice at this point according to your particular needs:

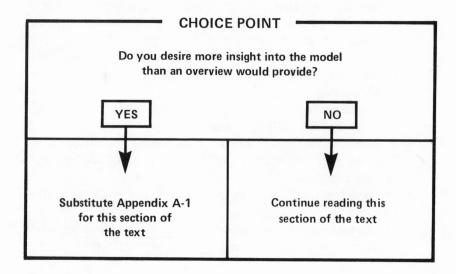

CHOICE POINT

Do you desire more insight into the model than an overview would provide?

YES

NO

Substitute Appendix A-1 for this section of the text

Continue reading this section of the text

This model is a synthesis of several diverse disciplines, theories, and points of view. Chief among these are concepts contributed by McLuhan ("hot" and "cool" media, 1964), Shannon and Weaver (mathematical information theory, 1949), Schroder, Driver, and Streufert ("environmental complexity," 1967), Neisser (cognitive psychology, 1977), Miller ("information chunk," 1967), and the rich tradition of classical rhetoric. Although these contributions will not be identified in this overview, their influence was central to the model's development.

This model can best be described in five stages. It begins by integrating two general models and continues through successive stages, as if we were focusing in on each with a higher-power microscope, until we reach the fifth stage. This last stage will be at the level of specificity required to use the process in its practical application of designing messages.

Stage 1: Integrating Communication and Cognitive Models

The conceptual framework for this model is created by integrating a simple *communication model* with a model of cognition. The communication model consists of a source, a message, and a receiver, which are related to each other through a primary channel and a feedback circuit. The *cognitive model* is characterized by three interactive elements: the stimulus, the organism, and the response. Although in their over-simplified representation, both models appear to be simple process models, they are in reality highly complex, interactive systems.

By creating a matrix, as illustrated in Figure 1, we emphasize that each element of the communication model is influenced by each element of the cognitive model.

That is, not only are the source and receiver (the human elements) governed in their cognition by stimulus, organismic, and response modalities, but the message element (if it is to serve the cognitive needs of the humans) must also reflect these modalities. In other words, this message-design model regards a message as having *s*timulus-dominated elements, *o*rganismic-dominated elements, and *r*esponse-dominated elements (S-O-R), each of which is controlled and designed in different ways.

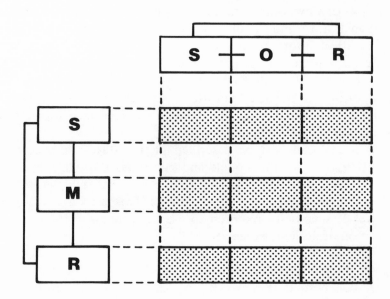

Figure 1. Integrating Communication and Cognitive Models.

Stage 2: Control of Message Elements by Source and Receiver

After the message source interacts with its environment, and through its cognitive processes selects a response pattern (a course of action), it wishes to communicate that decision to the receiver. As a consequence of that communication, the message source wishes to influence the receiver's response. The source's expectations or requirements must dominate the design of the *response* aspects of the message. But the design is not all one-sided. The receiver, through his or her organismic programming and capacity, imposes certain constraints upon the source's freedom to design the message.

Figure 2 illustrates these areas of dominance and suggests that the stimulus aspect of the message is most free from constraint, at least at this point.

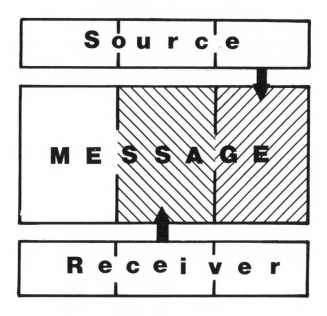

Figure 2. Control of Message Elements by Source and Receiver.

Stage 3: Separation of Information Load and Message Complexity

A fundamental relationship in this model was derived from information theory. It states that TIME (i.e., the duration of a message) is a function of the INFORMATION LOAD of a message divided by the COMPLEXITY of the message. The practical impact of this concept is that we can reduce the duration of a message either by reducing the amount of information or by increasing the message's complexity. That insight offers a message designer much control over the design.

In this stage of the model, we emphasize this relationship by dividing the message component of the model into a numerator and a denominator. This division, on top of the S-O-R division, creates a matrix consisting of six cells. Each of these cells represents a design domain, and this matrix provides the structure for Parts I and II of this book. (See Figure 3.)

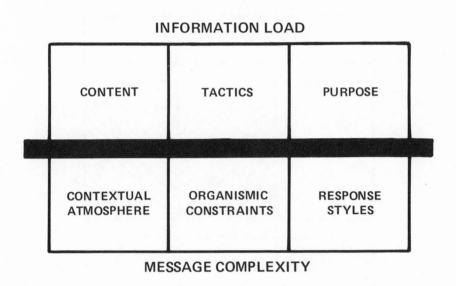

Figure 3. Separation of Information Load and Message Complexity.

Everything above the line (content, tactics, and purpose) relates to *information control* aspects of design and terminates with an estimate of the message's information load. Everything below the line relates to *message complexity*. Message complexity provides the context for the message content. The nature of that context is highly variable, but through careful design of complexity, the optimal context can be created to maximize the impact of the content. This function is at the heart of message design.

Stage 4: Specification of Message Complexity Elements
As we focus more closely upon the denominator of the model, we can specify six elements of message complexity. These six elements provide the basis for controlling message complexity in our designs.

The six elements are grouped in three pairs: two are related to the stimulus (or signal) functions of the model; two are related to the organismic constraints imposed by the receiver; and two are related to the source-controlled response element. More precisely, Diversity (DIV) and Density (DEN), which are signal properties, provide control over the "contextual atmosphere" generated by the message. Sophistication (SOP) and Readiness (REA) are estimates of the receiver-imposed organismic constraints upon the message. Aloofness (ALO) and Tension (TEN) control result in response styles compatible with the source's requirements.

These variables, when quantified and arranged into a bar-graph, comprise a "complexity profile" for the message, which reveals the "message prescription" that guides the design and production of the mediated message. Figure 4 relates the profile to the denominator of the model.

Stage 5: Operationalization of the Model

This theoretical model is easily applied to the practical design of messages by adding two more features: a set of matrices and a set of sequential steps. The matrices enable us to retain the inherent relationships among the model's elements, while avoiding complicated calculations and manipulations of the model's variables. The sequence of steps provides a useful guideline which insures attending to all of the considerations inherent in the design process. The steps are intended as a guide. In places the steps can be taken in a different order, but it is advisable to follow these steps until you are sufficiently familiar with the process to deviate without jeopardizing your successful outcome. Figure 5 suggests the sequence and indicates at which points matrices will be provided.

Figure 5, when its elements are elaborated, leads to the specification of the 21 steps in the design process. The following brief statements about each step will provide an overview of the process, and they will establish initial working definitions of the inherent concepts. Each step will be developed fully in the main text of the book.

Step 1. Select the Strategy. The first element of the all-important purpose statement is the identification of the message

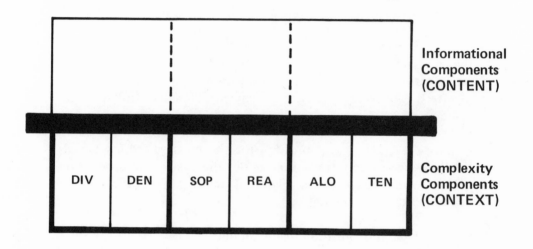

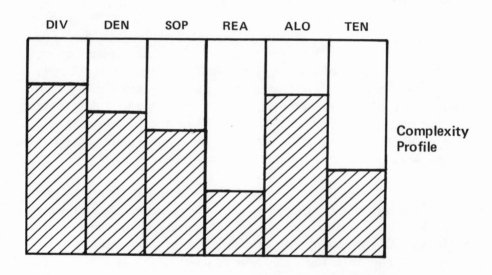

Figure 4. Specification of Message Profile Elements.

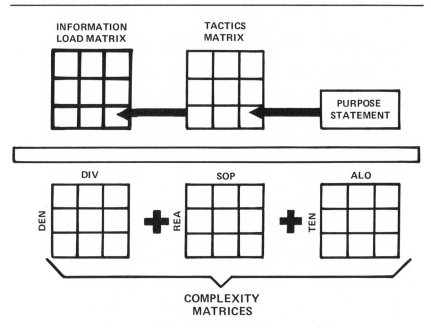

Figure 5. Operationalization of the Model.

strategy. This model offers nine strategic choices: to inform, to stimulate, to interpret, to instruct, to solve, to persuade, to argue, to entertain, and to transform.

Step 2. Profile the Receivers. Receivers are defined, as a part of the purpose statement, both in terms of their relevant knowledge, beliefs, and predispositions related to the topic, and also in terms of their cognitive styles that influence message development.

Step 3. Determine the Central Idea. This third element of the purpose statement defines and delimits the message content in a single, declarative statement.

Step 4. Establish Performance Objectives. Finally, the purpose statement specifies the performance or behaviors the receivers are expected to exhibit as a result of having received the message.

Step 5. Expand the Central Idea into a "Box-Outline." Analysis of the central idea provides an initial working structure of the message content. It is a graphic display of the points and subpoints.

Step 6. Identify the Appropriate Tactics. For each "terminal point" (the last level of division on the "box-outline"), support tactics are identified from a matrix appropriate to the message strategy.

Step 7. Calculate the "Obscurity Index." The obscurity index is an estimate of how much development is required by your receivers for each terminal point on the outline.

Step 8. Estimate the Information Load. Information load is scaled on a matrix which coordinates the amount of information in the message and the obscurity level. If the estimated information is inappropriate, given other design requirements, editing at the purpose statement level is required, and the process is repeated until the information load reaches the desired level.

Step 9. Select the Message-Body Organizational Pattern. A matrix matched to the information load matrix prescribes structural patterns and orders of presentation by which the message body should be organized.

Step 10. Check the Outline for Structural Weaknesses. Typically, the modified and refined "box-outline" of the message body is translated at this point into a full "sentence outline." A checklist is consulted to identify structural weaknesses in the body outline.

Step 11. Identify the Appropriate Diversity/Density Profile. A decision about the desired "contextual atmosphere" of the message is translated via a matrix into a diversity/density profile. This profile facilitates the selection of an appropriate presentational medium, and it suggests means of creating the desired contextual atmosphere.

Step 12. Select the Appropriate Dispositional Patterns. Given a sophistication/readiness profile (from the receiver profile), a number of refinements can be prescribed for the message content. The first consideration is dispositional pattern—the structure within which the message body is contained. A matrix is provided for reaching this decision.

Step 13. Select the Appropriate Graphics. Graphics selection is also a function of the sophistication/readiness profile. Matrices aid in the selection of appropriate graphics.

Step 14. Select the Appropriate Language Style. Again, matrices related to the sophistication and readiness variables provide guidelines for the selection of appropriate language style.

Step 15. Translate Desired Response Styles into an Aloofness/ Tension Profile. The purpose statement suggests the parameters of desired responses in specifying objectives. A matrix helps to refine the desired responses and translates their selection into aloofness and tension levels which, when designed into the message, should elicit the selected responses.

Step 16. Translate the Complexity Profile into a "Message Prescription." The conclusions drawn from the DIV/DEN, the SOP/REA, and the ALO/TEN profiles (combined into a "message complexity profile"), along with the content outline, translate directly into a detailed message prescription. This prescription reflects all of the critical design decisions.

Step 17. Translate the Message Prescription into a "Message Plan." A message plan is a kind of blueprint that visually coordinates time, content, and message complexity. The complexity variables can be identified in their proper balance for any given point in the message.

Step 18. Create a Storyboard. The message plan indicates, moment-by-moment, where verbal and visual material are required and what characteristics they should possess. The storyboard materializes the message from the message plan so that it takes on its first recognizable form.

Step 19. Write the Script. The storyboard translates directly into a script in the format that will be used by the production team.

Step 20. Coordinate the Production. While production specialists may be required to bring the message into its final presentable form, it is important for the designer to work closely with the production team to insure that all subtle design features are manifested.

Step 21. Trouble-Shoot the Message. After the message has been tested on the target or sample audience, any deviation of observed response from the expected response should be evaluated and perhaps corrected by working through the appropriate steps again.

Some Precautions, Exceptions, and Qualifications

Such a cursory presentation of the theoretical model and the process cannot avoid over-simplification (not to mention over-generalization), which leads to misunderstandings. A moment invested in correcting some potentially mistaken impressions seems in order.

You will be better able to use this approach to designing messages if you recognize that not all messages require such meticulous design as the full process prescribes. *Steps may be by-passed or truncated according to your unique needs.* For example, you may wish to employ a complexity profile of a message known to be successful with a similar audience, rather than generating your own profile. Or, you may have graphics from another source which, even though they do not meet the prescription perfectly, will work reasonably well and will save much time and money.

This process is intended to be employed at whatever level of precision is needed to meet your needs. Here is a good rule-of-thumb; *for messages that are costly to produce or for those for which the cost of failure is high, follow the process closely.*

You should also bear in mind that no model is a complete or perfect reflection of reality. We must distort in order to perceive. If you have a tendency to accept the products of this model as final and absolute, or if you believe that is the position I am coming from, you should keep this qualifier in mind: while the theoretical model upon which this process has been derived represents a logically defensible integration of many models, much research, and a lot of experience, the hypotheses derived from it have not been fully tested—although they *are* testable, if given the resources to test them.

A fairly common reaction I receive from those first exposed to this design approach is that it seems too mechanistic, too formulated, and sterile—that it seems to be a threat to personal creativity. Let me say that those who learn and *use* the process seldom make that complaint. I maintain that there is plenty of space for creativity within the process. It is true that the process systematically reduces the number of design possibilities available.

The reduction of "over-choice" is, to my mind, a virtue. But such constraints do not preclude creativity. On the contrary, I suspect they are prerequisite to creativity. One only has to examine the works of civilization's most celebrated creative artists to recognize that their imaginative genius has been expressed within the rigorous constraints of such "constraining" formats as the sonnet and the sonata.

"Message Design" and "Artistic" Approaches Contrasted

Please allow me to indulge in some over-generalization in order to make my point. Consider an artist's approach to creating a message. He or she begins with the decision to "do a film." Having made that decision, he or she may have to wait for the "muse" to visit. Once inspired, a feverish writing spree attempts to "capture the mood"—"just get it down on paper"—"it's only my first draft." This initial effort is followed by multiple rewrites, until "it feels just right." "I know I'm over budget, but you can't put a price tag on a true work of art." "Maybe we can put together a marketable piece from the out-takes to help defray costs."

Now, contrast the designer's approach. "I have a limited budget of both time and money. My job is to communicate this message to this specific audience as effectively as my resources permit. I must work within a fixed time block, and I must select the medium that best serves my specific objectives. I'll plan every minute before I start to write, and I'll make every shot count."

Beneath these brief vignettes are two differing sets of values. The *artistic approach* tends to judge success by:
- —whether it "feels right";
- —whether it has broad popular appeal;
- —how well it is received by the critics;
- —whether it exploits (or employs) the "state-of-the-art" technique; and
- —whether it achieves technical perfection.

On the other hand, the *design approach* judges success by:
- —whether it meets the source's requirements as specified by measurable performance objectives; and

—whether it achieves those objectives within the specified resources and situational constraints.

In general, these two approaches differ in their goals: The artistic approach strives for *perfection*; the design approach strives for *workability*.

These differing methods and criteria are reflected in costs. The artistic approach, with its rewriting and heavy editing in pursuit of perfection, generates very high costs. A network commercial, for instance, will cost several hundred dollars per second of finished product. The design approach, which minimizes the need for rewriting and editing by "up-front" planning, is able to cut costs remarkably on all such projects, without affecting adversely their impact on the audience.

The differing inherent costs result in vastly different final products. The high costs of the artistic approach require messages of such general (perhaps cosmic) content that they will appeal only to a popular or dilettante audience. The content must be general to attract a large enough audience over an extended time to justify the expense. On the other hand, the lower costs of the design approach allow the messages to serve specific audiences on matters of immediacy at whatever level of specificity is required.

The bias of this book is stated explicitly in its title: *Messages That Work: A Guide to Communication Design*.

Some Structural Features of MESSAGES THAT WORK

This book has been designed according to the precepts it advances. Accordingly, while profiling the anticipated readership, I discovered that the readers will probably group into several diverse clusters, with each cluster requiring something different from the book. To accommodate these heterogeneous requirements, I have organized the book so that it can be read at different levels of precision and exhaustiveness. A briefing on its structure will enable you to get from it what you want—and to do it efficiently.

First, take note that the book is divided into four main parts. Your special interests may cause you to disregard either Part III or Part IV. Parts I and II, however, are critical to the understanding of this model.

- PART I. Controlling the Informational Content.
- PART II. Controlling Message Complexity.
- PART III. Manifesting the Message.
- PART IV. Applications of the Design Process.

Subsumed under these main parts are the chapters relevant to them. You may wish to invest your time on the basis of chapter topics, rather than by major parts. The chapter organization should be most useful if you plan to use this as a handbook rather than as a textbook.

If you are process-oriented, perhaps you should read from step-to-step, disregarding the theoretical considerations. The step subtitles are superimposed upon the chapters and contrasted from chapter subtitles for easy recognition. The table of contents provides a quick reference to the steps treated in the various chapters.

Some will read this book for mastery learning. If this is your aim, you will find the learning objectives at the beginning of each chapter useful. I recommend reading the objectives before reading the chapter to provide a learning "set." Then after reading the chapter, return to the objectives to check your accomplishment. Chapter 9 will be of special interest to you because it provides objective-correlated exercises that have been classroom tested.

Throughout the book, I have employed stylized "choice points" to allow you to determine more readily what you should read for your special purposes. You have encountered a "choice point" already in this Introduction. Typically, they will direct you to one of the Appendices for greater elaboration than the general reader will find useful. The Appendices are organized in this manner:

Appendix A. *Theoretical Refinement.* Notes and elaborative material of a technical, theoretical nature are included here.

Appendix B. *Less Common Usages.* In order to retain exhaustive coverage of relevant topics, without exhausting the general reader, items that are less commonly used are assigned to this section.

Appendix C. *Extended Examples.* Enough examples are supplied in the main text to provide general comprehension, but some readers appreciate examples of larger scale so that they may see subtitles and interactions of features that are suppressed in brief examples.

My general strategic-reading recommendation for the serious reader is to read the book first at the general readership level. Then re-read it at the more specialized level that suits your needs. Finally, keep the book handy as a reference handbook to both theory and practice.

P.O.M.
October, 1982

PART I

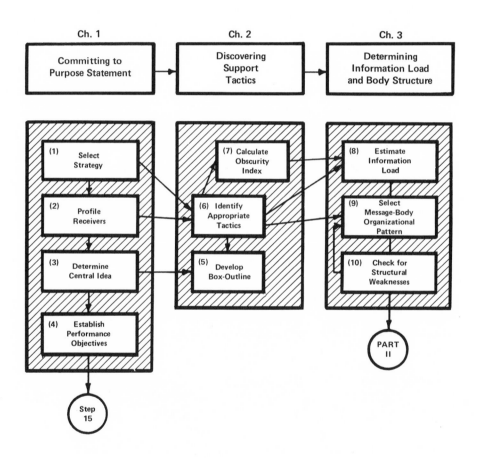

Ch. 1

| Committing to Purpose Statement |

Ch. 2

| Discovering Support Tactics |

Ch. 3

| Determining Information Load and Body Structure |

(1) Select Strategy

(2) Profile Receivers

(3) Determine Central Idea

(4) Establish Performance Objectives

(7) Calculate Obscurity Index

(6) Identify Appropriate Tactics

(5) Develop Box-Outline

(8) Estimate Information Load

(9) Select Message-Body Organizational Pattern

(10) Check for Structural Weaknesses

Step 15

PART II

1

Part I

Controlling the Informational Content

Part I is concerned with everything in the numerator of the basic model. Specifically, it includes Chapters 1, 2, and 3: Committing to the Purpose Statement, Discovering Support Tactics, and Determining Information Load and Body Structure, respectively. The first ten steps of the design process are directly related to controlling *what* is to be communicated in the message.

The management and control of message content is essentially a rhetorical consideration evolving from the classical rhetorical canons of "invention" and "disposition." Integrated into these rhetorical precepts are some precepts from the field of instructional development and some findings from the behavioral sciences. To this fundamental synthesis and interpretation, this model has contributed the concept of the "obscurity index" and a means of quantifying "information load."

Information control lends itself more readily to linear processing than does the message complexity portion of this model. One step tends to lead directly to the next in an orderly sequence. An overview of this process will provide a needed perspective to unite the separate steps into their appropriate *gestalt*.

The first major task of message designing is the specification of a purpose statement. That statement includes a strategy, a receiver profile, a statement of the central idea, and a list of performance objectives. By analyzing the central idea, the designer can construct a "box-outline," which must be consistent with, and exhaustive of, the central idea. The strategic choice isolates an array of support tactics which, when narrowed down through specific requirements of the receiver, will support the points of the box-outline. At the same time, selection of the tactics reveals the "obscurity index." The obscurity index and the supported outline provide the data necessary to calculate the information load. Given the information load and the supported box-outline, options can be considered for organizing the body of the message. After checking the refined body structure for weaknesses and making corrections where necessary, the information control phase is complete and we move to Part II. The performance objectives listed in the purpose statement will emerge again at Step 15.

"At a key point in the flight, a glider pilot must make a decision either to search for another updraft of air . . . or make a commitment to land. . . .

"Similarly, a message designer, at some point early in the planning, must make a commitment to a purpose statement. . . .

"This message-design process begins with making a commitment to a purpose statement."

Chapter 1

INFORMATION LOAD AND BODY STRUCTURE	SUPPORT TACTICS AND OBSCURITY INDEX	PURPOSE STATEMENT

CONTEXTUAL ATMOSPHERE	ORGANISMIC CONSTRAINTS	RESPONSE STYLES

Central Idea

By committing yourself to a purpose statement, you eliminate thousands of ways you could develop your message, thus providing direction and focus in your design; failure to make this commitment almost guarantees reduced message effectiveness.

Steps

1. Select the strategy.
2. Profile the receivers.
3. Determine the central idea.
4. Establish performance objectives.

Objectives

1. To recall the unique characteristics of each strategy defined in this chapter.
2. To interpret the results of an audience profile questionnaire in terms of its constraints on a message.
3. To scale an audience reliably on an audience profile scale.
4. To write a complete and appropriate central idea.
5. To detect improperly stated central ideas.
6. To write and evaluate performance objectives according to two models presented here.
7. To write and evaluate complete purpose statements.

Chapter 1

Committing to the Purpose Statement

At a key point in the flight, a glider pilot must make a decision either to search for another updraft of air (and prolong the flight), or make a commitment to land. The commitment to land is total. Once that commitment is made, the sailplane can only remain in the air a given number of seconds. The pilot has no option to "hit the throttle" and "go around." That commitment narrows the options dramatically and points clearly to the operations required to complete the task.

Similarly, a message designer, at some point early in the planning, must make a commitment to a statement of purpose. Once made, that commitment not only reduces the number of available options, but also it prescribes certain operations required to complete the task. Unless he or she is to abandon invested time and energy, the commitment is irreversible and ought, therefore, to be made with full deliberation. At the outset, there are literally thousands of options available for developing any given message. The problem is one of "over-choice." Yet, by the time the purpose statement is completed, the number of available options is only a small fraction of the original set. The purpose statement, like information, serves to reduce the uncertainty that prevails before a commitment is made.

This message-design process begins with making a commitment to a purpose statement. Then, one uses those basic choices to prescribe the operations that best serve that purpose at each of several subsequent choice points. Essentially, a purpose statement must accomplish four tasks. Foremost, it must insure that the requirements of the message's source (the sender) will be served;

this is achieved by the appropriate selection of a *strategy*. Then it must identify precisely the *intended receivers* so that receiver-imposed limitations can be accommodated within the design. Next, the message content must be defined and delimited according to the source's requirements, the receiver-imposed constraints, and the limitation of time and other resources. This condensation of content is manifested in a single, complete, concise statement called the *central idea*. And, finally, the purpose statement must specify the *performance objectives* the source establishes for the receivers, not only so that the message's effectiveness may be estimated, but also that they may contribute directly to appropriate design decisions.

A critic or a message analyst might well claim that any message has a purpose; it can be revealed or inferred through selected analytic processes. Indeed, a very useful critical tool is to compare and contrast the actual purpose with the ostensible purpose. Countless messages fail because the purpose and the attempt to achieve the purpose are incompatible. The best insurance against this common failure is to state the purpose explicitly and, once committed to it, to work within its constraints. Probably the most difficult aspect of message design is making a commitment to the purpose statement. Once done, the process guides your efforts to completion. But misjudgments at this crucial point have far-reaching impact.

Step 1. Select the Strategy

A strategy, stated with an infinitive, identifies the method the source employs to elicit the desired performance specified in the objectives. The strategy defines the task of the source, whereas the objectives define the behaviors of the receiver. Any of numerous infinitives might serve as a strategy descriptor, but nine standardized ones serve this process well; they are: to inform, to stimulate, to interpret, to instruct, to solve, to persuade, to argue, to entertain, and to transform. Each strategy requires different means of development and therefore must be defined rather precisely and perhaps arbitrarily.

To inform. In the strategy "to inform," the source explicitly provides the receiver with new information in an effort to enable the receiver *to recognize* it. Recognition implies the ability to discriminate an item from other items in a set. Given several instances or items, an informed person would recognize or identify the appropriate one.

To stimulate. In the strategy "to stimulate," the source attempts to elicit or prompt the receiver to recognize intuitive knowledge which may be fanciful or even false; the effort is *to elevate* implicit thoughts from the experience level to the explicit level.

To interpret. In the strategy "to interpret" (educe), the source attempts to create a context which enables the receiver *to retrieve* tacit knowledge. Michael Polanyi (1966) has defined tacit knowledge precisely, but in essence, it means that we know more than we are able to tell. Interpretation enables the receiver to retrieve and then to communicate what was originally unaccessible and uncommunicable knowledge.

To instruct. In general, in the strategy "to instruct," the source guides the receiver in the acquisition of knowledge, attitudes, or skills which may be performed by recall or demonstrated at will. Since the tactics of such guidance are differentiated, three subtypes of instruction are defined: To instruct (*details*) involves forming associations; to instruct (*concepts*) involves forming classifications; to instruct (*relationships*) involves forming relationships.

To solve. In the strategy "to solve," the source guides the receiver through a selected process in an effort to identify a solution which reduces the gap between the desired state and the actual state of affairs. This strategy seeks to prevent further complaint or search after the "solution" is identified.

To persuade (to promote). The strategies "to persuade" and "to promote" are similar with only one essential difference. In the strategy "to persuade," the source makes plausible intellectual and/or emotional appeals in an effort *to change* selected attitudes, beliefs, or values already held by the receiver. The change can be in either strength, direction, or both. The best evidence of change is the unsolicited change in behaviors related to the changed beliefs, attitudes, or values. The strategy "to promote" differs only in that it seeks *to mobilize* the changed attitudes, beliefs, or values to achieve a specific, desired action. Evidence of the desired action's performance is the criterion.

To argue. In the strategy "to argue," which is defined here more narrowly than in popular usage, the source submits a reasoned case in support or in refutation of a particular proposition in an effort *to test* the case's adequacy against the receiver's most critical response. Successful argument means that the receiver has been unable to debilitate the source's case. The crucial differences between the strategies "to argue" and "to persuade" lie in their differing goals and methods. Persuasion attempts *to change* the receiver; argument attempts *to test* the case. Persuasion uses all available appeals; argument employs only reasoned discourse.

To entertain. In the strategy "to entertain," the source attempts *to hold* the attention or interest of the receiver in an effort *to divert or amuse.* Literally, to entertain means "to hold between," which connotes tension and suspense. The most general categories of amusement are probably inspiration, portrayal, and down-play. Evidence of having entertained takes various forms depending upon the category involved.

To transform. In the strategy "to transform," the source guides the receiver through processes intended to cause the receiver *to reframe* his or her perceptions of the self and the situation or context so that his or her everyday activities in life reflect the reframed perceptions. This strategy is sometimes therapeutic and may lead to what Castaneda (1974) calls "enlightenment." Its accomplishment is typically characterized by behavior changes on several dimensions.

Your ability to classify strategies accurately is essential to your ability to use this message-design process effectively. You may wish to study the identification drill provided in Chapter 9.

Step 2. Profile the Receivers

Two errors are common in efforts to profile audiences. Probably most common is the tendency to want to reach too broad an audience. After all, our most prevalent models are presented on the mass media. Yet, in order to reach the mass audiences, all of the receivers' uniquenesses must be peeled away so that only blank stereotypes remain. Messages designed from stereotypes are of necessity more mundane and superficial than those that incorporate the individuals' experiences and cognitive styles into the message design. The other common error is to collect so much information on the audience, usually at an inappropriate level of abstraction, that it confuses rather than clarifies the design efforts. Incidentally, I believe it is better to create an image of oneself *designing* a message for an audience, rather than *adapting* a message for an audience. The difference is subtle, but the different images will probably be reflected in the end-products.

The receiver profile is an inherent part of the design process; it is not merely a step taken to adapt an established message to an audience. Many design decisions will be made on the basis of your profile. It is important to define your audience as narrowly as will serve your needs and to select only the information about your receivers that contributes directly to your design. The receiver profile focuses on the essentials of: general demographics, strategy-related variables, and cognitive style.

General Demographics

One basic approach to defining an audience is to specify the demographics arbitrarily and then let the message find its way to the predetermined audience. Another basic approach is to take a given audience and identify its demographics. Both approaches are appropriate, depending upon the source's purpose.

The demographic information provides a basis for creating a mental image of the audience. Like any composite construct, it is subject to error, yet if inferences are carefully drawn from the data, the mental image, especially if personified, provides the designer someone on whom to test supports and stylistic treatment. One magazine, for example, conducted a survey of its readers to discover that: 70% were between the ages of 18 and 44; 87% had attended college, 73% had graduated, and 46% held advanced degrees; 46% of household incomes were $15,000 or over; 78% had bought a hard-cover book within the last three months, 31% had bought five or more; 72% held credit cards; 90% owned life insurance, 28% owned mutual funds, and 45% owned corporate stock.

From these data (and more), the publisher concluded that the readers are generally younger, brighter, more prosperous, responsible, and classier than the readers of any magazine of its type. Authors, keeping this profile in mind, make subtle and perhaps subconscious choices to fit the image.

One more example should suffice to illustrate the utility of demographic data. This profile defines the audience for whom a series of instructional radio programs was designed (Koegel and Marsh, 1979).

> The typical student enrolled in the ON/AIR Project classes was between 18 and 30 years of age, an upper-division student, Caucasian, female, and single. This student maintained a reported GPA of 310 or higher, worked ten or more hours per week, and took the course to fulfill a requirement.

It should be apparent that even such a brief sketch as this produces a much clearer image than merely identifying the receivers as "typical college students."

The specific demographic categories are variable according to the nature of the message, but age, sex, occupation, education level, socioeconomic status, cultural heritage, and social affiliations are standard, almost universal, categories. Some books are useful for translating demographic information into inferences and composites. For example, Gail Sheehy's *Passages* (1974) profiles common patterns in adult life according to age and sex. Also, Milton Rokeach's *The Nature of Human Values* (1973) profiles various patterns of values according to several demographic variables.

Strategy-Related Variables

For each strategy that we discussed earlier, there is a matrix we will use later for determining appropriate tactics to employ in the design. Each matrix is defined by two variables, so it is essential to determine where the receivers are identified on appropriate continua in order to use each matrix. Table 1.1 identifies the variables associated with each strategy.

The strategies *to inform, to stimulate, to interpret*, and *to instruct* share the variables of "receivers' knowledge level" and "receivers' awareness of knowledge level." Obviously, these two variables differ: the "knowledge level" is an estimate of what the receivers know about the message topic. This might be measured directly by an achievement test, or perhaps it could be estimated by someone acquainted with the receivers. It is not appropriate to ask the receivers directly for an estimate of their knowledge level, however, because of the subjectivity involved. It is appropriate to ask how *confident* the receivers are in their knowledge level, but even that is not the same as *awareness* of knowledge level. To determine that, we must look at the "receivers' confidence/receivers' knowledge" ratio. In other words:

$$\text{Receivers' awareness of knowledge} = \frac{\text{Receivers' confidence in knowledge}}{\text{Receivers' actual knowledge}}$$

Table 1.1

Strategy-Related Variables

Strategy	Variables
To inform	a. Receivers' knowledge level
To stimulate	b. Receivers' awareness of knowledge level
To interpret	
To instruct	
To solve	a. Desired state: level of goal definition
	b. Actual state: level of goal attainment
To persuade	a. Receivers' acceptance level
(To promote)	b. Sources' acceptance level
To argue	a. Receivers' willingness to grant
	b. Sources' argument
To entertain	a. Receivers' seriousness level
	b. Sources' seriousness level
To transform	a. Receivers' left-brain strength
	b. Receivers' right-brain strength

The strategy *to solve* is concerned with the relationship of the desired state of affairs to the actual state of affairs. Estimates of these values may be made either by the source or by qualified observers. Specifically, we seek estimates of "level of goal definition" (how precisely a goal is defined) and "level of goal attainment" (how effective efforts have been to reach the goal).

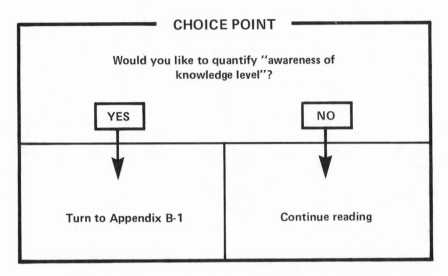

The strategy *to persuade* (to promote) focuses upon the "stasis" or pivotal point in a controversy. Stasis is determined by comparing "receivers' acceptance level" with "sources' acceptance level." Only the person who accepts or rejects is in a position to reveal those positions, so we must get the estimates directly from those involved. Carefully constructed attitude scales provide the best means of attaining these estimates, but simpler means are available at the expense of precision.

The strategy *to argue* also seeks the stasis; but since it is not concerned with gaining acceptance, its relevant focus is upon the receivers' willingness to grant the adequacy of the source's argument. The stasis is discovered by: (1) analyzing the source's argument, and (2) estimating the receiver's willingness to grant the various elements. The "willingness" estimates might be made by a critic or a "devil's advocate."

The strategy *to entertain* derives its tactics from the relative levels of seriousness shared by receivers and source. Estimates of both are required to use the matrix. These estimates may come from any reliable source.

Finally, the strategy *to transform*, one of the more difficult to understand and employ, requires estimates of what Castaneda

(1974) calls the "tonal" and the "nagual." The closest translation I can provide is "left-brain strength" and "right-brain strength." Ornstein (1972) elaborates and offers support for the theory that the left and right hemispheres of the brain serve fundamentally different functions. By estimating the degree of balance resulting from receivers' dominant tendencies in brain usage, we can determine appropriate tactics to facilitate transformation experiences. Estimates of brain-sidedness strength are best made by directly observing an audience sample and then scaling your impressions on a scale discussed below, under "Left-Brain/Right-Brain Scale."

Cognitive Style

Ausburn and Ausburn (1978) have defined cognitive style thus:

> In general, the concept of cognitive style refers to psychological dimensions that represent consistencies in an individual's manner of acquiring and processing information. In other words, it concerns individual differences in the processes of *cognition*, which generally include all processes by which knowledge is acquired: perception, thought, memory, imagery in the "picture-in-the-mind" sense defined by Fleming (1977), and problem solving. The motion of variation in *style* of cognition implies more than degrees of skill or ability in these cognitive processes; it implies the existence of individual differences and preferences in actual *modes* or *manners* of gaining, storing, processing, and using information as well. There is thus a qualitative, as well as a quantitative, variation in mental functioning that underlies the concept of cognitive style.

Since several critical design decisions will be made on estimates of cognitive style when we consider the influence of organismic constraints imposed on message complexity and subsequently upon the stylistic refinement of the content, it is essential to identify selected aspects of the receiver's cognitive style in the purpose statement. This design process requires two aspects of cognitive style to be isolated: level of *sophistication* (SOP) and level of *readiness* (REA).

Sophistication is the more constitutional part of cognitive style; it is the more stable, habitual part that suggests the degree of cognitive maturity. We can estimate sophistication level from estimates of the receiver's preferred level of *abstraction*, the degree of *implicitness* at which the receiver can function, and the degree of *precision* the receiver habitually employs.

Readiness, by contrast, is the more temporal or situational aspect of cognitive style. Even if a person were highly sophisticated, the situational conditions might cause him or her not to be receptive to a message. An effort to modify the message by reducing its sophistication level in this case would be misdirected. The receiver's readiness level would be the more appropriate target. The readiness level is estimated by determining: how much *framing* of the message is required by the receiver; how much the *relevance* of the message should be emphasized; and how much *mnemonic* (memory) assistance is needed.

Gathering Information About Receivers

You should use any source of information that provides the information you need to profile your receivers, but preference should be given to the most efficient sources. Three commonly used methods are: the questionnaire, an informant, and direct observation.

The Questionnaire. The questionnaire given to a representative sample of your receivers, or to all of them if the number is small and well-defined, can provide most of the information required for an effective design. This is perhaps the best way of profiling an audience. The questionnaire should be carefully constructed so that: it can be completed in a short time; it covers the essential items; it avoids ambiguity and confusion for both the person taking it and for the interpreter. Sometimes it is important to determine the reliability of the questionnaire (that is, the degree to which it elicits consistency of response), and that can be determined with standard statistical reliability techniques.

An Informant. When an audience cannot be sampled and questioned directly, you may need to rely upon the estimates of a secondary source—an informant. An informant may be a member of the audience or a person who has had ample opportunity to observe the receiver's behavior. Based upon synthesized impressions, the informant can answer items that would normally be included on a questionnaire. Sometimes an informant is able to detect patterned perspectives that may not be directly apparent from questionnaire responses. To the extent that this is so, this method compensates for the loss of precision provided by the questionnaire.

Direct Observation. Especially if the designer has a specific list of items in mind (a prepared schedule is advisable), direct observation of the receivers is informative. This is especially so when the receivers are collected into an audience in their usual environment. Granted, the single visit represents only a limited sample, yet the first-hand observation provides a store of tacit knowledge that can unconsciously augment the answers to more explicit inquiries.

Several other approaches to gathering profile information are available, especially if the value of achieving the purpose justifies the additional costs. As an economic consideration, we should recognize that the cost of additional information accelerates the closer we get to complete information. Typically, such costs are unjustified if we can get most of the needed information at a fraction of the cost. Some of these techniques include: public opinion polling, psychoanalytic interviewing, pupilometric studies (observing the dilation of eye pupils), skin conductivity tests, and many more. Typically, the more general methods discussed above are adequate and economical.

Useful Instruments for Profiling

The characteristics from selected techniques can be combined into instruments that serve your particular needs. Several are briefly illustrated and should be modified according to the dictates of your purpose.

SOP/REA Rating Scale. This scale covers the essential dimensions of sophistication and readiness. More items could be included if checking reliability or indirect query were important.

(Low) 1 2 3 4 5 6 7 (High) 1. Indicate the level of *abstraction* at which you function best.

(Low) 1 2 3 4 5 6 7 (High) 2. What level of *implicitness* serves your purposes best?

(Low) 1 2 3 4 5 6 7 (High) 3. Indicate the level of *precision* you normally employ.

(High) 1 2 3 4 5 6 7 (Low) 4. At what level do you find it most useful
to have subject content *framed* in con-
text?
(High) 1 2 3 4 5 6 7 (Low) 5. How *relevant* do you perceive this topic
to be to you?
(High) 1 2 3 4 5 6 7 (Low) 6. To what extent do you need assistance in
remembering new subject matter?

An average of items one to three yields a sophistication
estimate; an average of items four to six yields a readiness
estimate.

Attitude/Knowledge Profile Scale. A convenient device for
visualizing the distribution of scaled information is illustrated
below. Either an attitude statement or a question about the
content can be used, and when the seven-point scale is printed on
the edge of the paper, the stack of responses can be fanned out to
reveal the distribution profile. Figure 1.1 illustrates the profile
derived from such questions as this:

Answer each question by circling the correct answer, *and* then indicate your
level of confidence in your answer by blacking in the appropriate scale value
at the right.

1. The three basic elements of the Toulmin model are:

	Confidence
a. Stimulus—organism—response	(Low)
	1
b. Data—warrant—claim	2
	3
c. Major premise—minor premise—conclusion	4
d. Symptom—cause—solution	5
	6
	7
	(High)

Token/Field Profile. Figure 1.2 displays a profile of a governor

ITEM   PROFILE

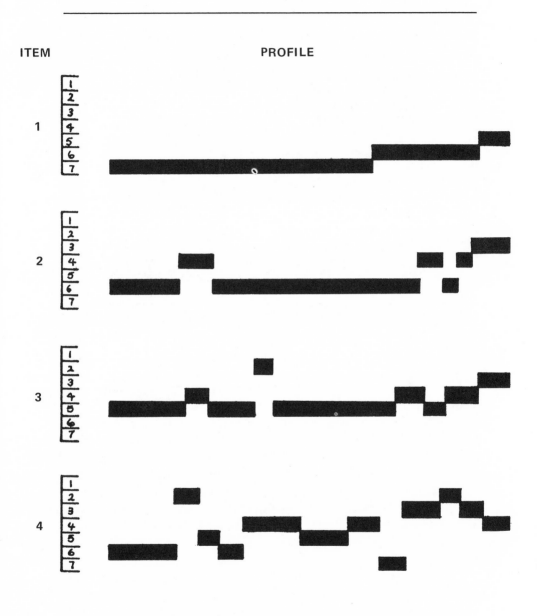

Figure 1.1. Attitude/Knowledge Profile Scale.

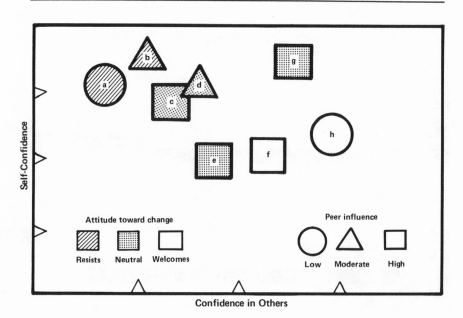

Figure 1.2. Token/Field Profile.

and his cabinet which was created for me by an informant. The informant arranged tokens on the field (defined by levels of confidence in self and in others) to represent the audience members. The tokens were selected by shape and color to represent individuals according to their attitudes toward change on their influence upon the other members of the cabinet. By interpreting the tokens' placement on the field by such theories as Harris' (1967), I was able to infer certain character traits. And, with the added information provided by the tokens themselves, it was an easy task to determine where various persuasive thrusts should be aimed.

Left-Brain/Right-Brain Scale. This scale is useful in conjunction with the strategy "to transform." The higher the score, the greater the right-brain influence. A score of four represents a balance. The ratio between the sum of scores above zero and the sum of scores below zero when the scale is transformed indicates both the direction and degree of dominance. Positive scores indicate right-brain dominance. Scale transformation is made by:

1	2	3	4	5	6	7	original score
-3	-2	-1	0	+1	+2	+3	transformed score

Directions

Indicate the place on each scale that best describes your habitual or dominant orientation.

1 2 3 4 5 6 7

Sequential	_ _ _ _ _ _ _	Simultaneous
Linear	_ _ _ _ _ _ _	Relational
Mathematical	_ _ _ _ _ _ _	Artistic
Verbal	_ _ _ _ _ _ _	Spatial
Analytic	_ _ _ _ _ _ _	Holistic
Logical thought	_ _ _ _ _ _ _	Ready integration
Vague body image	_ _ _ _ _ _ _	Clear body image
Poor face recognition	_ _ _ _ _ _ _	Good face recognition
Good name recognition	_ _ _ _ _ _ _	Poor name recognition

Reinforcement Preference Scale. Ask your sample audience to indicate its preference for various reinforcements (rewards) for a job well done. Have them circle one number for each reinforcement type. The higher numbers represent higher preference.

1 2 3 4 5 6 7   *Recognition* (Someone acknowledges your success either to you or to others.)

1 2 3 4 5 6 7   *Payment* (You receive a tangible reward for your successful efforts.)

1 2 3 4 5 6 7   *Tension Reduction* (You experience a reduction of
                           pressure or tension following a successful effort.)

1 2 3 4 5 6 7   *Participation* (You are allowed access to greater
                           challenges or adventures following a successful re-
                           sponse.)

The more vividly you can "image up" your audience from the
profiled information gained by these various methods and instruments, the better you will be able to design your message to meet
their uniqueness. An imaging exercise is provided in Chapter 9.
After working through that exercise, you will be able to create
your own drills, which when practiced a few times, should enable
you to "try out" your ideas on that surrogate audience.

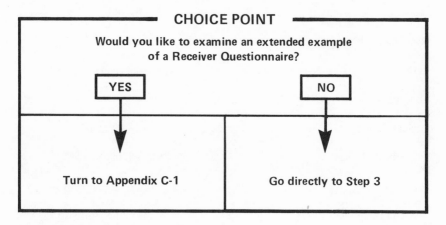

CHOICE POINT

Would you like to examine an extended example
of a Receiver Questionnaire?

YES

NO

Turn to Appendix C-1   Go directly to Step 3

Step 3. Determine the Central Idea

A *central idea* is a single, complete, declarative sentence which
summarizes the essence of the message. It is the whole message
abstracted to one sentence. The central idea once established
serves as a regulator or "gate-keeper" by determining the relevance
or irrelevance of anything included in the message body. It may be
thought of as a seed, or an egg, or a DNA molecule which contains
all and only the elements required for the message's full
development.

A central idea is stated in a *single* sentence so that the scope and essence of the message can be perceived at once—as a whole. Within that single sentence, you may emphasize and subordinate in order to establish the desired balance of meaning. You may be tempted to believe that some topics are too complex to be reduced to a single sentence. This example may refute that notion:

After reading *Zen and the Art of Motorcycle Maintenance* (Pirsig, 1974), I wished to define the term "Quality" as Pirsig had used it throughout the book. First, I listed all of the sentences where the term was used significantly. Then, I highlighted all of the significant words that formed the context for its usage. The next step was to list and categorize these highlighted words. Four categories emerged, and I wrote a paragraph using as many of the words as I could from each category. Then, with much painful editing, I reduced each paragraph to a single sentence. I now had a four-sentence paragraph defining "Quality," but I wanted a one-sentence definition, so with even more painful editing, I reduced the four sentences to one. Granted, it is one of the most dense sentences I have ever read, but it is proof that even very obscure and complex ideas can be abstracted to a single sentence. This is the result of that exercise:

> Quality is a perception-preceding event which provides direction for caring, tranquil, and confident persons in order to facilitate their ability to distinguish and integrate entities, to select and rearrange information, to identify goals and purposes, and to judge importance and excellence to the end of taming the system (Marsh, 1975).

A central idea is a *complete* sentence. A complete sentence represents a complete thought, whereas a sentence fragment or phrase only indicates a target for thought. Before you can present your message, your thought must be complete—predicated; your "homework" must have been done. The real work of designing a message (possibly the hardest aspect of the process) resides in cleaning up and structuring the thought behind the message. Committing yourself to the central idea becomes your "moment of truth."

A central idea is a *declarative sentence*. Asking a question does not require a commitment, and a central idea requires a commitment to your message content. There can be no hedging at this step. The declarative mode serves to emphasize that commitment.

The central idea determines what is *relevant* and what is irrelevant to the message. Anything developed in the message, except for a deliberate digression, is irrelevant if it is not rooted in the central idea. The central idea must be broad enough to cover everything that needs to be in the message, but narrow enough to exclude related, but non-essential, items.

The central idea's primary function is to guide your design of content. If you present the central idea to your receivers, it is likely you would want to paraphrase it into the appropriate style. In that case, you could develop it as a single sentence or in several; it could be declarative, interrogatory, or exclamatory. The point to remember is that even though your receivers may never be exposed to your working central idea, you can hardly design an effective, efficient message if you do not write it out and keep it before you.

Examples and Non-Examples of Central Ideas

Examples. The central idea at the beginning of this chapter meets all of these criteria. Here it is for your closer examination: By committing yourself to a purpose statement, you eliminate thousands of ways you could develop your message, thus providing direction and focus in your design; failure to make this commitment almost guarantees reduced message effectiveness.

The frontispiece for each chapter in this book displays its central idea. They are collected to facilitate synthesis and review in Chapter 9. These should provide ample examples.

Non-examples. A "non-example" is an instance which does *not* exemplify the concept. Some non-examples will help you refine the limits of the "central idea" concept. These non-examples are typical of those submitted by students upon their first attempt to write central ideas:

1. Sole proprietorship, the most common type of ownership in America, and its advantages and disadvantages. (This is not a central idea because it is not a complete sentence.)
2. Is it not better to have loved and lost than never to have

loved at all? (This is not a central idea because it is not a declarative sentence.)

3. Except in the case of cost-push inflation, inflation is caused by an overabundance of aggregate demand for goods and services. It can be controlled by the appropriate fiscal or monetary policy, or by some combination of both. (This is not a central idea because it is not a single sentence.)

4. To inform a model student audience how to recognize an abstract, philosophical idea concerning the "radiance of reality." (This is not a central idea, not only because it is an incomplete sentence, but also because it confuses the functions of a central idea and a statement of strategy. A good "rule-of-thumb" is that if an alleged central idea begins with an infinitive, it is probably a strategy statement. A safeguard against this type of error is to be sure that your message topic is the sentence subject of your central idea.)

Approaches to Discovering Central Ideas

Analytic Approach. Often a formal definition, process, or principle serves as a central idea. For example: (*Definition*) "Murder is the unlawful killing of a human being by another with malice aforethought, either expressed or implied" (Black, 1968). (*Process*) "There is only one way in which a person acquires a new idea: by the combination or association of two or more ideas he [or she] already has into a new juxtaposition in such a manner as to discover a relationship among them of which he [or she] has not previously been aware" (Sparke and McKowen, 1970). (*Principle*) "The amount of change in energy necessary to effect a just-noticeable difference varies directly with the initial amount of energy present" (Fleming and Levie, 1978).

The analytic type of central idea is easily divided (or analyzed) into its component elements which are ultimately developed as points. The message elements are inherent in the principle, definition, or process employed as a central idea.

The Synthetic Approach. Rather than beginning with a definition, process, or principle, you may simply have a list of ideas related to your topic that you want to include in your message. It is somewhat like a grocery list with random arrangement. To formulate a central idea, you should group items into categories, then include all of your categories into a single, declarative sentence. The example of defining "Quality" presented above incorporated this approach. Each category thus becomes an element of the message which will be developed into points later.

Many messages go awry because of inadequate central ideas. Small faults at this level become catastrophies later. The exercises in Chapter 9 are designed to help you discriminate between adequate and inadequate central ideas and to provide guided practice in writing your own.

Step 4. Establish Performance Objectives

Performance objectives, which specify what the receiver is expected to be able to *do* after receiving the message, serve both to guide the design and to evaluate the final message product. The underlying assumption here is that every message seeks some kind of change in the receiver—emotional, cognitive, psychomotor, etc. But since thinking or feeling cannot be witnessed directly, we must rely upon behavior that can be witnessed in order to infer the presence or absence of the thought or feeling. If behavior is displayed that we would expect to accompany our desired changes in mental states, we can be more confident that our message has worked. It should be obvious that the more precisely we define the desired behaviors, the better we will be able to determine whether our efforts to produce them were successful.

Less obvious perhaps is the role performance objectives play in guiding the design of the message. Until we know precisely what we are trying to accomplish, we are likely to accomplish it only by accident, if at all, and even then we are unlikely to recognize that we have succeeded. There is no role for tacit objectives at this stage. They must be stated clearly and explicitly. Mager (1975, p. 53) goes so far as to say: "If you give each learner [or any receiver for that matter] a copy of your objectives, you may not have to do much else." The statement of objectives is particularly important in this process of message design in directing the content, selecting appropriate response styles, and assessing the message success.

The elements of performance objectives are essentially stable, but they may be identified differently. Mager (1975), for example, identifies three elements: the overall behavioral act, the conditions (and/or restrictions) under which the behavior is to occur, and the criterion of acceptable performance. The behaviors, conditions, and criteria are identified in the following examples.

1. (Condition) Given five minutes to review his or her notes after receiving the message,—
   (Behavior) the receiver will list from memory the elements and scaling dimensions of the complexity model—
   (Criterion) with no errors on the elements and no more than five errors on the dimensions.

2. (Condition) Given a list of 50 words,—
   (Behavior) the receiver will underline the ones of Anglo-Saxon origin—
   (Criterion) with 90 percent accuracy.

3. (Condition) Given attitude scales before and immediately after receiving the message,—
   (Behavior) the receivers will score higher on the second scale—
   (Criterion) by an average of at least three scale points.

Kibler *et al.* (1974) discriminate between the actual behavior and the result of that behavior. They also list as an element the person(s) who perform(s) the behavior, thus they identify five elements: (1) *who* performs the behavior, (2) the *actual behavior*, (3) the *result* of the behavior, (4) the *relevant conditions*, and (5) the *standard* of acceptance. Here are some examples:

1. (Who) Those receivers wishing college credit—
   (Actual behavior) will write—
   (Result of behavior) an essay on diffusion of innovation through mass media—
   (Relevant conditions) after given an opportunity to discuss the message with a classmate for 20 minutes.
   (Standard) The essay must be between 800 and 1,000

words and develop at least four of the six main ideas of the message.

2. (Who) The members of the test audience—
(Actual behavior) will deposit reaction questionnaires—
(Result of behavior) indicating their enjoyment of the message—
(Relevant conditions) given no opportunity to discuss their reactions with others—
(Standard) with the average rating of five or above on a seven-point scale and a 4:1 ratio of positive fill-in comments.

Early in this chapter, we recognized that designing a message is often plagued with "over-choice." You should see more clearly now that the carefully prepared purpose statement helps to focus on the more plausible possibilities. Indeed, the commitments made at this level will close many less productive avenues and bear directly upon decisions you will make in each of the subsequent steps.

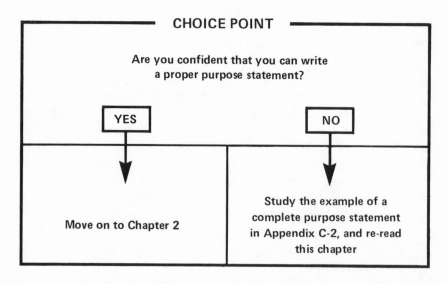

CHOICE POINT

Are you confident that you can write
a proper purpose statement?

YES

NO

Move on to Chapter 2

Study the example of a
complete purpose statement
in Appendix C-2, and re-read
this chapter

"In designing messages, we pack smaller ideas in large categories, and pack those into even larger points, and finally, pack the main points into one large "central idea crate."

* * * * *

". . . when you start planning a summer camping trip, you may refer to a topographical map of some wilderness area where landmarks are not well established. . . . In a similar manner, we will employ matrices to pinpoint the tactics appropriate to our selected strategies and audiences."

Chapter 2

INFORMATION LOAD AND BODY STRUCTURE	SUPPORT TACTICS AND OBSCURITY INDEX	PURPOSE STATEMENT

CONTEXTUAL ATMOSPHERE	ORGANISMIC CONSTRAINTS	RESPONSE STYLES

Central Idea

With the information provided in your purpose statement and the appropriate matrix, you can expand your central idea into a "box-outline," identify the appropriate tactics for developing the outline, and calculate the "obscurity index," which will be useful later in determining the appropriate information load.

Steps

5. Expand the central idea into a "box-outline."
6. Identify the appropriate tactics.
7. Calculate the "obscurity index."

Objectives

1. To analyze a central idea into its elements.
2. To structure the central idea elements into a "box-outline."
3. To select appropriate tactics from a matrix by which the box-outline can be developed.
4. To calculate an "average obscurity index" for a given message.

Chapter 2

Discovering Support Tactics

Two familiar images will help you understand and retain the fundamental considerations involved in discovering support tactics. Here is the first one. In tidying up after opening Christmas presents, you may want to save all of the nice boxes for another season. Since your storage space is limited, you "nest" the smaller boxes into the shoe boxes, and then pack the shoe boxes neatly into larger cartons, and finally pack the cartons into one large crate. In designing messages, we pack smaller ideas in large categories, and pack those into even larger points, and finally pack the main points into one large "central idea crate." Thus, we create a "box-outline."

For the second image, when you start planning a summer camping trip, you may refer to a topographical map of some wilderness area where landmarks are not well-established. You have to locate your campsite by a system of coordinates. First, you identify the appropriate range and township (vertical and horizontal belts six miles in width). Where they intersect, you can identify a 36-square-mile area. Each of the 36 sections of land can be identified by a conventional numbering system. When you have identified the "section" of interest to you, you can further pinpoint your campsite by dividing that section into quarters, and the selected quarter can again be divided into quarters. The entire "address" can thus be given: "T2W, R4N, Section 23, southwest quarter of the northeast quarter." In a similar manner, we will employ matrices to pinpoint the tactics appropriate to our selected strategies and audiences.

Step 5. Expand the Central Idea into a "Box-Outline"

We stated earlier that the central idea regulates the message content and that it is analogous to a seed, an egg, or a genetic code. Our object here is to "crack that code" and to identify its components. By analyzing a central idea, we can not only detect the components, but also we can establish their relationships. Examine this central idea used as an example in Chapter 1: "Murder is the unlawful killing of a human being by another with malice aforethought, either expressed or implied." The components of this sentence can easily be identified and related in terms of our "box" image. The large crate is the central idea. The cartons can be labeled: (1) *unlawful* killing, (2) killing *of a human,* (3) killing *by a human,* and (4) killing with *malice aforethought.* The fourth "carton" contains two "shoe boxes" labeled: "expressed" and "implied." This analysis lends itself to easy diagramming—a practice with several practical advantages—as illustrated in Figure 2.1.

Figure 2.2 illustrates a more complicated box-outline derived from the synthetically derived definition of "quality" presented in Chapter 1. Compare the definition with the outline and note that the outline is inherent in the central idea. See Figure 2.2.

These examples reflect some general rules of outlining which should be understood and used as a checklist with your own outlines.

Rule 1. All main points are rooted in the central idea. The main points are the "cartons" that fit into the "crate." Main points are traditionally labeled with Roman numerals (I, II, III, etc.).

Rule 2. All subpoints are rooted in their superior points. If the subpoints are of the first degree, they are traditionally labeled with capital letters (A, B, C, etc.). Second-degree subpoints are traditionally labeled with arabic numerals (1, 2, 3, etc.). The labeling hierarchy is: I., A., 1., a., (1), (a): Boxes nested in boxes.

Rule 3. Every point has a coordinate point. The function of a point is to divide. It divides the central idea into its component points, or it divides a point into its subpoints. After a division, there must be at least two parts; after dividing a central idea, or another point, there must be two points or two subpoints. Points

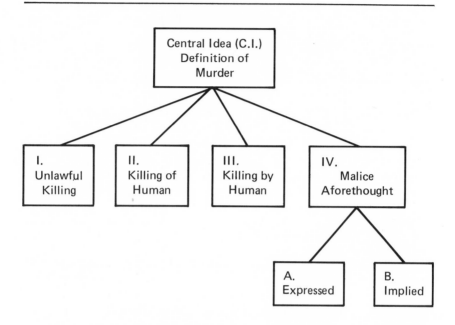

Figure 2.1. "Box-Outline" Based on a Definition of "Murder."

at the same level of division are coordinate points and share the same labeling system. In other words, if you have a point labeled "I," you must also have a point labeled "II." If you have an "A," you must have a "B." If you do not have a II or a B under these conditions, neither the I nor the A is a point: it may simply be a paraphrase of the central idea or point, or it may be a mislabeled support used to illustrate, prove, or emphasize the point.

Rule 4. Supports, which are added to the "terminal points," may be of any number. The specific roles and types of supports will be developed in Chapter 3. It is important to consider now only where they are used and in what quantity. In general, a support functions to amplify—not to divide—a central idea or a point. Since a single, well-chosen example can amplify (that is, elaborate or illustrate) a point, a support, unlike a point, may stand alone. A point may have one or several supports attached to

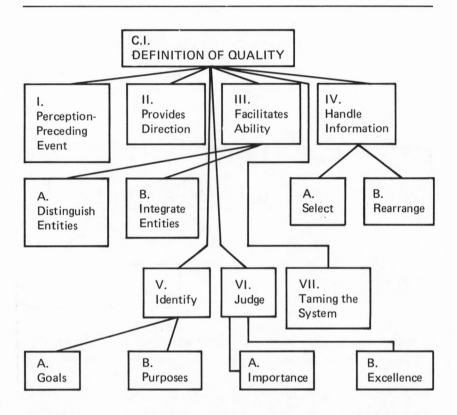

Figure 2.2. "Box-Outline" Based on a Definition of "Quality."

it. Supports, with a few exceptions, are used only at the "terminal-point" level. A terminal point is the result of the last level of division. For example, in Figure 2.2, point II is a terminal point as is point VII because they are undivided. Points III, IV, V, and VI are not terminal points because they are divided. See Chapter 9 for outlining exercises.

Step 6. Identify the Appropriate Tactics

The tactics by which you can develop your box-outline's terminal points are identified on a *matrix*. The appropriate matrix is selected according to the strategy commitment made in the purpose statement. In your purpose statement, you have also identified certain characteristics of your audience which must be referred to now in order to enter the matrix. Notice again how critically important the purpose statement is to the design process.

General Matrix Characteristics

Before examining the actual design matrices, let us consider some characteristics of a matrix in general. The derivation of the word "matrix" provides some insight into its nature. Webster (1959) defines "matrix" thus:

> ma . trix (ma'triks, mat'riks), n. [pl. MATRICES, MATRIXES], LL., womb, public register, origin; L., breeding animal—stem of *mater,* a mother/, 1. originally, the womb; uterus; hence, 2. that within which, or within and from which, something originates, takes from, or develops;. . .

The matrix "gives birth" to its offspring—its cells. To push the analogy a bit further, a matrix requires two inputs to produce one output. Input variables from each of two axes intersect to create a cell, or output. Since we will rely heavily upon matrices throughout this design process, not only for selecting tactics, a digression to consider some general characteristics of the matrices used here seems to be in order.

All matrices employed here are of the 3 x 3 variety. This means that a matrix is made up of three rows (running horizontally) and three columns (running vertically). The three categories on each axis suggest that the variable is continuous rather than dichotomous, as a 2 x 2 matrix would suggest. It is important to remember that these are intended to represent continuous variables and that they are simplified to only three intervals to aid comprehension. This is an instance of reducing reality artificially to a manageable size. Figure 2.3 illustrates a generalized matrix.

To enter a matrix, we will typically select a value for both variables and identify the cell where they intersect. For example, if Variable A were "low" and Variable B were "high," we would identify cell L-H, the shaded one in Figure 2.3. There will be times when we identify a characteristic in a matrix cell that we desire to

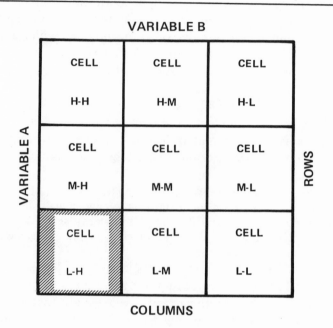

Figure 2.3. A Generalized Matrix.

design into a message. In that case, enter the matrix through the cell and identify the variable values associated with that cell.

Because the variables are continuous, and are only represented as categorical, you may wish to interpolate if the 3 x 3 format seems too constricting. I have arbitrarily assigned values of 2, 4, and 6 to the categories of high, medium, and low, respectively. This is to facilitate translation into a seven-point rating scale. In Figure 2.4, Cell Y is interpolated at value 5 half-way between categories 4 and 6 on both variables. This cell would represent a kind of "hybridized" content drawing from each of the inter-sected cells. Cell X interpolates Variable B but not Variable A to produce values of 4 and 1 for A and B, respectively.

The Matrices

Each of the strategies identified in Chapter 1 is related to a matrix. Each matrix is presented and explained in this section.

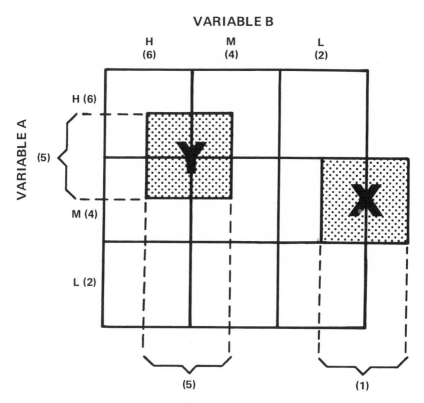

Figure 2.4. Illustration of Interpolation on a 3 x 3 Matrix.

A. To Inform, to Stimulate, to Interpret

This first matrix serves three strategies, as illustrated in Figure 2.5: *To inform* (explicit knowledge sequence), *to stimulate* (intuitive knowledge sequence), and, *to interpret* (tacit knowledge sequence).

Consider first the strategy *to inform*. Its function is to present *explicit knowledge* in such a way that the receiver will be able to recognize it; thus, it follows the *explicit knowledge sequence*. This sequence involves the tactics: imagine, associate, divide, amplify,

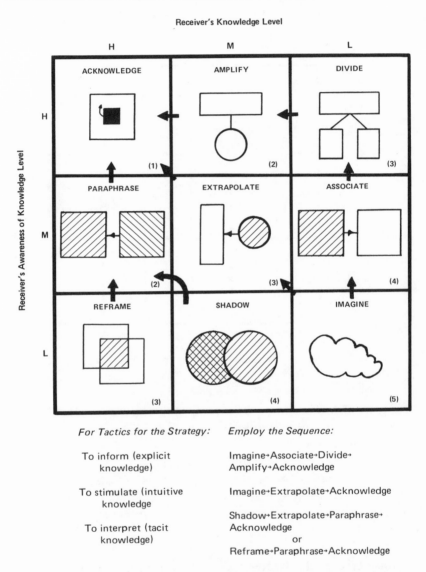

Receiver's Knowledge Level

For Tactics for the Strategy: *Employ the Sequence:*

To inform (explicit   Imagine→Associate→Divide→
  knowledge)   Amplify→Acknowledge

To stimulate (intuitive   Imagine→Extrapolate→Acknowledge
  knowledge

To interpret (tacit   Shadow→Extrapolate→Paraphrase→
  knowledge)   Acknowledge
                                         or
                                   Reframe→Paraphrase→Acknowledge

Figure 2.5. Tactical Matrix for Strategies: To Inform (Explicit Knowledge Sequence), To Stimulate (Intuitive Knowledge Sequence), To Interpret (Tacit Knowledge Sequence).

and acknowledge. The sequence may begin at any of these cells (according to your assessment of the receivers) and then proceed in sequence to "acknowledge." Each cell contains both a strategy name and a symbol, which will be explained below. The symbols, if used consistently, provide a useful shorthand, as we shall see later.

Imagine. In this tactic, you invite your receiver to create an image in his or her mind and from his or her experience according to your prompting. The image typically need not be factually accurate. It need only to provide an appealing starting point. Suppose I should say to you: "Close your eyes and picture yourself sitting where you are. Get a good image. See yourself vividly in every detail. Now, stand up and walk outside by the nearest exit. You find a free-flight balloon waiting for you there. Get into it. Untie the anchor rope and feel yourself beginning to rise. See the spot below you in sharp detail. As you rise, see other buildings come into sight. Now see the whole town, and as you rise higher see the town diminish into the terrain of the country. . ."

We could continue, but this illustrates the nature of this tactic. If your receivers are low both in knowledge of your topic and in their awareness of their lack of knowledge, this tactic provides involvement and arousal while introducing the topic in a non-threatening, non-technical way. The cloud symbol suggests this "airy" quality.

Associate. You may move to this tactic from "imagine," or you may initiate the sequence at "associate." In this tactic, you associate the known with the unknown in order to establish a *gestalt* or ill-defined image of the whole. The symbol in this cell suggests movement from the "known" (shaded box) to the "unknown" (white box). This tactic is essentially metaphoric or analogical. You extract the structure or essence from the familiar object or experience and relate it to the unfamiliar. For example, I might say: "Your bird's-eye-view of the terrain below you, as you see it from the balloon, is similar to what happens in language as we move up the abstraction scale and farther and farther away from the objects below. Their particular features are lost—they may even disappear altogether—but at this expense, we gain a broader view."

Our affinity for association is as great as our affinity for imagination. We cannot engage in cognitive activity without involving both to some degree, yet the tactic "associate" enables us to focus more precisely on the explicit knowledge we wish to communicate than mere imagination allows, so it is higher in the sequence.

Divide. Given a *gestalt,* whether provided for the receiver or brought with him or her, the next tactic is to divide that vague conception into its elemental components. This "teasing-out" process adds definition to the *gestalt.* This is the same process we have discussed in relation to dividing a central idea into its points, except now we are talking about dividing a terminal point. Of course, if we divide a terminal point, we will establish at least two new terminal points. In Chapter 3, we will see how that affects information load and how we may have to alter the scope of the message as a result. But, for now, it is enough to recognize that if the receiver's knowledge of a terminal point is low and he or she knows it is low, then a division of it into smaller pieces is indicated. Note that the symbol in this cell suggests division.

Amplify. Amplification is accomplished by adding supporting material to a terminal point. I have mentioned supports above and will develop them in detail in Chapter 3. Subpoints and supports are often confused, yet their functions are opposites. Remember that *points divide* and supports *amplify,* elaborate, illustrate, vivify, document, but do not divide. A terminal point may be supported with one or several supports to form what we will call an *information chunk.* More will be said about information chunks in Chapter 3, yet now I should mention that a part of their effectiveness stems from their using both right-brain and left-brain functions. With moderately knowledgeable receivers, who recognize their knowledge level, terminal points may be supported directly without employing the other tactics of this sequence.

Acknowledge. Sometimes a receiver already knows about the content of the terminal point. Even though it is appropriate to include that point in your outline for the sake of structural

integrity, no amplification is needed. This provides an opport
to "stroke" your receivers by mentioning the terminal point ...u
then acknowledging their knowing it. It tends to validate the
receivers and reinforce their attentiveness. If acknowledgment is
omitted; or, even worse, if such a terminal point is developed with
any of the other tactics, the impression received might be that you
are needlessly telling them what they already know. That
impression in itself tends to erode interest and attention.

The symbol for acknowledgment is one I have for several years
used to represent the figure of speech known as *synecdoche*. This
figure refers to a part of something in order to elicit the whole
image in the mind of the receiver. An example: "The pen is
mightier than the sword" specifies particulars in order to jog the
recall to interpret much more than was said, and it is the receiver's
existing recall that is jogged. Synecdoche only stimulates and
acknowledges it.

Now consider the strategy *to stimulate*. This strategy, rather
than relating to explicit knowledge, relates to intuitive knowledge.
Intuitive knowledge implies instantaneous apprehension; it is the
knowing of something without the conscious use of reasoning or
instruction. The process entails translation of a vicarious experience into a sharable state. If the sequence is entered at the
beginning, the tactic of "imagine" is used as with the strategy "to
inform." But once activated, the source helps the receiver
"extrapolate" meaning from the imagined experience rather than
associating it with his or her preconceived topic.

The symbol for "extrapolate" suggests movement from a
known (shaded) specific support (image) to an unknown generalized point. A more generalized meaning is drawn from the
imagined experience. Assigning meanings to dreams would be an
example of this. Once the point is discovered, acknowledgment
follows.

Finally, we will consider the strategy *to interpret*. This strategy
is concerned with tacit knowledge. It assumes the existence of
prior knowledge and attempts to elevate what is known only in a

holistic, unencoded way to the explicit level. Tacit knowledge accounts in part for the "schemata" Neisser (1976) asserts are prerequisite to perception. Polanyi (1966), who has written a definitive work on tacit knowledge, concludes:

> Statements explicitly derived from identifiable premises can be critically tested by examining their premises and the process of inference which led to them. But if we know a great deal that we *cannot tell,* and if ever that which we know and *can* tell is accepted by us as true only in view of its bearing on a reality beyond it, a reality which may yet manifest itself in the future of an indeterminate range of unexpected results,. . .then the idea of knowledge based on wholly identifiable grounds collapses, and we must conclude that the transmission of knowledge from one generation to the other must be predominantly tacit.*

Since tacit knowledge, by definition, is present and only requires being made explicit, the tactical sequence disregards the "low" column of the matrix. If one's tacit knowledge level is estimated to be moderate, the sequence is: shadow, extrapolate, paraphrase, and acknowledge. But if the level of tacit knowledge is estimated to be high, the sequence is: reframe, paraphrase, and acknowledge. Of course, tacit knowledge is not directly verifiable, so an estimate of its level must be made subjectively either by the source or by the receiver. Greater confidence is gained when both source and receiver are in agreement.

Shadow. This tactic is based on a facilitative communication technique where the facilitator, who is more expressive than the receiver, describes various possible states of knowing or feeling. The receiver is required only to state whether any given description matches what he or she knows or feels. After several "hypotheses" have been confirmed, and typically many more have been denied, a pattern or profile of the tacit knowledge begins to emerge.

Extrapolate. Shadow moves in sequence to *extrapolate*; and, since I have defined this tactic already, I will not repeat it here.

Reframe. The definitive work on reframing is by Goffman (1974). He sees a framework as a mental construct that renders what would otherwise be a meaningless aspect of the scene into something that is meaningful. By reframing, one changes the

---

*From *The Tacit Dimension*, by Michael Polanyi. New York: Doubleday & Company, Inc., 1966.

framework so that a different meaning is attributed to the same scene. Watzlawick (1978) provides this example of reframing:

> It is a typical problem of many students that they cannot concentrate their attention on study matters because they are distracted by almost incessant thoughts about the many much more pleasant things they could do if they did not have to study. . . . Frequently, an almost immediate improvement can be achieved if they can be brought to set themselves a reasonable time limit for the completion of their daily tasks, after which they may do anything they wish to do *except* study. Leisure and pleasure are thus reframed as a punishment and thereby lose their charm in very much the same way as we may find ourselves wide awake on Sunday mornings while on work days we could sleep for hours and hours.*

Paraphrase. While reframing tacit knowledge allows us to perceive it differently, paraphrasing allows us to capture an allusive thought by avoiding the mischief caused by the language in which it is cast. Rogers (1942) has developed this technique as a means of preventing misunderstandings in interpersonal communication. The receiver states a position, then the source paraphrases that position until the receiver is satisfied that the restated version matches the intended message. The process moves tacit, ill-defined knowledge to a more explicit level after which acknowledgment is all that remains.

B. To Instruct

1. To Instruct (General). Instruction differs from informing in that it seeks to enable the receiver to *recall* rather than merely to *recognize* the content. The tactics for instruction differ according to the nature of the content being taught: *concepts, details,* or *relationships* (networks and processes). The general matrix for instruction in Figure 2.6 classifies different types of learners and prescribes general tactics for each. More specific tactics are developed in the textual elaboration of the matrix according to the types of instruction.

Sophomoric. This receiver does not know, but does not know

*From *The Language of Change: Elements of Therapeutic Communication*, by Paul Watzlawick. Copyright © 1978 by Paul Watzlawick. By permission of Basic Books, Inc., Publishers, New York.

Receiver's Knowledge Level

Receiver's Awareness of Knowledge Level

	H	M	L
H	*PROFOUND* Knows; knows he or she knows ------------------------ 1. Acknowledge 2. Proceed to next item (1)	*COGNIZANT* Knows some; knows what he or she does not know ------------------------ 1. Acknowledge known areas 2. Isolate weak areas 3. Accelerated treatment (2)	*INGENUOUS* (Novice) Does not know; knows he or she does not know ------------------------ 1. Build confidence in process 2. Full treatment (3)
M	*KNOWLEDGEABLE* Knows; suspects knowledge is inadequate ------------------------ 1. Probe suspicions 2. Quiz at terminal level of the accel. treatment 3. Reassure of adequacy (2)	*DILETTANTISH* (Amateurish) Knows some; suspects he or she knows only some ------------------------ 1. Quick assessment 2. Confirm suspicion 3. Isolate weak areas 4. Accel. treatment (3)	*NAIVE* Does not know; suspects he or she does not know ------------------------ 1. Quick assessment 2. Confirm suspicion 3. Full treatment (4)
L	*DORMANT* (Sleeper) Knows; does not know he or she knows ------------------------ 1. Quiz at terminal level of accel. treatment 2. Deny ignorance 3. Reassure of adequacy (3)	*SUPERFICIAL* Knows some; does not know he or she knows only some ------------------------ 1. Begin at terminal level 2. Confront weaknesses 3. Accel. treatment (4)	*SOPHOMORIC* Does not know; does not know he or she does not know ------------------------ 1. Begin at terminal level 2. Confront ignorance 3. Full treatment (5)

Sequences are within cells, not among cells.

The function of instruction is to facilitate recall.

Figure 2.6. Matrix for Strategy: To Instruct/General.

he or she does not know. The tactical sequence is: (1) Begin instruction at the terminal level in order to demonstrate to the receiver the immensity or complexity of the task. In other words, overwhelm the receiver. (2) Confront the receiver with his or her ignorance, not to humiliate, but rather to establish the existence of a knowledge gap. (3) Present the full instructional treatment. The "full treatment" is prescribed below according to the type of instruction involved.

Naive. The naive learner does not know and suspects he or she does not know. The tactical sequence is: (1) Take a quick assessment of knowledge. (2) Confirm the suspicion of ignorance tactfully. (3) Present the full instructional treatment.

Ingenuous. This novice learner does not know and knows he or she does not know. The tactics are: (1) Build confidence in the process, and (2) present the full treatment.

Superficial. The superficial receiver knows some, but does not know that he or she knows *only some.* The tactical sequence is: (1) Begin instruction at the terminal level. (2) Confront the receiver with his or her areas of weakness. (3) Present the accelerated treatment.

Dilettantish. The amateur learner knows some and suspects he or she knows only some. The tactical sequence is: (1) Take a quick assessment. (2) Confirm the suspicion of partial knowledge. (3) Isolate the areas of weakness. (4) Present the accelerated treatment.

Cognizant. The cognizant receiver knows some and knows what he or she does not know. The tactical sequence for the cognizant receiver is: (1) Acknowledge the known areas. (2) Isolate the weak areas for concentrated treatment. (3) Present the accelerated treatment.

Dormant. The "sleeper" knows, but does not know he or she knows. Use this tactical sequence with the dormant receiver: (1) Quiz briefly at the terminal level of the accelerated treatment. (2) Deny ignorance. (3) Reassure the receiver of his or her adequacy.

Knowledgeable. This receiver knows, but suspects that his or her knowledge is inadequate. The tactical sequence is: (1) Probe the suspicions. (2) Quiz at the terminal level of the accelerated treatment. (3) Reassure the receiver of his or her adequacy.

Profound. The profound receiver knows and knows he or she knows. The tactic is simply to acknowledge the knowing and proceed to the next item.

After consulting the general matrix for tactical sequences, you will need to consult the treatment sequences according to the type of instruction you have selected. For each type of instruction, a "full treatment" and an "accelerated sequence" are specified.

2. To Instruct
(Concepts)

Merrill and Tennyson (1977) have defined a concept as: ". . . a set of specific objects, symbols, or events which are grouped together on the basis of shared characteristics and which can be referenced by a particular name or symbol." They develop the process of teaching concepts in detail; I have abstracted and simplified their process for the present tactical purposes.

Full Treatment. When the full treatment is prescribed in the general matrix, it refers to this sequence:

  a. *Present definition.* Define the concept formally as, for example, a "concept" is defined in the paragraph above.
  b. *Present an initial matched set.* The "matched set" refers to an example (which exemplifies the concept) and a non-example (an example which fails to exemplify the concept). At this level, the matched set should be *easy* (uncomplicated) and *divergent* (easily discriminated).
  c. *Isolate critical attributes.* A "critical attribute" is a necessary condition to be a member of the class. Not only is it appropriate to identify the critical attributes in the examples, but also to identify their absence in non-examples.
  d. *Present practice matched set.* Given a matched set, encourage the receiver to *inquire* about attributes and provide helpful feedback after discriminations are attempted.
  e. *Present terminal level matched set.* The terminal level sets are similar to the initial matched set except that the instances are *hard* (complicated) and *convergent* (very similar except for a critical attribute).

Accelerated Treatment. Reference to the accelerated treatment in the general matrix prescribes the following sequence:

a . *Present a matched set* (hard and convergent).

b . *Isolate the critical attributes.*

c . (Terminal level) *Present concept definition.*

3. To Instruct
(Details)

Instruction aimed at the recall of details requires a different set of treatments. Instead of learning concepts, the receiver is asked to learn specific dates, names, formulas, symbols, vocabulary words, etc. The emphasis here is upon mnemonic technique and reinforcement of correct responses.

Full Treatment. The full treatment incorporates six steps:

a . *Preview the whole.* Present the whole set of details sequentially without elaboration in order to establish a mental set and to recognize familiar items.

b . *Conduct recitation.* After initial exposure, repeat the sequential presentation asking the receivers to respond to the stimulus.

c . *Isolate the problem areas.* Group all of the incorrect responses together to form a "problem-set."

d . *Suggest mnemonic devices.* Examine the problem-set item-by-item and suggest (or stimulate the receivers to create) memory aids for each.

e . *Drill with problem-set using reinforcement.* Present the stimulus for an item in the problem-set, get a response, reinforce a correct response with praise, payment, privilege, etc., and withhold reinforcement for incorrect responses. The reinforcement ideally follows the response immediately. Then proceed to the next item.

f . *Conduct recitation to criterion.* Return to the whole set and progress sequentially. Continue recitation until the predetermined level of achievement is met.

Accelerated Treatment.

a . *Drill with reinforcement.* Present the whole set one item at a time, and reinforce correct responses immediately.

  b. *Provide the correct response* for each error immediately.
  c. *Conduct recitation to criterion.*

4. To Instruct
(Relationships: networks, processes)

Relationships, including networks and processes, involve both elements and interaction among those elements. Often, the interactions take place simultaneously, thus defying a linear examination or explanation. They tend to be complex and difficult to instruct. Merrill (1977) has developed a "concept elaboration theory" that lends itself nicely to the instruction of concepts. It is by its nature rather complex, though. His treatment is more strategic than we need for our tactical purposes, so I have adapted his process to our needs by simplifying the procedure somewhat.

Full Treatment.

  a. *Identify the terminal task.* State for your receiver what the learning objective is for this terminal point in your outline. The time required to develop this tactic limits the number of terminal points you can accommodate in your message.

  b. *Present an overview of the complete network or process.* Describe in some detail the conditions under which the terminal performance will be demonstrated.

  c. *Identify the governing rule or underlying principle.* State concisely and abstractly the relationship among the elements.

  d. *Present the simplist usable case.* All of the elements and relationships must be present in this case, but with no complications or exceptional characteristics. Its function is to reduce complexity to its lowest level in order to reveal the inherent structure.

  e. *Isolate the elements of that case.* This is similar to identifying "concept attributes" as discussed above. Its function is to insure recognition and to give emphasis to the elements.

  f. *Present increasingly complex cases* in which the elements are identified until the target level of complexity is reached.

g. (Terminal level) *Present an elaborated rule or underlying principle.* This should match the expectations of the initial objective in terms of completeness.

Accelerated Treatment.

   a. *Present a complex case of the network or process.*

   b. *Isolate the elements of that case.*

   c. *Identify the relationships of the elements.*

   d. *Present elaborated rule or underlying principle.*

C. To Persuade (To Promote)

Persuasion (and its special cases of promotion and dissuasion) incorporate tactics on the basis of the comparative acceptance of an issue by the source and the receiver. Three basic instances should be delineated: First, when the source's acceptance of position is high, he or she will attempt to *persuade* the receiver to accept that position with similar intensity. Second, when the source moderately accepts a position, he or she will attempt to move the strong believer (or strong disbeliever) to a more moderate or qualified position. Third, when the source rejects a position he or she will attempt to *dissuade* the receiver—that is, to reject the position.

Since I have discussed the techniques of achieving these objectives elsewhere (Marsh, 1967), I will concentrate here only on the tactical sequences, rather than upon the nuances of the tactics. (See Figure 2.7.)

Acceptance sequence. Given a high degree of source acceptance of a position, the receiver may agree, have reservations, or disagree with the source. If the initial position is strong disagreement, the tactic should be "to move" the passions by appealing to the *pathos* (feelings, emotions). Given the appropriate emotional framing and a reserved acceptance, the next tactic is "to prove." I have subscripted "Prove" on the matrix to distinguish between two types of reasoned proof. Prove$_1$ employs the classical rhetorical proofs of the *enthymeme* and the *example*. The enthymeme is a "popular" form of reasoning where the "warrant" or major premise is often granted by the receiver, thus requiring no support. It may also take the form of a truncated syllogism which leaves

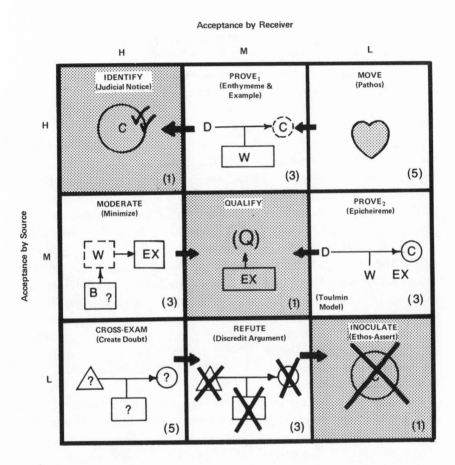

*Figure 2.7. Matrix for Strategies: To Persuade/Dissuade;
To Promote*

one element out to be supplied by the receiver, thus achieving commitment of ownership. The "example," as used in this context, is a truncated form of induction where a general conclusion is granted on the basis of a sample of one or two instances which appear to the receiver to be typical. Rhetorical proofs of these types inherently involve the receiver's intimate participation in the process.

Finally, in this sequence, the tactic is to establish *identity* of positions. Stressing the "common ground" or "consubstantuality," as Burke (1950) calls it, reinforces the changed position. If identity of position is the initial condition, the position can merely be noted for "judicial notice" (assuming acceptance unless challenged) without further effort.

Moderation sequence. When the source regards the appropriate stance to be a qualified one and the receiver is only moderately accepting, the tactic is to specify the appropriate qualifications; when done, the task is accomplished. If the receiver's position is one of strong acceptance, the tactic should be to *moderate* that position by minimizing the strength of the warrant (major premise). Toulmin, Rieke, and Janik (1979) explain how warrants that relate to the "real world" must have *exceptions* because they are *validated* only by inductive (and therefore incomplete) *backing.* To minimize the credibility of an overstated position, the tactics to employ are to *challenge the backing* and *to demonstrate exceptions* to the warrant.

In the instance of disbelief where moderate acceptance seems appropriate, prove$_2$ is the indicated tactic. Toulmin's reasoning model, which attempts to reconcile inductive and deductive models to produce a practical and cautious method, requires documented data (inartistic proof), backing and exceptions to the warrant, as well as qualified claims. Because it is grounded in externally verifiable data and warrants, this model generates enough credibility to justify qualified acceptance. Its prototype, the *epicheireme*, was well-established in classical rhetoric in Quintilian's *Institutio Oratoria* (Butler, 1921).

Dissuasion sequence. Given a strong believer in a position rejected by the source, the tactic "cross-examination" is employed to generate some degree of doubt in the receiver's mind. Wellman (1948) and McBath (1954) offer suggestions for practicing this tactic in more detail than space permits here. Once doubt is present in the receiver's mind, direct *refutation* is effective for dissuasion. *To refute* means to invalidate an existing argument by destroying any element that is essential to the holding of that position. It is generally good advice to avoid "overkilling" if it is your receiver's argument you are refuting. It is typically better to identify a critical weakness and concentrate your efforts on it.

If a receiver already rejects a position that is likewise rejected by the source, a tactic called "inoculation" is appropriate. Its function is to reinforce disbelief in order to resist better the subsequent efforts of others to gain acceptance for that position.

The use of *ethos* is important in efforts to inoculate. "Ethos" is a kind of persuasive appeal that emanates from the perceived character, intelligence, or good will of the source; from his or her charisma or credibility if you prefer. Often an unsupported assertion by a person with such credibility carries the weight of a demonstrated claim. McGuire (1964) is generally accepted as the definitive authority on inoculation.

D. To Entertain

The dominant tactic of the strategy *to entertain* is established by the source's level of seriousness. If seriousness is high, the tactic will be to *inspire*; if moderate, to *portray*; and if low, to *play down*. The shades of each of these tactics are determined by the receivers' seriousness levels. These shades are identified in Figure 2.8 by the nine cell descriptors. These descriptors and their synonyms may be sufficient to suggest the appropriate tactical development, but if nuances are desired, you should consult a good dictionary.

For example, if you were the featured banquet entertainer at a "Save the Albatross" convention, you should begin by analyzing seriousness levels. Assume that their level is high and your level is low. Your best tactic would be to "play down" their proposals with satire.

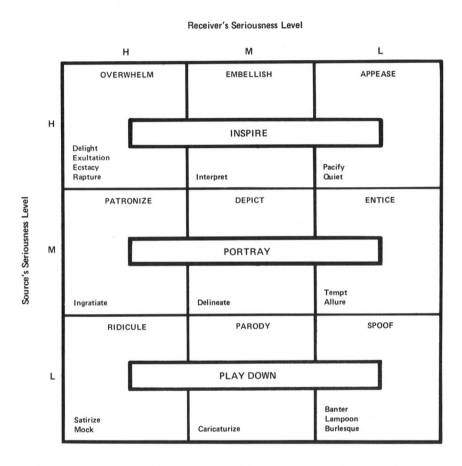

NOTE: Obscurity indexes are not employed in this matrix because entertainment is not primarily concerned with information, propositions, or processes.

Figure 2.8. Matrix for Strategy: To Entertain.

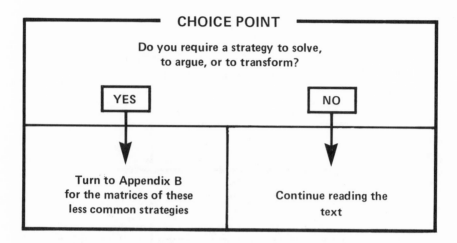

Having discovered the appropriate tactics and/or tactical sequence for your strategy and your audience, list them under the appropriate terminal points on your box-outline. They will guide the refinement of your content in subsequent steps.

Step 7. Calculate the "Obscurity Index"

"Obscurity" is the quality of not being easily perceived, not easily understood. It connotes being vague, cryptic, or inconspicuous. The "obscurity index" attempts to quantify the degree to which the message content is initially obscure for the receiver. The more the meaning is obscured for a given receiver, the more tactical support is required to make that meaning salient. Since more time is required to develop the tactics for more obscure content, less content can be communicated within a fixed time. This condition consequently influences the message's information load.

The obscurity index is located within parentheses in the matrix cells. The one exception is the matrix for the strategy "to entertain." Obscurity indexes are not employed in that matrix because entertainment is not primarily concerned with information, propositions, or processes. A subjective estimate must be employed for this matrix.

Consider this example: If it were your task to persuade a

receiver on one issue of the message where his or her acceptance is low and the source's acceptance is high, the appropriate tactic for that issue would be to move from the use of pathos to the use of enthymemes or examples and then, to identification. The process begins in the upper-right cell of the matrix, and that cell has an "obscurity index" of five. If, however, your receiver were only moderately resistant, you could have begun at the *proof* stage where the index is only three. In other words, the more you have to work with your receiver at any given terminal point, the higher the obscurity index will be.

When the index for each terminal point has been identified, you should average them. That average obscurity value will be required to calculate the information load in Step 8.

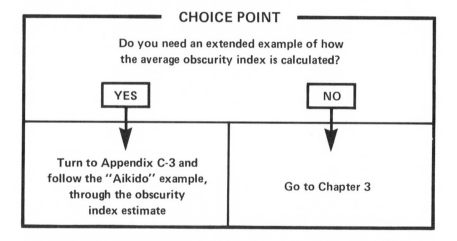

CHOICE POINT

Do you need an extended example of how the average obscurity index is calculated?

YES

NO

Turn to Appendix C-3 and follow the "Aikido" example, through the obscurity index estimate

Go to Chapter 3

Chapter 3

INFORMATION LOAD AND BODY STRUCTURE	SUPPORT TACTICS AND OBSCURITY INDEX	PURPOSE STATEMENT

CONTEXTUAL ATMOSPHERE	ORGANISMIC CONSTRAINTS	RESPONSE STYLES

Central Idea

Given the tactical choice and the obscurity index for each terminal point, you can: first, estimate (and modify, if desirable) the message's information load; then, select an appropriate organizational pattern for the message body; and, finally, complete the information control phase of the process by inspecting the body for structural weaknesses.

Steps

8. Estimate (and modify, if desirable) the information load.
9. Select the message-body organizational pattern.
10. Check the outline for structural weaknesses.

Objectives

1. To recall the definition of an "information chunk."
2. To describe the different functions of supports and points.
3. To discriminate between points and supports in an outline.
4. To recognize the commonly used support types.
5. To determine the information load of a message.
6. To describe strategies for modifying message information load.
7. To classify organizational structures into hierarchical categories.
8. To recognize the uses for various orders of presentation.
9. To use the "body-structure matrix" for structural decisions.
10. To identify structural weaknesses in a message outline.

Chapter 3

Determining Information Load and Body Structure

Recall a time when you stood at a hotel registry and scanned the pigeonhole mail slots behind the desk. If you were to scan the names assigned to each slot only once, what would the greatest number of them be that you could recall immediately after glancing away? You might be surprised. Let me use a simpler illustration: Turn back to any one of the 3 x 3 matrices in Chaper 2; read each cell only once without delay; turn away and reproduce the matrix. How many cells can you fill in correctly?

Miller's (1967) research supports the prediction you will do no better with the mail slots than you will with a 3 x 3 matrix. In fact, if you get all nine cells in the matrix, you will probably be operating at the most optimistic estimate of your channel capacity. Miller identified, in a number of varied experiments, the human channel capacity for both attention and immediate memory to be seven items. Individual differences produce enough variance to cause him to set the upper limit at 7 ± 2; that is, from five to nine items. If you have thought the use of 3 x 3 matrices in this model to be too simplistic, consider that position in light of the 7 ± 2 principle. The image of the 3 x 3 matrix is a good one to keep in mind while designing a message because it represents the maximum number of slots you have to work with in structuring an effective message under normal conditions.

Bruner (1966) offers this suggestion for working within these restrictive limits:

> My colleague George Miller has proposed a magic number 7 ± 2 as the range of human attention or immediate memory. We are indeed limited in our span. Let me only suggest here that

compacting or condensing is the means whereby we fill our seven
slots with gold rather than dross.

This chapter focuses upon how to select our limited number of
slots, how to fill them with gold, and how to arrange them to
maximize their impact.

Step 8. Estimate the Information Load

Information load is a function of both the number of
"information chunks" (slots) in the message and the average
"obscurity index." The obscurity index was defined in Chapter 2.
We must now define an information chunk in order to understand
the information load matrix.

I have borrowed Miller's (1967) concept of "chunk" and have
modified its magnitude while retaining its essence. Miller introduces the notion this way:

> Absolute judgment is limited by the amount of information.
> Immediate memory is limited by the number of items. In order to
> capture this distinction in somewhat picturesque terms, I have
> fallen into the custom of distinguishing between *bits* of informa-
> tion and *chunks* of information. Then I can say that the number
> of bits of information is constant for absolute judgment and the
> number of chunks of information is constant for immediate
> memory. The span of immediate memory seems to be almost
> independent of the number of bits per chunk, at least over the
> range that has been examined to date. (p. 36)

Miller's units were smaller than is useful to consider in designing
a whole message, but the principle is the same: it is the number of
"ideas," not the size of the ideas, that is critical. The "information
chunk" I employ is defined as a *terminal point* from a box-outline
plus the supporting material that amplifies that point. There may
be one or several supports associated with a point; in either case,
there would be only one chunk. Since a chunk consists of a point
(or subpoint) and support, it is critical to distinguish their
respective functions—otherwise quantification will not be reliable,
and structure will be confused.

In our discussion of box-outlines in Chapter 2, I stressed that
the function of a point is *to divide*. By contrast, the function of a
support is *to amplify*. Supports not only provide redundance to

ease the cognitive strain of processing terse, abstract points, but also they tend to provide concreteness, vividness, and specificity. Points are processed predominately with the left brain; supports tend to have an affinity for the right brain. An information chunk therefore blends the two functions into an efficient and integrated unit. Figure 3.1 illustrates this distinction graphically with symbols I shall use consistently throughout the book. I arbitrarily assign number and letter labels to points and verbal descriptions to supports in order to prevent their confusion on an outline.

Types of Supports

Listing several common support types will illustrate the diversity of possibilities and help to refine their function. No suggestion of exhaustiveness is intended, although these are the most commonly encountered supports.

Repetition. Repetition is a form of support that provides emphasis and redundancy by stating the point again in exactly the same words. Repetition is a form of support that provides emphasis and redundancy by stating the point again in exactly the same words.

Paraphrase. Like repetition, paraphrase provides emphasis and redundancy, but it does so by restating the point in different words. In other words, paraphrase by-passes the confusion that may beset one way of saying something, yet it runs the idea through the nervous system for a second time.

Description. A description is a technique of creating a vivid picture in words which allows the receiver to experience vicariously the thing described. For example:

> The portrait of the Achieving Manager which emerges from our study is that of an individual employing an integrative style of management, wherein people are valued just as highly as accomplishment of production goals . . . wherein candor, openness, sensitivity, and receptivity comprise the rule in interpersonal relationships rather than its exception . . . wherein participative practices are favored over unilaterally directive or lame duck prescriptive measures. Moreover, from a motivational standpoint, the Achieving Manager needs to find meaning in his [or her] work and strives to afford such meaning to others. Higher order,

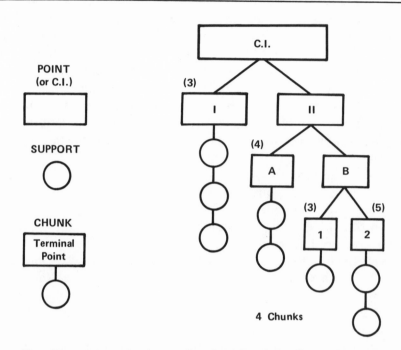

Note: Disregard the numbers in parentheses during first viewing. They will be explained later in reference to the Information Load Matrix.

Figure 3.1. Information Chunks.

constructive incentives are his [or her] motivational preoccupations, while his [or her] less-achieving comrades remain mired in fantasies of defense and self-preservation (Zemke, 1979).

Narration. A narration is a description that moves through time creating a sense of "story" as it progresses. Can you remember a time when you sat on your mother's lap as she read a children's story to you? You squirmed as she began. You were more interested in thumbing through the book just looking at pictures. But as the action began to unfold, you sat quietly while your mental images drew you into the adventure. You grew impatient to see the pictures on the pages she had not reached yet. By the time of the story's climax, you had been completely transported from your mother's lap into the hero's role.

We have a special affinity for narration—we have grown up with it.

List of brief examples. A list, if it is not divided and elaborated, may serve as a single support. It should be used cautiously, however, because there is often a temptation to crowd subpoints into an already fully-loaded message and pass them off as a support. But, if a list is presented without development, it serves as a support; for instance: a list of names or places, a list of key-words, a list of principles, a list of steps in a process, etc.

Explanation. An explanation entails an accounting for, or the giving of reasons for, an occurrence. It is an effective support when properly applied *because* it satisfies the receiver's curiosity by moving beneath the surface inquiry of "what" into the underpinning question of "why."

Numerical data. Statistics and other numerical data are often required as documentary support, but they are difficult to comprehend and retain because of their abstractness. When it is possible and appropriate to do so, they should be translated into more familiar images: The ratio one to one billion is as one second is to about 34 years.

Quotation. "Quotation" used as a support connotes more than merely quoting testimony; it entails a particularly refined selection of words from another to express your idea with the emotional intensity of a literary passage. Minnick (1979) provides an example of a quotation imbedded in a quotation which in turn is imbedded in a quotation which in turn is imbedded in his words:*

> Winston Churchill used quotation appropriately and well. In a wartime speech on May 19, 1940, he used as a conclusion a stirring and inspirational quotation. He had taken the helm of the British nation just at the moment when the Germans broke through the Maginot Line and were threatening to destroy both the French and the British armies. Having noted the gravity of the situation, he concluded his call for sacrifice and courage with the following words:
>
> "Today is Trinity Sunday. Centuries ago words were written to be a call and a spur to faithful servants of truth and justice.

*Reprinted by permission from *Public Speaking*, by Wayne C. Minnick, Copyright © 1979, Houghton-Mifflin Company, Boston.

"Arm yourselves, and be ye men of valor, and be in readiness
for the conflict, for it is better for us to perish in battle than to
look on the outrage of our nation and our altars. As the will of
God in Heaven, even so let Him do."

Authoritative opinion (testimony). In the authoritative opinion
of the court in the Weeks v. Bailey case (33 N.M. 193, 263, P. 29,
30): "'Testimony' is that species of evidence which is produced
through language of witnesses."

In a less restrictive usage, authoritative opinion may be
paraphrased and used as a support.

Document. Quoting from a formal document rather than from a
literary passage (or from a witness) generates a form of support
used primarily as evidence rather than for clarification or
emphasis. For example: Amendment V of the United States
Constitution insures that: "No person shall be held to answer for a
capital, or otherwise infamous crime, unless on a presentment or
indictment of a Grand Jury . . ., nor shall any person be subject
for the same offense to be twice put in jeopardy of life or
limb . . . ."

Example. A vivid, extended example allows the receiver to
sample, although not necessarily representatively, the concept
being offered. While a sample of one is usually suspect, a single
example gains effectiveness if it appears to the receiver to be
representative. While a list of brief examples may appear more
representative, a single, vivid example generates a greater degree of
vicarious experience and consequent engagement.

Comparison. This support type includes both figurative and
literal analogies as well as direct comparisons. The direct comparison is illustrated thus: The support types of quotation, testimony,
and document are similar in one vital respect—they all rely upon
words supplied by someone other than the speaker.

Contrast. Contrast is the counterpart of comparison. Rather
than seeking similarities among cases, contrast identifies differences or exceptions. A "non-example" is an established support
type which employs contrast. The illustration used for "comparison" above is an instance of a non-example of "contrast." A direct
contrast of "quotation" and "testimony" might focus upon the

literary quality of quotation contrasted from the evidential quality of testimony.

Definition. By "definition" I mean a statement of limits; a boundary. A definition sets down boundaries or shows the precise outlines of the thing defined in order to make it clear. A formally defined statement may be used as a support for a more vaguely or abstractly stated point.

Visual support. Anything that is processed visually and used as a support qualifies as a visual support. The form may vary widely to include: charts, photographs, film clips, maps, drawings, models, or physical objects, etc. Figure 3.2 is a visual support for our present topic of consideration.

It is important to remember the distinction between points and supports. Chapter 9 includes some exercises to develop the ability to discriminate them reliably. Remember that *supports amplify points* in order to clarify, to prove, to render impressive, to provide emphasis, to gain attention, or to arouse emotional responses. Also, remember that a terminal point with its supports constitutes an information chunk—the basic building unit of a message.

The Information Load Matrix

Having grasped "information chunks" and the "obscurity index," the defining variables of the information load matrix, you are now able to calculate the information load of a message. Figure 3.3 displays the matrix. To enter the matrix, count the information chunks on your box-outline and enter the corresponding column. Next, average the obscurity indexes from each initial terminal point on your box-outline and enter the appropriate row. (The final number of terminal points may be greater than the initial number after the tactics have been implemented.) The cell identified by the intersect will indicate the information load on a seven-point scale. The scale-value 4 is the mid-point on the scale and represents an "average" load. Light information loads range from 3 (slightly below average) to 2 (definitely light) to 1 (extremely low). The heavy loads range from 5 (slightly above average) to 6 (definitely heavy) to 7 (extremely overloaded).

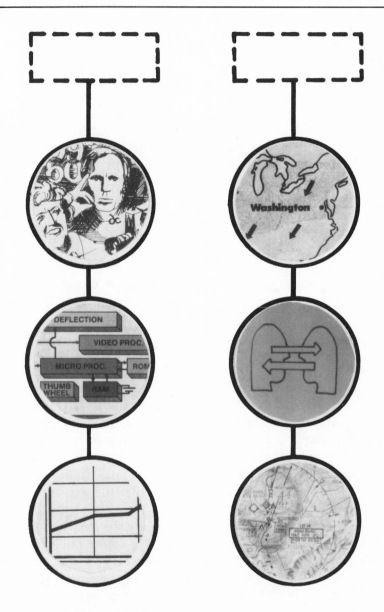

Figure 3.2. Sample of Visual Supports.

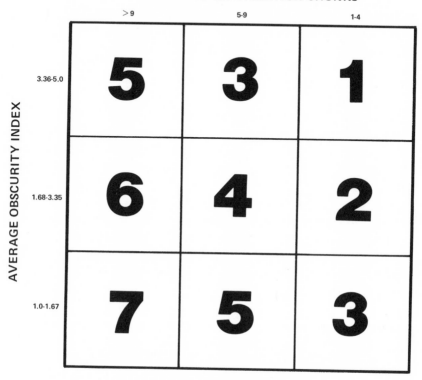

Figure 3.3. Information Load Matrix.
(Cells indicate information load indexes.)

Take an example from Figure 3.1 and assume the following obscurity indexes: I = 3, II A = 4, II B 1 = 3, II B 2 = 5. Since there are four information chunks, enter the column labeled "1-4." Now, enter the row labeled "3.36-5.0," because the average obscurity index is 3.75. The cell value "1" indicates that the information load of this message is extremely below normal. If we were to choose to design the message at a "normal" information load, we could either add more information chunks, or develop the chunks at lower obscurity levels. Of course, changing to a lower obscurity level would change your assumption about your audience. Notice that you cannot detect simply by looking at the box-outline that this is an extremely low information load. We could retain that box-outline and change the obscurity index to 3.0 and thereby raise the information load a whole scale point; that is, we could raise the information load from extremely low to definitely low.

A more common need is to reduce the amount of information permitted into a message. In that case, editing is indicated. There are two basic editing choices: edit by narrowing the scope of the message, or edit by reducing the structural depth. Figure 3.4 illustrates these options.

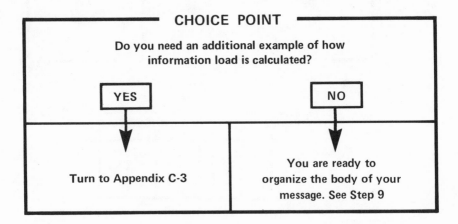

CHOICE POINT

Do you need an additional example of how information load is calculated?

YES

NO

Turn to Appendix C-3

You are ready to organize the body of your message. See Step 9

A.

Editing by Narrowing Scope (The central idea would be modified to reflect the narrower scope.)

B.

Editing by Reducing Structural Depth (Supports would be added directly to points I and II, after the editing.)

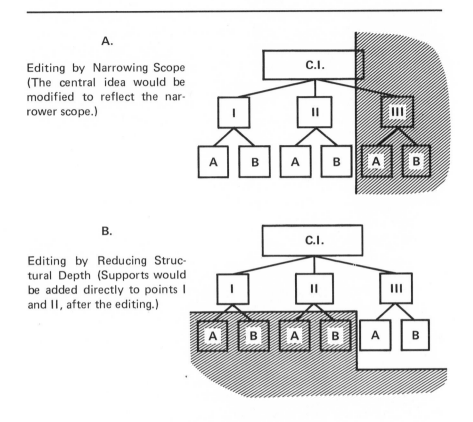

Figure 3.4. Editing Options.

Step 9. Select the Message-Body Organizational Pattern

We have used the box-outline up to this point for our own analytical purposes. For instance, it has served us: to insure that our points have exhausted the central idea, to count the information chunks, to calculate the obscurity index, etc. In other words, it has aided us in making critical design decisions. But we have not yet considered whether this structure and order of presentation (arrangement) are appropriate to the needs of our receivers. This is the time to face those considerations.

Body Structure

In many cases, the strategy will dictate a general pattern for organizing the message body. By the time you have completed your box-outline, you will probably sense the level of structural depth and complexity that will be appropriate. Table 3.1 will assist you in classifying structural options according to the "structural hierarchy." A brief description of each pattern in the structural hierarchy will clarify Table 3.1.

Low-Level Patterns

- *Amplification* develops the central idea directly with supports so that the message body becomes one large information chunk.
- *Topical* organization amplifies several discrete topics treated as an integrated unit.
- *Clustered* structure is the simplist kind of grouping of items according to a shared common quality.
- *Simple Narrative* structure presents a series of simple events sequentially in a "chronological order."
- *Simple Spatial Sequence* represents a line in space presented from one end to the other.
- *Simple Problem-Solution* patterns juxtapose problem and solution without detailed analysis of either.
- *Syllogistic* structure builds main points on the premises and conclusion of any type of syllogism.
- *Simple Comparison/Contrast* organization compares similarities and differences among the readily apparent qualities of two or more things.

Medium-Level Patterns

- *Nested Categories* are similar to clusters, but are more refined and are of greater structural depth. Both a matrix and a categorical outline illustrate nested categories.
- *Flow Chart* structure represents linear sequences with more precision and definition than the simple narrative pattern. It allows branching, converging, and feedback.
- *Spatial Layout* identifies events or items on a planar field rather than in linear sequence.

Table 3.1

The Structural Hierarchy

BODY ORGANIZATION PATTERNS

HIGH LEVEL	MEDIUM LEVEL	LOW LEVEL
Taxonomical	Nested Categories (matrix, categorical)	Amplification Topical Clustered
Circuit	Flow Chart	Simple Narrative (sequential events)
Exploded	Spatial Layout	Simple Spatial Sequence
Algorithmic	Problem-Solving Sequence	Simple Problem-Solution
Imbedded Toulmin Layout	Complete Toulmin Layout	Syllogistic
Pattern/Isolate Transformation	Reframed Structure	Simple Comparison/ Contrast
Compounded	----------------------------------	----------------------------------

- *Problem-Solving Sequence* follows a prescribed pattern of steps leading from problem to solution.
- *Complete Toulmin Layout* involves all seven elements of the Toulmin model (discussed in Appendix B-3) structured so that the claim is the central idea.
- *Reframed Structure* extracts the essential structure from

one situation and uses that structure for representing a different situation. An analogy is such a structure.

High-Level Patterns
- *Taxonomical* structure consists of highly refined nested categories arranged hierarchically.
- *Circuit* structure is a specialized flow chart which incorporates "and-gates" and "or-gates" to regulate necessary and sufficient conditions.
- *Exploded* structure isolates the items of a spatial layout retaining a suggestion of their relationships while emphasizing the characteristics of the parts.
- *Algorithmic* structure is a taxonomical pattern with "choice points" added at every juncture so that each choice dismisses further consideration of the rejected options.
- *Imbedded Toulmin Layout* incorporates a Toulmin pattern as the overall organization pattern, then supports the elements with claims drawn from subordinated Toulmin patterns.
- *Pattern/Isolate Transformation* involves the amplification of an isolate until it is perceived as a pattern, then an element of the pattern is selected as an isolate and the process is repeated. This structure operates in the reverse direction as well.
- *Compounded* structure incorporates two or more structures into one grand structure; for instance: A circuit structure connects two Toulmin layouts through an "or-gate." The warrant of each layout is organized as a matrix, and the data elements are clustered.

Although these lists are not exhaustive, their combinations can create countless patterns for structuring messages. The organizing principle governing the formation of these lists has been to identify the most basic relationship of elements and then to extrapolate that pattern to accommodate increasingly complex relationships. You can add your creations to the lists similarly.

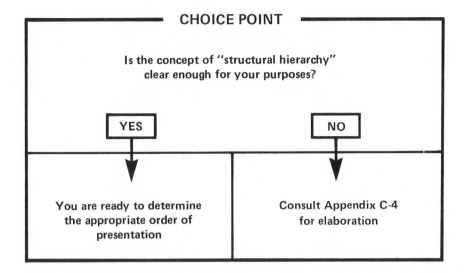

CHOICE POINT

Is the concept of "structural hierarchy" clear enough for your purposes?

YES → You are ready to determine the appropriate order of presentation

NO → Consult Appendix C-4 for elaboration

Order of Presentation

In addition to determining the basic organizational pattern of your message, it is often important to consider the order in which the elements of that structure should be presented. In the case of sequential structures, the order is often obvious, but the cognitive impact caused by different orders of presentation can vary considerably. In some cases, it is enough to be aware of the possibility of considering alternative orders. Other cases require more systematic refinement than intuition permits.

The "Body Structure Matrix" (Figure 3.5) is useful in determining which structural level to use and what order of presentation is probably best for your message. The inputs for this matrix are "information load" (which we have already determined) and "readiness" (which we have estimated in our purpose statement's receiver profile). The cell identified by the appropriate intersect will prescribe five conditions: (1) the level of *structural* complexity, (2) the pattern for *arranging* points, (3) the order for developing *information chunks,* (4) the degree and order for *supports,* and (5) the use of *transitions.* A brief elaboration of each of these items will enable you to use the matrix.

Structure. The principal structural options have been discussed

READINESS	INFORMATION LOAD 6-7	3-5	1-2
H	1. High structure 2. Climactic arrangement 3. Direct support 4. Minimal support a. Specific b. Literal 5. Minimal transitions	1. Medium structure 2. Climactic arrangement 3. Direct support 4. Moderate support a. Mixed b. Mixed 5. Minimal transitions	1. Low structure 2. Climactic arrangement 3. Direct support 4. Full support a. General→specific b. Figurative→literal 5. Minimal transitions
M	1. High structure 2. Mixed arrangement 3. Mixed support 4. Minimal support a. Specific b. Literal 5. Moderate transitions	1. Medium structure 2. Mixed arrangement 3. Mixed support 4. Moderate support a. Mixed b. Mixed 5. Moderate transitions	1. Low structure 2. Mixed arrangement 3. Mixed support 4. Full support a. General→specific b. Figurative→literal 5. Moderate transitions
L	1. High structure 2. Anti-climactic arrangement 3. Implicative support 4. Minimal support a. Specific b. Literal 5. Elaborate transitions	1. Medium structure 2. Anti-climactic arrangement 3. Implicative support 4. Moderate support a. Mixed b. Mixed 5. Elaborate transitions	1. Low structure 2. Anti-climactic arrangement 3. Implicative support 4. Full support a. General→specific b. Figurative→literal 5. Elaborate transitions

General Rules:

1. The higher the information load, the higher the structural complexity should be.
2. High readiness indicates a need for climactic structure.
3. High readiness indicates a need for direct support development.
4. Low information load indicates a need for full support (developing from general to specific and from figurative to literal).
5. Low readiness indicates a need for elaborate transitions.

Figure 3.5. Body Structure Matrix.

in Table 3.1. A cell prescribes either high, middle, or low structural patterns as categorized in that table.

Arrangement. "Arrangement" refers to the order in which the points are presented. Three choices are offered: climactic, anti-climactic, and mixed. The *climactic* arrangement is one which presents the less impressive or less significant points first and continues by adding the next more weighted point, and so on, until the final, most powerful point climaxes the arrangement. The *anti-climactic* arrangement presents the most significant points first and, by increments, finally presents the less impressive points. The *mixed* arrangement presents the strongest points at the beginning and at the end and hides the less significant points in the middle.

Information chunk development. An information chunk, you will recall, is a terminal point with its attendant supports. *Direct* support requires first stating the point then offering the supports. *Implicative* support calls for presenting the supports first and then "inducing" the point from them. *Mixed* support allows for both direct and implicative development within the message.

Degree and order of support. A chunk may have one or several supports. When the support of a point is *minimal*, the supports should be both specific and literal. When *full* support is given to a point, the supports should be presented from the more general to the more specific and from the more figurative to the more literal. *Moderate* support allows some points to be supported fully and others to be supported minimally.

Transitions. Transitions bridge the thought from point to point, and they may be accomplished verbally, visually, musically, etc. The prescriptions in this matrix are related to the transitions' degree of elaboration. *Minimal* transitions may be simply a word, or brief phrase, or perhaps a pause. *Elaborate* transitions may take the form of a story that bridges the thought gap, or perhaps more commonly, a brief summary of the present point and an introduction or framing of the next point. *Moderate* transitions are typically just a sentence or two in length.

Step 10. Check the Outline for Structural Weaknesses

The type of outline you need will vary with the kind of message and the level of development your communication task requires. Some "quick and dirty" messages may need only the original box-outline; others may call for a fully developed box-outline; still others may require a formal complete-sentence outline. Some structural qualities are common to all forms, and those qualities should be examined with care at this point because structural weaknesses, while changeable at this stage, will become locked-in to the design as the process continues if not corrected here.

Assuming that your message requires the full treatment, your outline will evolve through these stages: The original box-outline, derived from analyzing the central idea, will be adapted to accommodate the appropriate tactics. After calculating the information load, you might have to alter the number of information chunks. The body structure must be selected, and the order of presentation for central idea, points, and supports. Finally, that modified and refined box-outline should be translated into a complete sentence outline.

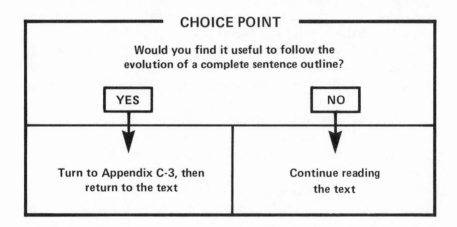

CHOICE POINT

Would you find it useful to follow the evolution of a complete sentence outline?

YES   NO

Turn to Appendix C-3, then   Continue reading
return to the text   the text

Checklist for Structural and Formal Weaknesses

Even when using the models, many students of message design make common errors in their early efforts. I have identified in

Table 3.2, the errors I have found to be most common. Some of the prescriptions on the checklist are obviously fundamental; others may appear arbitrary, yet my experience leads me to believe that precision in structuring a message, even in matters of form, can prevent confusion and oversight. If you examine your outlines in light of each item on the checklist and make the necessary corrections, your message body should be adequately designed in terms of information control. We are now ready to place the body into an appropriate context and to refine its design in terms of message complexity.

Table 3.2

Checklist for Structural and Formal Weaknesses

DESCRIPTION OF WEAKNESS	VISUAL CUES	
	INCORRECT	CORRECT
1. Central idea is missing.		
2. Central idea is labeled as a point rather than verbally.		
3. Item which does not divide is labeled as a point.		
4. Attempt is made to divide a point with supports.		
5. Terminal points are left unfinished. They should terminate either with support or acknowledgment.		
6. Information chunks are appended to a support.		
7. Too many points are left unnested.		

Table 3.2 Continued

---

8. Labels are used improperly.

     A. _____
       I. _____
         a. _____
           1. _____

     I. _____
       A. _____
         1. _____
           a. _____

9. A point standing alone indicates absence of a division.

     I. _____
     A. _____
     II. _____
     A. _____
       1. _____

     I. _____
     A. _____
     B. _____
     II. _____
     A. _____
       1. _____
       2. _____
     B. _____

10. Unindented points imply confused subordination.

     I. _____
     A. _____
     1. _____
     2. _____
     B. _____
     II. _____

     I. _____
     A. _____
     1. _____
     2. _____
     B. _____
     II. _____

11. Supports are improperly labeled. Reservation of alphanumeric labels for points prevents confusion of points and supports.

     (A) – (B) – (C)

     (EX) – (DEF) – (QUO)

12. Incomplete sentences encourage guessing and may result in ambiguity or vagueness.

     I. Single word or phrase   II. A sentence completes the thought.

PART II

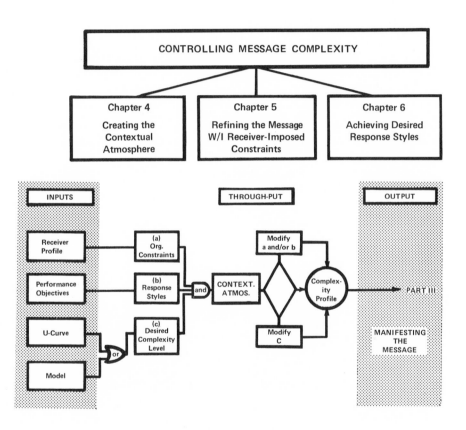

CONTROLLING MESSAGE COMPLEXITY

Chapter 4	Chapter 5	Chapter 6
Creating the Contextual Atmosphere	Refining the Message W/I Receiver-Imposed Constraints	Achieving Desired Response Styles

INPUTS

THROUGH-PUT

OUTPUT

Receiver Profile

Performance Objectives

U-Curve

Model

(a) Org. Constraints

(b) Response Styles

(c) Desired Complexity Level

or

and

CONTEXT. ATMOS.

Modify a and/or b

Modify C

Complex-ity Profile

PART III

MANIFESTING THE MESSAGE

Part II

Controlling Message Complexity

Part II is concerned with everything in the denominator of the basic model. Specifically, it includes Chapters 4, 5, and 6: "Creating the Contextual Atmosphere," "Refining the Message within Receiver-Imposed Constraints," and "Achieving Desired Response Styles," respectively. Steps 11 through 15 are directly related to *how* the message context is to be created.

The rhetorical canons of invention and disposition are of primary concern for the management and control of message content. But the canons of memory, disposition, style, and delivery are more appropriately considered in relation to message complexity.

This model has categorized numerous findings from the psychology of perception, learning, and cognition into six clusters. These clusters, "the elements of complexity," are systemically interactive, yet they "center" conveniently into the stimulus, organismic, or response components of the model. This organization of a large number of psychological concepts and principles into six main concepts not only has resulted in the selection of the relevant findings, but also has rendered them manageable. By slicing the conceptual "apple" along different axes, relevant and manageable pieces have emerged.

This identification of message complexity elements enables us to view messages in terms of their complexity profiles, and in doing so, allows us to visualize the more subtle aspects of a message and to compare that message with another along the same subtle dimensions. Not only does the ability to compose messages at this pattern-level enable us to design messages more effectively, but also it permits us to make meaningful comparisons and controls in our empirical research efforts.

It may be helpful in conceptualizing message complexity to think of it as the *context* which contains and shapes the *content*. The same wine may be displayed in either a dusty green bottle or in a cut-crystal decanter. The context often influences the perception of the content. The complexity of a message characterizes non-verbally the many assumptions the source has made about the receiver and the situation.

The information-control considerations of a message can be approached sequentially, as we have seen in the linear model which introduces Part I. Complexity control, however, is less susceptible to such a process treatment. Complexity is better managed when viewed as a system rather than a process; thus, the "steps" at this stage are more of a convenience than a necessity.

Some working definitions of the complexity elements will clarify the following explanation of the schematic frontispiece for Part II, thus providing an overview for the next three chapters.

With these basic working definitions at hand, we can now explore the frontispiece schematic. The receiver profile, drawn from the receiver-description in the purpose statement, provides sophistication/readiness input which identifies restrictions on the design referred to as organismic constraints. The performance objectives from the purpose statement also provide input to enable desired response styles to be translated into the aloofness/tension dimensions. A third input into this system prescribes an optimum total complexity level. This prescription may be derived from empirically plotted "U-curves" or from profiles of successful model messages.

These three inputs exhaust the available degrees of freedom so that the contextual atmosphere (defined by diversity/density) is a fixed quantity. However, within this fixed quantity, trade-offs can be made to allow diversity and density to vary. If the resulting profile is unsatisfactory and the overall complexity level is unchangeable, then adjustments must be made in either the organismic variables, or in the response variables. Changes in either of these should be reflected in a revised purpose statement. But if changes are unacceptable in either of these categories, the only alternative is to change the target complexity level. Once an acceptable trade-off is discovered, the message complexity profile can be completed, and we can exit the system and go on to Part III.

We should note that because of the systemic interactions among these complexity components, the schematic presented here is only one of several acceptable ones. As was mentioned earlier, the "process" is only a convenience at this stage, and it is not to be regarded as rigid or inflexible. A designer could begin with given values for the contextual atmosphere and organismic constraints, for example, and derive the values for response style. Given any two values and a total complexity level, the third value can be derived.

Chapter 4

INFORMATION LOAD AND BODY STRUCTURE	SUPPORT TACTICS AND OBSCURITY INDEX	PURPOSE STATEMENT

CONTEXTUAL ATMOSPHERE	ORGANISMIC CONSTRAINTS	RESPONSE STYLES

Central Idea

The structured content of your message, achieved through the information-control processes, can be placed into the desired "contextual atmosphere" created by the selection of appropriate levels of diversity and density.

Step 11. Identify the Appropriate Diversity/Density Profile.

Objectives

1. To recognize the role of "set" in the perception of message content.
2. To recall the descriptors for each cell in the contextual atmosphere matrix.
3. To recognize the cognitive patterns associated with the cell descriptors in the conceptual atmosphere matrix.
4. To recognize exemplar social contexts associated with cell descriptors in the contextual atmosphere matrix.
5. To scale diversity and density reliably.
6. To recognize strengths and weaknesses of various contextual atmosphere profiles.
7. To recognize the relationship between the contextual atmosphere profile and the total message complexity level.

Chapter 4

Creating the Contextual Atmosphere

When a professional proofreader scans a page of print, misspellings, broken type, and awkward spacing seem to spring off the page into his or her attention. A novice would have to search for the errors and even then would probably miss some. The difference between the proofreader and the novice is that the proofreader has established a psychological "set" or predisposition to perceive the errors. Similarly, if you become hungry when driving, you develop a "set" to perceive signs and billboards of eating establishments. When someone is unconfident, he or she may pick out innocent remarks from the conversation and interpret them as insults. The point of these examples is that we perceive our environment according to our psychological set. We see our world through an "idiosyncratic set of goggles."

The concept of "set" is a well-established psychological phenomenon. Its relevance to designing messages is that by controlling certain qualities of the signal, we can create a context which predisposes our receivers to perceive our message content in somewhat predictable ways. Consider the non-verbal cues (signals) we experience in a courtroom, or a nightclub, or a rock concert, or a wrestling match. Each of these environments or "atmospheres" almost compels a different pattern of emotion and cognition. And these contextual atmospheres are functions of the signal characteristics of diversity and density. Since every message has some degree of each of these elements, every message contributes in part, at least, to the psychological set through which receivers filter the message content. The "contextual atmosphere matrix" suggests guidelines for creating an environment, through the message itself, which will increase the probability of achieving the source's purpose.

The Matrix

The Contextual Atmosphere Matrix (Figure 4.1) is defined by the signal characteristics of diversity and density. Its nine cells require only brief elaboration. Let us examine each cell in turn according to the kind of atmosphere created by the various combinations of diversity and density levels.

Ecstatic

An ecstatic atmosphere is generated by high levels of both diversity and density. A multi-media barrage in which a great deal of information is presented in a short time through several audio and video channels can have an almost "electrifying effect." Often after only a few moments in this sensory-overloaded environment, people report "tripping-out" or (in a more classical term) being "transported." They cease being aware of the technology that creates the signal and begin to view the content almost hallucino-genically. To be ecstatic means to come out of oneself—to be extended beyond the present moment or place—to become enraptured.

Under what motivation would a message designer deliberately place receivers in this state? It is fairly obvious that critical powers are at a minimum under these conditions. Persuasion, conversion, transformation, and "bandwagoning" are much more easily accomplished when the receiver is in a state of ecstasy. But sometimes message designers generate this state for less manipulative ends. It may be desirable to force receivers to break out of the conceptual blockages caused by a preoccupation with the "iso-lates" of a situation and to view the matter from a "pattern-level" view. *Pattern recognition* is the dominant cognitive activity, while *rapture* is the dominant emotional state.

A specific case will illustrate how pattern recognition was achieved through a highly diverse and dense message. In an introductory theory course in communication studies, my col-leagues and I wanted to create an awareness of the major patterns

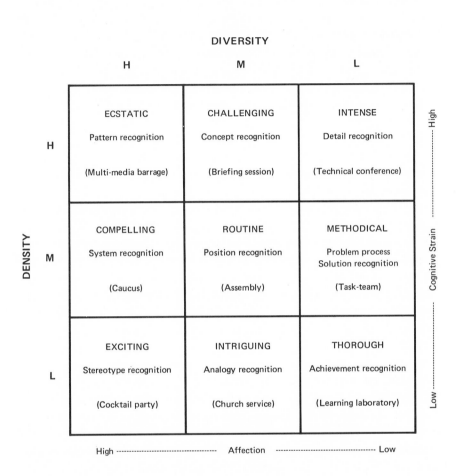

Figure 4.1. Contextual Atmosphere Matrix.

and connections of communication theory as they evolved through 4,000 years of western civilization. We accomplished this pattern-view in 45 minutes with five screens and stereophonic recording. We chose not to present a shallow overview of six or seven major contributions, but rather we employed hundreds of slides of specific historical personages, scenes, and artifacts. Our students appeared to grasp the overview we were trying to create and they reported being "transported" in the process.

Challenging

When density is held at a high level and diversity is reduced to a moderate level, the dominant cognitive process is concept recognition. To process a dense message with only moderate diversity is challenging because the receiver must rely more upon himself or herself than upon the signal to generate images fast enough to keep up with the content flow. Formal briefing sessions are *challenging* in this respect and facilitate *conceptualization*. Concept recognition, in this usage, lies between pattern recognition and detail recognition. A simple analogy assigns concept recognition to the naked-eye domain, where detail and pattern recognition are assigned to the domains of the microscope and the telescope, respectively.

I was once contracted to create a course on briefing techniques for the U.S. Army Corps of Engineers. The goal of the course was to train briefing officers to enable visiting Generals and Senators, etc., to conceptualize existing and future projects in a very brief time period. An examination of the successful briefing sessions revealed signal characteristics of high density and only moderate diversity. Usually the diversity was achieved through a live speaker, an overhead projector, a few maps, and a series of projected slides.

Intense

Defined by high density and low diversity, the cell descriptor "intense" is associated with the cognitive processes related to *detail recognition*. Visualize a conference of technicians, academics, or scientists where technical papers are presented to their colleagues. The attention devoted to precision and detail far exceeds the level normally appropriate for a popular audience. Now visualize one of the speaker's presentations: it is being read from a manuscript with little vocal variety; you are able to see only a speaker behind the lectern and an occasional chart or graph, yet within 12 or 15 minutes he or she reports on a study that required a year to conduct. We have here high density, low diversity, and an atmosphere of great *intensity*.

Compelling

By reducing the density of an otherwise ecstatic atmosphere, the designer can generate a compelling mood. A caucus at a political convention illustrates this environment. Business is conducted efficiently under the pressure of time, so the density is moderate, and there is high diversity among the people's appearance, vocal quality and patterns, thought processes, etc. A clear process is obscured by the numerous *systemic interactions* and *transactions* taking place. It is much easier to recognize the complex system under these conditions than it is to follow a linear process to its conclusion. The "all-at-onceness" system *compels* rather than directs one's attention and involvement.

Routine

In an assembly with a central focal point, such as a stage or an elevated position for a person presiding, as contrasted with a caucus, the moderate diversity modifies the compelling into the routine. It is relatively easy under these *routine* conditions to *recognize positions* taken by different spokespersons. If a message designer has no other basis for diversity, for density, or vice versa, trading off this balance is probably the most appropriate choice. At least, it is comparatively safe.

Methodical

The methodical atmosphere which is compatible with a task-group's or production team's efforts requires moderate density of content, but little distraction caused by even moderate diversity. By keeping diversity low under these conditions, the cognition can be rather linear. Linearity, of course, is a prerequisite to employing sophisticated processes and logical sequences.

An accrediting team examining the curriculum and administration of a university requires this kind of *methodical* atmosphere, as does a medical team attempting to *diagnose* a particular case. A level of density that provides information at a rate too rapid for complete assimilation would be as inappropriate as not getting enough information or having it trickle in at time-wasting rates.

Exciting

The high diversity and low density of a cocktail party conversation provide the conditions for an exciting atmosphere, but notice that "exciting" connotes less potency than either "compelling" or "ecstatic." This atmosphere is typically pleasant, yet typically "lightweight." One has to spread himself or herself too thinly in order to be sociable to be able to delve into any topic requiring high or moderate density. In the cocktail party environment, cognitive processes seem to be set to generate as well as to function at a level of hasty generalization and over-generalization. The *creation* and *recognition of stereotypes* are fostered under these conditions.

Perhaps you remember the format of the original "Laugh-In" television show. The overall format was highly diverse, but quite low in density. But the cocktail party feature of that format was particularly illustrative of this *exciting* atmosphere.

Intriguing

By reducing some of the diversity of a cocktail party but retaining a moderate amount through order of service, trappings, costumes, paraphernalia, music, etc., conservative church services create an intriguing atmosphere. And in this context, the *intrigue* is heightened by the use of *analogies* and *parables*, which have a special compatibility with the cognitive processes used to process the typically low density messages. Some *avant garde* church services create more excitement than intrigue, and some evangelistic services strive for rapture and ecstasy. Yet, as these environmental contexts change, so do the emotional and cognitive processes involved.

Thorough

To create a context in which knowledge, skills, habits, etc., can be recognized and then acquired, the designer should, if all other conditions are equal, strive to incorporate a low density/low diversity profile into the message. The *thoroughness* required to perform at this cognitive level of *achievement recognition* requires slow movement through the content, with a lot of redundancy and often only surface analysis. At the same time, distractions should be kept to a minimum.

Recall a learning laboratory with students seated in carrels at computers, working their way through programmed learning material. Or, visualize a student in a language laboratory listening to a redundant treatment of German declination on a tape cassette while looking at a printed list of examples. Both diversity and density are as low as is appropriate for the cognitive task at hand.

Two rules-of-thumb should be kept in mind when using the contextual atmosphere matrix. First, the degree of *cognitive strain* experienced by the receiver tends to increase as message density increases. In other words, denser messages require the receiver to think harder. The second general rule is that the degree of *affection* experienced by the receiver tends to increase as diversity is increased. Receivers tend to like a lot of variety in their messages, even though high diversity is not always appropriate to the conceptual task or the emotional state. In some cases, diversity and density should be "traded off" in order to keep the overall complexity total within fixed limits. But when more freedom is available within the complexity total, it is often useful to increase diversity (to heighten appeal) as the subject matter requires increased density. In one study (Koegel and Marsh, 1979), we found that the best profile for the composite value of both "liking" and "learning" the message was high diversity and high density, coupled with high aloofness and low tension.

The Diversity Scale

Diversity, as is so with each of the other complexity elements, is scaled along three defining dimensions. By separating out these dimensions, our estimates become more reliable. Each dimension is assumed to be of equal importance to the concept, thus allowing us to average our estimates to find the overall diversity value. Incidentally, all complexity elements and their dimensions are scaled on a seven-point scale.

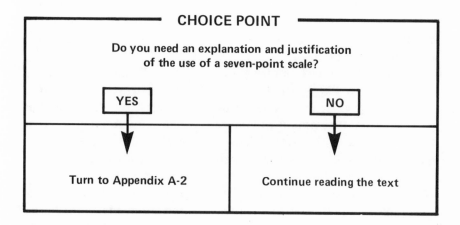

Let's begin with a working definition of diversity and then refine it by defining its dimensions:

Diversity is a measure of how much *variety* is manifested within the total message context. It is conveniently estimated by scaling *audible variety, visual variety*, and *structural variety*.

Audible Variety

A single, monotonous voice on a tape recording would be very low in audible variety. By interspersing live-voice comments by a different speaker with rich tone and varied inflection, we would increase the audible variety of the message. We could increase it even more by adding an array of live voices (male, female; young, old; rich, thin; etc.). Further, we could add some sound effects and mood music, and vary the recording speed. Finally, to achieve a very high level of audible variety, we could distort the sound with filters and echo chambers, or we could have sounds coming from more than one direction or displayed simultaneously instead of sequentially. It is impossible to present an exhaustive checklist of ways to identify audible variety (or any of the other dimensions, for that matter). But by understanding the concept, you can soon develop such an awareness of audible variety that you will be able to discriminate one signal from another with reliably scaled estimates.

Visual Variety

Start with the simplist visual array you can generate that might accompany a verbal message. Perhaps it would simply be an illuminated projection screen or a blank wall. Add to that a color (either projected or printed). Then alternate colors, mix colors, create dynamic color patterns with projected emulsions of various color combinations. Next add a person, then a chorus dressed in different costumes. Next project a photograph on a screen, then a motion picture. Add further, multiple screens, split screens, stage props, spotlights, mood lights, modeling lights, make-up, banners, posters, and words projected on the screen. Pass out to your audience printed programs or handouts, including cartoon characters, printed material in a variety of type faces, montages, collages, schematic drawings, etc. With each addition, you increase visual variety. Your message becomes "busier" because of the increased activity in the visual perceptual system. Of course, you can generate such visual diversity that its interaction with other sensory systems will increase the total message diversity. For example, by blurring images, using strobe lights, and simulating motion visually you could activate the basic-orienting sensory system and cause your viewer to lose his or her balance or even to lose a recent meal. Again, there are so many possibilities for creating visual variety that no checklist could be adequate. It is better to understand the concept and then to practice scaling every chance you get.

Structural Variety

Less obvious than either audible or visual variety is the range within which a signal can be structured. Perhaps the simplist case would be a static display of a single, plain object. But even the addition of another identical object changes the structural characteristics. The two objects could be viewed as a pair or as two separate objects. The way objects, images, thoughts, words, paragraphs, etc., are displayed can vary by the way they are framed, grouped, sequenced, nested, gridded, iterated, repeated, etc.

Contrast, for example, the simple musical motif of "Happy Birthday to You" with a classic sonata. Rather than being limited to a single, simple structure, the sonata gains diversity by being structured into various movements, which are themselves structured differently on several dimensions. The first movement might be *allegro* (quick) and structured with three different themes, each with its internal structure of introduction, development, and conclusion. The second movement might be *largo* (slow) and developed in an A-B-A pattern. The third movement, traditionally in dance tempo, might be structured with an exposition, a development, and a reiteration. And, finally, the fourth movement could be rapid tempo, with a structure which develops several variations on a theme. Aside from other musical qualities, like diversity of instrumentation, timbre, etc., the structure of the composition provides an important source of diversity.

An excellent example of structural diversity in a film is Saul Bass's *Why Man Creates* (1968). Each of several episodes making up the total message is structurally unique. Some are narrative in structure, some topical, some montaged, others logical, and some poetic. Some episodes state a point explicitly and then support it; others develop examples and merely imply the point. At places transitions are employed; at other places they are omitted. Then, overall there is a superimposed structure which integrates the various episodes into one harmonious whole. A wide range of structural variety thus increases the overall message diversity.

The scale we use in measuring (estimating) diversity takes this form:

DIVERSITY   1 2 3 4 5 6 7

Audible Variety	Low _ _ _ _ _ _ _ High
Visual Variety	Low _ _ _ _ _ _ _ High
Structural Variety	Low _ _ _ _ _ _ _ High

The Density Scale

A working definition provides an appropriate perspective before defining the dimensions for scaling density:

Density, diversity's counterpart, is a measure of how "heavy" the message is psychologically. Density is conveniently estimated by scaling rate of change, redundancy, and structural depth. In other words: how frequently does the style, topic, or delivery change? How much repetition (at any level of structure) is there? How finely are ideas analyzed into their components?

Rate of Change

A low-density message might leave the receiver with the impression that it "dragged." It might seem to dwell on a topic overlong. It might be accompanied by a feeling of wanting it to move along more rapidly to its conclusion. These are not the feelings experienced by an instrument-rated pilot, however, when he or she attempts to copy a flight clearance from a busy air traffic controller. Such clearances are of vital importance; they are precise and very brief. A pilot has to practice copying and comprehending clearances because of their high density in general and their very rapid rate of change in particular. Read this example as quickly as you can to get a feel for rapid change rate.

> *Memphis Ground*: ATC CLEARS ZEPHYR THREE FOUR FIVE SIX JULIET TO NASHVILLE AIRPORT VICTOR FIVE FOUR SOUTH, VICTOR SEVEN. MAINTAIN FOUR THOUSAND UNTIL FIFTEEN MILES SOUTHEAST OF THE MEMPHIS VOR. MAIN FIVE THOUSAND, OVER.
>
> You: (Read back the clearance clearly, concisely, and with no errors—it says here.) (Kershner, 1977)*

"Rate of change" is an estimate of the message's "activity" dimension in the terms of Osgood and Tannenbaum's "semantic space." Its value increases as transitions are omitted and topics or moods change abruptly. It often seems staccato or choppy. There is no "slack time" provided. This rapid change rate contributes directly to the overall density of the message.

Redundancy

Redundancy is characterized by a super-abundance or superflu-

---

*Reprinted by permission from *The Instrument Flight Manual*, Third Edition, by William K. Kershner, Copyright © 1977 by The Iowa State University Press, Ames, Iowa.

idity—an overflowing of symbols to express the meaning intended. It is also characterized by a high degree of repetition, reiteration, restatement, paraphrase, and restatement. Notice the redundancy in this paragraph. It makes the same point over and over again.

Consider the visual redundancy in this example. Cover the lower part (below the line) of the word printed below, and then ask someone what the word is. He or she will probably be able to identify it. The part of the word that was covered was therefore redundant, not essential; but the redundancy may reduce the cognitive strain involved:

EXAMINATION

But notice that there is redundancy even in the part that is above the line. Try quizzing a different person now by covering up everything after EXAM as well as everything below the line. The chances are good that even that fraction of the original visual stimulus can also be identified.

Redundancy can take place at several different levels: Supports provide redundancy for points. Introductions and summaries provide redundancy at a different structural level. The grammar is another source of redundancy as in: "The old man had lived a full life before he died at ninety." Visual channels can be redundant of sound tracks. Seeing the word and hearing it simultaneously also creates redundancy.

By becoming aware of the redundancy in the messages we receive, we can begin to establish a sense of what is a normal amount or what is an excessive or an impoverished amount. The point to remember about redundancy's role in contributing to the density element of message complexity is this: density increases as redundancy is *reduced.*

Structural Depth
Under diversity, we discussed structural variety, which is

different from structural depth. Structural variety is concerned with how many different organizing patterns are contained within a message, but structural depth is related to how much division, or nesting, or interlocking there is in the message.

Wang (1970) has found "mean linguistic depth," the number of "self-embedded structures," and the number of "conjoining transformations" in the derivational history of the sentence to be good predictors of sentence comprehensibility. But beyond the structural depth at the sentence level, the degree to which the content is analyzed also affects comprehensibility by regulating message density. By paraphrasing Wang and extending her findings to the domain of message structure rather than to sentence structure, we can clarify the concept of structural depth. Thus, we can infer these general rules:

1. The same information presented in two separated messages has a lower level of structural depth than if it were presented in one message.
2. Points separated and treated sequentially have a lower level of structural depth than when they are "nested" within the same unit.
3. Points that are supported directly are of a lower level of structural depth than ones which are sub-divided before they are supported at the terminal division level. Figure 4.2 attempts to illustrate these ideas graphically.

Density Scale

Estimates of the density dimensions are conveniently quantified with the following seven-point scale:

1 2 3 4 5 6 7

Rate of Change	Low _ _ _ _ _ _ _	High
Redundancy	High _ _ _ _ _ _ _	Low
Structural Depth	Low _ _ _ _ _ _ _	High

Complexity-Scale Reliability

There is likely to be a wide range of variance among raters and

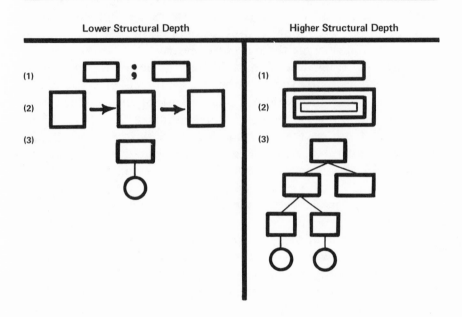

Figure 4.2. Visual Representation of Structural Depth.

even between subsequent ratings of the same message by the same raters until the working definitions presented here become enriched with practice. A method I have found effective for reducing the variance of judgment is to have a group rate a message on all complexity dimensions. Then I identify the highest and the lowest raters on each dimension and have them present the rationales for their choices. This kind of dialogue refines the working definitions more with each repetition. The whole group acquires a tacit-knowledge definition of each concept through this process. Even though no one can define explicitly what these refinements are, the raters can make finer and more consistent discriminations as a result of this interaction. I have trained novices in six hours to rate the complexity of messages where one standard deviation was .37 scale points on the seven-point scale. In other words, 68 percent of the group's judgments clustered within a range of .74 scale points. This level of precision renders this scaling instrument very useful for message designing.

Step 11. Identify the Appropriate Diversity/Density Profile

It should be obvious by now that the contextual atmosphere created by a message is the function of the diversity and density relationship and that that relationship is controllable by the message designer. There are some advantages to representing this relationship graphically in the form of a bar-graph I call a "profile." Not only does the profile help the designer communicate better with other designers, directors, or producers, but it also enables him or her to compare one message with other segments. In other words, the contextual atmosphere of a message can be quickly compared with the organismic constraint segment or the response requirement segment of the message in order to determine where "trade-offs" are possible if the overall complexity level must be adjusted. Figure 4.3 illustrates two diversity/density profiles (scaled on a seven-point scale) for quick comparison. By interpreting these profiles with the DIV/DEN Matrix, you can see quickly how the messages create different contextual atmospheres.

Message profiles can be identified in either of two ways. First, you can determine what values to assign to each of the diversity or density scale dimensions, average the dimension values, then plot them onto a profile scale. Or, you can begin with a given profile and translate it into scale-dimension values required to manifest that profile. The "given" profile may be the product of a decision reached after consulting the contextual atmosphere matrix, or it may be the profile of a message you have scaled for use as a model.

Selecting the Medium for Your Message

There are several factors that influence the choice of the medium by which your message design will become a reality. Some considerations are imposed by external conditions such as availability, cost, durability, convenience, etc. Those concerns, while they certainly influence the choice of medium and conse-

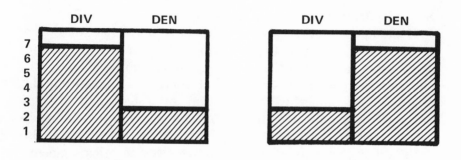

Figure 4.3. DIV/DEN Profiles on Seven-Point Scale Provide Quick Comparison.

quently the message design, do not emanate from the more fundamental considerations of message design itself. The relative advantages of various media are adequately discussed elsewhere and therefore lie beyond the scope of this book. I believe it is generally more desirable, unless the external considerations are a "given," to select the medium according to requirements of the particular message content and message complexity properties.

Table 4.1, summarized and interpreted from Travers (1970), provides a useful basis for making media decisions. Before selecting a medium, you should determine whether the audible or the visual channel should be dominant. Follow that decision with a determination of the required level of diversity. Now you are in a better position to select the most appropriate medium.

Table 4.1

Guidelines for Selecting Audible or Visual Channels

Use the:

AUDIBLE CHANNEL	VISUAL CHANNEL
1. When immediate attention is required. (Crucial information is better insured of reception when the audible mode is used.)	1. When messages are complex.
	2. When referability is important.
	3. When messages are long.
2. When a relatively simple arrangement is employed.	4. When environment is noisy.
3. When fewer dimensions are required. (Audible dimensions include: frequency, amplitude, complexity, duration, and localization.)	5. When arrangement is complicated.
	6. When precise spatial discrimination is important.
4. When precise spatial discrimination *is not* required.	7. When simultaneous presentation is desired.
5. When sequential presentation is appropriate.	8. When more dimensions are required. (Visual dimensions include: two spatial coordinates, intensity, wavelength time, depth, color, and motion.)
6. When electronic amplification, transmission, or recording is possible or desired.	

Chapter 5

INFORMATION LOAD AND BODY STRUCTURE	SUPPORT TACTICS AND OBSCURITY INDEX	PURPOSE STATEMENT

CONTEXTUAL ATMOSPHERE	ORGANISMIC CONSTRAINTS	RESPONSE STYLES

Central Idea

Your assessment of your receivers' levels of sophistication and readiness can guide your choice of dispositional patterns, graphics, and language style for the further refinement of your message.

Steps

12. Select the Appropriate Dispositional Patterns.
13. Select the Appropriate Graphics.
14. Select the Appropriate Language Style.

Objectives

1. To scale sophistication and readiness reliably.
2. To recall the cell descriptors of the General SOP/REA Matrix.
3. To assign a list of cell descriptors to blank SOP/REA Matrices.
4. To recall and define Quintilian's dispositional elements.
5. To assign a given message to its appropriate dispositional matrix cell.
6. To recognize guidelines for graphic and photographic composition.
7. To recognize rules-of-thumb for selecting graphics.
8. To recall the characteristics of the Basic Graphics Matrix.
9. To assign a given graphic to its appropriate cell.
10. To recognize four basic language styles.
11. To quantify a given message reliably for difficulty and interest.
12. To prescribe a language style for a given audience and strategy.

Chapter 5

Refining the Message
Within Receiver-Imposed Constraints

Think for a moment of how you might tell a story differently to a trial lawyer and again to a junior high school student. You would surely present two different messages, and they would differ according to your estimate of your receiver's differing levels of *sophistication*. Sophistication is one of the constraints imposed upon a message by the receiver. Another major constraint on your freedom to design a message is the *readiness* level of your receiver. To explain readiness, I will refer to a study by Trabasso (1968), who plotted learning curves for both fast and slow learners. After the curves were generated, he plotted them backwards from a common terminal point in time. (Originally, the learning tasks were plotted as beginning simultaneously and ending at different times.) The results were unexpected but provided a very plausible explanation of the difference between the fast- and slow-learner groups.

Figure 5.1 illustrates that the curves were almost identical except for the long "tail" on the "slow" group's curve. Trabasso concluded that since the association activities were practically congruent between the two groups, the difference lay in the preparation phase that precedes association. In other words, the slow learners took longer to *prepare* for doing the learning task, but when they were *ready* they performed as efficiently as the "fast" group. The fast group, therefore, had higher *readiness* than the slow group. Instruction, it seems, should be concentrated on developing readiness, rather than on association, in order to improve the performance of the slow learners.

103

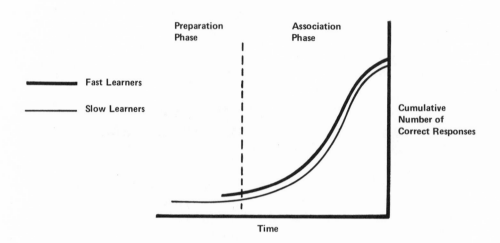

Figure 5.1. Learning Curves Plotted Backwards to Illustrate Differences Between Fast and Slow Learners. (This curve has been simplified for illustrative purposes; it is not based on Trabasso's actual data.)

An examination of the working definitions for sophistication and readiness will prepare you to understand the generalized SOP/REA Matrix as it relates to message refinements dictated by the receivers' capabilities and limitations.

Sophistication. Sophistication is paired with readiness to determine what kinds of constraints the receiver imposes upon the message design. The sophistication level of a receiver is rather constitutional in that, although changeable, it tends to be stable. It is similar to one's cognitive style and native ability combined. We can estimate sophistication by scaling the ability and willingness to handle abstraction, implicitness, and precision. Actually, sophistication describes a state of the receiver rather than a characteristic of the message. A message designed to accommodate a sophisticated receiver would be more properly identified as "erudite," but this term often seems more awkward than "sophistication."

Readiness. The counterpart of sophistication is readiness. Even though a receiver may be sophisticated, he or she may not be able to process a message effectively because of some temporary emotional state or cognitive blockage. Readiness is an estimate of how much preparation within the message is required to render the receiver "ready" to process the message content. Specifically, we look for how much framing of the topic is needed, how much the relevance of the topic to the receiver should be stressed, and to what degree memory aids are needed to achieve the objectives. Technically, the receiver is "ready," and the message adapted to him or her is an "austere" message.

The General SOP/REA Matrix

Just as a matrix was useful in helping us to make design decisions about creating the desired contextual atmosphere of our messages, matrix structure provides insights into ways of refining our messages according to the sophistication and readiness of our receivers. We will examine specifically how to make decisions about the overall structure (disposition) of messages, about appropriate graphic styles, and about appropriate language styles. Since all of these applications are functions of sophistication and readiness, it will be useful to examine first the generalized properties of the cells created by the SOP/REA general matrix presented in Figure 5.2.

Message Correlates to Sophistication

When we define the complexity components of the message as constrained by the receiver, we should more properly use terms that describe the message rather than the receiver. "Sophistication" and "readiness" are actually properties of the receiver. "Erudition" and "austerity" are properties of a message that correlate with the needs of sophisticated and ready receivers, respectively.

If we design "high austerity" messages to serve "high sophisticated" receivers, we can establish the continuum that defines the *columns* of the general matrix. By defining that continuum with three cell categories, we have:

SOPHISTICATION

	H	M	L
H	ERUDITE/ AUSTERE	ELEGANT/ AUSTERE	PLAIN/ AUSTERE
M	ERUDITE/ SUBTLE	ELEGANT/ SUBTLE	PLAIN/ SUBTLE
L	ERUDITE/ FULL	ELEGANT/ FULL	PLAIN/ FULL

READINESS

Figure 5.2. General SOP/REA Matrix.

Sophistication

High	Middle	Low
ERUDITE	ELEGANT	PLAIN

Erudite. An erudite message is one cast in the learned style of scholarship. It is the style appropriate to a graduate seminar, a professional conference presentation, or an advanced textbook.

Elegant. An elegant message is one cast in a gracefully refined style. It is a middle style between erudite and plain and thus supplies the neglected aspects of each of those styles. It is pleasingly contrived, but not studied. It displays a somewhat homey quality, but it is sharpened. Often cleverness and wit are associated with elegance.

Plain. A plain message is cast in a simple, common, homey style. It is down-to-earth, conversational, concrete, and spontaneous.

The Sophistication Scale

The sophistication level of an audience is easily estimated by scaling three dimensions: *abstraction, implicitness,* and *precision.* A brief definition of each, as it is used here, will facilitate your using the scale.

Abstraction. To abstract means to extract from several tangible instances their common qualities. For instance, one can abstract the qualities of trunks, branches, leaves, and roots from several experiences with different trees and then begin to think in terms of "treeness" rather than in terms of oak tree or pine tree. An even higher level of abstraction would involve regarding abstracted "concepts" in terms of their relationship to one another. This operates in developing "propositions," whether syntactical or mathematical. Even greater abstraction is involved when one relates these propositions to one another to create a "system." When we rate a person on the abstraction scale, we are attempting to define the scale point which best represents the dominant or most comfortable abstraction level in that person's mental habits.

Implicitness. Some people can see more easily than others

beneath the surface meaning of a statement, a picture, or an event. Some can see even more deeply beneath the surface to pick up unexpressed meanings from symbolic poetry, non-representational art, or *avant garde* music. This ability to understand without having everything "spelled out" for them is defined by this scale as "high implicitness."

Precision. Perhaps the extreme positions on the precision dimension are "sloppy" and "fussy." The precision scale attempts to estimate to what degree a person requires precisely stated, highly defined, definite, and exact treatment of information. It is a way of estimating to what degree one can tolerate uncertainty or error. A person scored at a level seven might commonly be regarded as compulsive.

When abstraction, implicitness, and precision values are averaged from the following scale, we have a working estimate of our receivers' sophistication level:

SOPHISTICATION (ERUDITE)   1 2 3 4 5 6 7

Abstraction	Low _ _ _ _ _ _ _	High
Implicitness	Low _ _ _ _ _ _ _	High
Precision	Low _ _ _ _ _ _ _	High

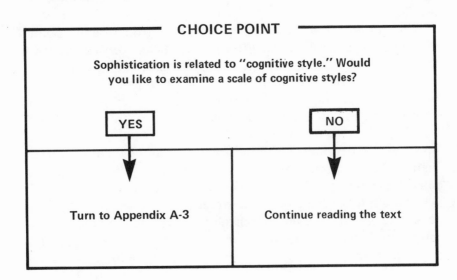

CHOICE POINT

Sophistication is related to "cognitive style." Would you like to examine a scale of cognitive styles?

YES

NO

Turn to Appendix A-3

Continue reading the text

Message Correlates to Readiness

The continuum that relates appropriate message qualities with receivers ranging from high to low readiness consists of "austerity" gradations. This continuum is represented on the matrix in the rows. When we divide these gradations into categories, we have:

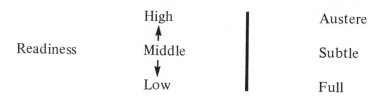

Austere. A message marked by austerity is one characterized by its serious, disciplined, severely simple manifestation. It is "bare bones." It is without ornament. A person who is highly ready to receive a message is likely to be impatient with "frills." Right-to-the-point structure, graphics, and language without motivational appeals, digressions, or "extras" are message qualities appropriate to such receivers. You must not confuse austerity with plainness, discussed above. A message can be both plain and austere, or it could be austere and erudite, as the matrix indicates.

Subtle. As the midpoint between the extremes of "austere" and "full" development, the message of subtle development is characterized by delicate, fine, or faint suggestions, which require a moderate degree of mental acuteness, penetration, and discernment. The "subtle" message points the receiver in the right direction and gives him or her a shove, but neither sends the receiver off on his or her own, nor leads him or her by the hand to the destination.

Full. The "full" development does lead the receiver by the hand to the destination. This treatment employs whatever device is required to render the receiver ready to perceive the source's meaning. It involves elaborated structuring, motivation, and emphasis.

The Readiness Scale

We estimate an audience's readiness by attempting to determine how much *framing* of the message, *emphasis on relevance,* and *assistance with memory* is needed. If our task were to estimate the degree of austerity possessed by a given message, we would scale the message (not the receiver) according to how much these dimensions were reflected in that message. A brief elaboration of each will clarify the use of this scale.

Framing. The degree of framing is a function of establishing a perspective and providing guidance through the message. In designing a message, we attempt to determine how much framing is required by the receiver. In analyzing a given message for framing, on the other hand, we estimate how much was provided. An example of framing would be to set your topic of inflation into the context of the post-World War II economy, then into the perspective of the last decade, and finally, into the frame of the current economic cycle. A person of high readiness would be ready for your topic without this framing. Framing also includes the function of providing continuity through the message as, for example, with well-developed verbal transitions or pointers (in graphics) that direct the course of focus and movement. Goffman (1974) must be credited for this concept which he developed in his definitive work, *Frame Analysis.*

Relevance. When we estimate the degree of relevance we think our audience will require, we look at something related to motivation. A motivated person is more apt to see the relevance of a point than one who is less ready. By stating explicitly why the topic is relevant to the receiver's interest and how a given point or support fits into the larger scheme of things, we provide relevance. Any teacher who has had a pupil hold up a hand and ask, "Why do we have to study this?," should have some insight into the need for making the topic relevant. Indeed, "relevancy" was a battle cry of the militant students of the '70s who were attempting to reform their educational institutions. College professors and administrators had been remiss in estimating the students' need to understand the relevance of such traditional subjects as history and English. The students were so low in readiness, they refused to participate.

Mnemonics. Another dimension that helps to define readiness is the amount of assistance the receiver requires in order to remember important material. The assistance can be rendered in such a simple way as speaking slowly and pausing now and then to allow time for the short-term memory to become fixed in the long-term memory. Or, it may be direct aid, as when the speaker provides a memory aid such as: "You will always be able to remember William Shakespeare's wife's name if you just remember the sentence: "Ann hath a way." There are many techniques and many levels at which they can be employed, but our concern here is with the extent to which they are required by the receiver.

Readiness is the average of our framing, relevancy, and mnemonics estimates, which are easily scaled with this instrument:

READINESS (AUSTERITY)   1 2 3 4 5 6 7

Framing (Required/provided)	High _ _ _ _ _ _ _ Low
Relevance (Required/provided)	High _ _ _ _ _ _ _ Low
Mnemonics (Required/provided)	High _ _ _ _ _ _ _ Low

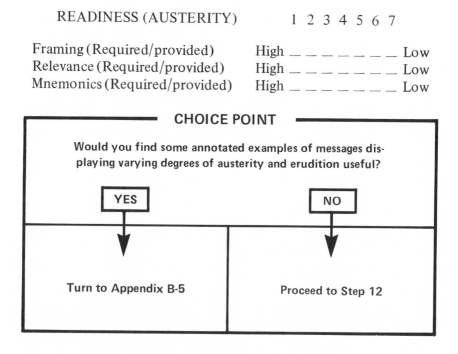

CHOICE POINT

Would you find some annotated examples of messages displaying varying degrees of austerity and erudition useful?

YES

NO

Turn to Appendix B-5

Proceed to Step 12

Step 12. Select Appropriate Dispositional Patterns

Dispositional Patterns
Disposition, the second canon of classical rhetoric, was original-

ly conceived as that source of persuasion which resides in arrangement of persuasive appeals. Classical rhetoric was exclusively concerned with persuasive public speaking. Even though our interests in designing messages carry us well beyond those limitations, there is some traditional wisdom in those ancient precepts. When they are interpreted loosely enough to apply to messages of various strategies, they provide valuable guidelines for making design decisions.

The canon of disposition includes both the arrangement of the major segments of the whole message, as well as the structure and order of presentation of information and appeals within the body of the message. Since we have already considered the selection of message-body organizational patterns, our concern here is with the selection and arrangement of major message components. Since Quintilian's pattern is best defined, I will use his terminology to describe the most common dispositional elements. After defining each concept, we will examine a SOP/REA matrix which facilitates our making design decisions.

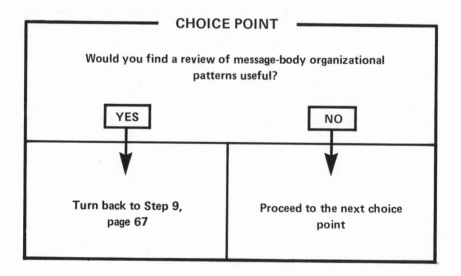

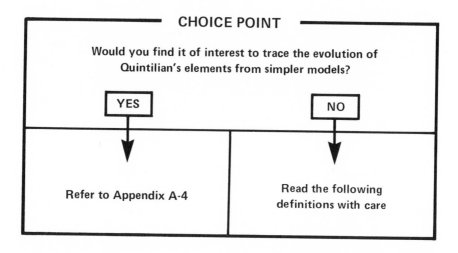

The Exordium. The exordium is that portion of a message's introduction which renders the receivers receptive to the message. Its main function is to predispose the receivers to be attentive. It is a kind of transition from where the receivers have been in their thoughts and activities to concentrated and focused attention on the message proper. Consequently, it may begin anywhere, but it must focus on the message's topic reasonably quickly. Not only does the attention have to be focused quickly, but the receivers' interest should be made at this stage to enhance the credibility of the source (ethos) and to establish identity or common ground between source and receiver.

For many receivers, there is a moment of discomfort or at least uncertainty at the onset of a message which stems from questions about the relevance of the topic, the credibility of the source, the probability of understanding the message, the risk of being manipulated, or simply receiving a fair return on the time invested. Until these uncertainties are quieted, they will continue to distract the receiver from the source's message. It is often advisable to clear these discomforts up before attempting to develop the topic or position.

The Narration (Expository Background). Traditionally, a speaker would present the basic facts which set the case into perspective in the form of a narration. He or she would tell a story in an effort to "reconstruct the crime," for instance, in an appeal to the jury. Story-telling, even when based upon historical fact, lends itself to both slanted presentation and to the building of tension to a climax. It enables the source to provide the expository background the receiver needs in order to understand the main message that is yet to come, and it provides enough time to create the emotional atmosphere or mood which is most conducive to a favorable reception.

I have chosen to refer to this stage as an *expository background* because it need not be narrative in form. Nor is it limited to persuasive applications. Its essential function is to provide an appropriate informational base which will allow the receiver to understand the message that follows. Because its function is to prepare the receiver for the main message, the expository background is a part of the introductory stage.

The Proposition (Central Idea). The central idea of a persuasive or argumentative message is more precisely called a proposition. A proposition is an assertive statement which demands proof or demonstration. Since we are extending these dispositional concepts beyond mere persuasion, I prefer the more generic term "central idea." Since we have discussed the function of the central idea in some detail, further definition at this point is not needed. But one caution is appropriate. A common error in message design is to present the central idea before the receiver is psychologically prepared to grasp it. Since the central idea states the essence of the message in one statement, it is critical that the receiver understand and retain it. Premature exposure can render it ineffective.

The Division. In a persuasive message, the division typically follows the statement of the proposition immediately, and its function is to list all of the issues that are inherent in the proposition. This list, because it is exhaustive, provides an abstract of the persuasive case which follows. It serves not only to emphasize the proposition by elaborating it, but also to preview the message body.

In non-persuasive messages, the division serves those functions as well except that rather than listing issues, it outlines the main points to be developed in the body. This preview helps to orient the receiver for better following the source's thought. It helps to generate a sense of engagement in the message, because it activates a set of expectations which will either be actualized or not. If the message follows the expectations, there is a built-in reward for having guessed correctly. If the anticipations are not met, there is a conflict which sharpens the attention until it is resolved. Notice that the division provides a lot of redundancy which in turn reduces message density.

The Confirmation (Body). It is in the confirmation that the persuasive message (the case) is presented and developed with a variety of proofs or appeals. This is the substance of the message—its heart. In non-persuasive messages, the body identifies and supports the message content in the ways we discussed in detail in Part I.

The Refutation. The refutation is appropriate only in persuasive and argumentative messages. Its function is to destroy the receiver's confidence in the opposing positions. The term "rebuttal" is sometimes confused with refutation. Technically, a refutation discredits opposing beliefs while a rebuttal attempts to rebuild a case or an argument after it has been refuted.

The confirmation and refutation together comprise the body of a persuasive message. Typically, the confirmation precedes the refutation, but not necessarily so. Generally, the trauma of giving up a security-lending belief is reduced if a new belief is compared with an established one and gradually becomes more appealing. Thus, when the older belief is rejected, the "void" has been avoided. But, in some extreme circumstances (especially where the receiver is under the continuing physical control of the source), it is more effective to destroy confidence in an existing belief first and then fill the void with a counter-position. A drowning person will grasp for any straw.

The Peroration. The peroration, technically speaking, is the conclusion for a persuasive speech. It has several functions to perform in order to provide closure on the persuasive effort: The receiver's memory should be aided by summarizing the main contentions and emphasizing the proposition. The receiver must be left with reduced tension, resolved conflicts, and some kind of reward for having adopted the source's belief or position. It must create a sense of finality and commitment. It must provide ready-made defenses or rationalizations to resist subsequent appeals from the opposition and the receiver's own second thoughts.

I prefer to retain the term "peroration" rather than to use the more common "conclusion," even when discussing non-persuasive messages. The term "conclusion" too often connotes merely reaching the end of a line of thought or presenting a summary of main points and a restatement of the central idea. There are instances where those functions are adequate, but the term "peroration" reminds us that selected psychological factors often might need to reach closure in addition to topic termination.

The Transition. Beyond Quintilian's basic seven parts are two that are optional and without a specified position in the basic sequence: the transition and the digression. The transition provides increased continuity from one thought to another. Transitions may be employed between major structural components (e.g., exordium and expository background), or between main or subpoints, or between supports. In other words, transitions (bridges) can be built wherever the designer believes the receiver needs to be led by the hand from point-to-point. A transition can provide a brief respite or a temporary tension reduction without letting the attention stray.

The Digression. The digression also provides a break in the otherwise intense statement of the message. It can be used at any point where such relief is thought to be needed. The break can provide the receiver with time for integration of previous points, or it can provide the source with time to alter the contextual atmosphere or emotional environment. The digression differs from the transition in that it departs from the patterned development of thought; it allows the attention to stray off the topic. The departure can be off on an associated tangent, or it may take the form of a complete break in the line of thought.

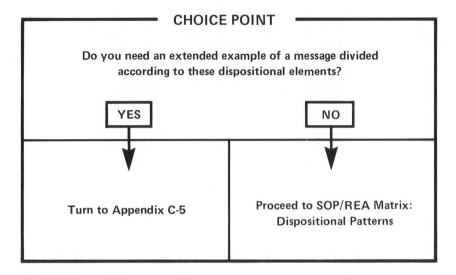

Dispositional Patterns Matrix

The Dispositional Patterns Matrix (see Figure 5.3) has the same general characteristics as the General SOP/REA Matrix. Instead of erudite/austere cell descriptors, however, this matrix employs more commonplace descriptions of the receivers defined by the cells. Then, for each audience type, there is a suggested prescription for the overall structure of a message. When this matrix is used in conjunction with the general matrix (Figure 5.2), the cell entries are rather self-evident. Rather than elaborating on each cell, therefore, I will select a single cell for explanation.

The cell labeled "Rank and File," which is defined by moderate sophistication and low readiness, will serve our purpose nicely. This audience represents a generalized cross-section of the country's adult workforce. First, note that the corresponding cell on the general matrix prescribes an *elegant* and *full* treatment. We will expect to include all or most of the traditional dispositional elements to create "fullness," and the elegance prescription suggests a pleasingly contrived, but not studied, structure.

More specifically, we should plan a fully developed *exordium* in an effort to compensate for low readiness. The moderate sophistication level allows us to spend less time on the *expository*

READINESS	SOPHISTICATION H	SOPHISTICATION M	SOPHISTICATION L
H	ELITE (Expert) C.I. Full Body	PROFESSIONAL (Responsible) Brief Expos. C.I. Full Body	OVER-ACHIEVER (Dedicated) Full Expos. C.I. Full Body
M	DISPLACED EXPERT (Quick Starter) Brief Exord. C.I. Full Body Brief Peroration	MODAL (Competent) Brief Exord. Brief Expos. C.I. Body Div. or Trans. Brief Peroration	LAY AUDIENCE (Popular) Brief Exord. Full Expos. C.I. Div. Body Trans. Brief Peroration
L	UNDER-ACHIEVER (Slow Starter) Full Exord. Brief Expos. C.I. Body Brief Peroration Optional Digres.	RANK and FILE (Adult Workforce) Full Exord. Brief Expos. C.I. Div. or Trans. Full Peroration Optional Digres.	MASS AUDIENCE (Common Denominator) Full Exord. Full Expos. C.I. Brief Body Full Peroration Optional Digres.

Figure 5.3. Dispositional Patterns Matrix.

background than we would with a mass audience, for example, and that segment could be developed somewhat cleverly. The *central idea* should be stated clearly and explicitly, and it could be followed immediately with a *division* element. Actually, well-developed *transitions* between the main points could be used instead of the division, but this audience does not require both. A *body* of moderate information load and the structure determined at Step 9 will be appropriate. *Digressions* are optional but should be used only to achieve specific tactical ends. Finally, the peroration should be fully developed and strong to accomplish both desired cognitive and desired affective states.

With these structural decisions made, the sentence outline begun in Part I can be completed, and the message assumes its completed skeletal form.

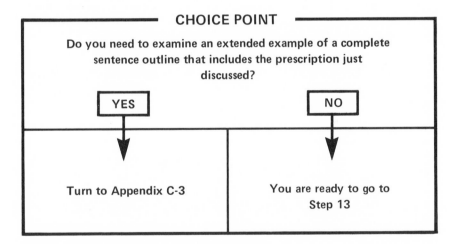

CHOICE POINT

Do you need to examine an extended example of a complete sentence outline that includes the prescription just discussed?

YES

NO

Turn to Appendix C-3

You are ready to go to Step 13

Step 13. Select the Appropriate Graphics

The first designing decision to make in connection with selecting graphics for a message is whether to use them or not. Sometimes they are appropriate, and sometimes they are not. This point *per se* illustrates the importance of selecting the medium according to the task requirements, rather than beginning with the decision "to do a film on the topic of X."

In a one-to-one communication situation, you can often determine whether visual supports (including graphics) are appropriate by listening carefully to your receiver's responses. By listening carefully to his or her metaphors, you can pick up clues as to how he or she prefers to process your message. For example: Your conversation partner might say: "I don't seem to be *hearing* what you're really trying to tell me." This metaphor suggests that he or she is processing information aurally and needs a verbal paraphrase of your position or point. But, he or she might say: "I'm sorry, I just don't *see* what you mean." This metaphor implies that the cognitive processing is predominantly visual and that either an actual or a verbally descriptive visualization would facilitate the communication. Some researchers (Bandler *et al.*, 1979) have attempted to correlate such metaphors with a subject's eye movements, thus claiming that where a person looks, when glancing away, provides a clue to whether the information is being processed in the left or the right hemisphere of the brain.

On a more general level, we can often infer whether to rely upon the visual channel for communicating our primary information by referring to some general rules (see Table 4.1, p. 101). Typically, we should use the visual channel as our dominant channel when our message is long or complex; when the arrangement is complicated; when referability and spatial discrimination are important; when the environment is noisy; when simultaneous presentation is desired; or when several dimensions are required to represent several interacting variables.

Having decided that visual or graphic development is appropriate, how do you decide from the thousands of possible choices which to employ? Let us first look at some somewhat universal criteria for selecting graphics and then examine more specifically how our receivers' levels of sophistication and readiness should influence our design decisions.

General Criteria for Selecting Graphics
Photogenic Quality. Andreas Feininger (1965) has distilled from his vast professional photographic experience several dimensions which define the extent to which a subject is photogenic. I have (I

hope without distorting his meaning) compressed his advice to a convenient scale. Table 5.1 displays a semantic-differential type scale which allows one to estimate the photogenic quality of a given photograph. This scale says in essence that photogenic quality is enhanced by capturing: (1) very simple order and clarity, (2) high contrast, (3) sharp detail, (4) life-giving surface texture, (5) bold form, (6) crisp outline, (7) patterns created by the repetition of related forms, (8) an illusion of depth generated by receding lines or interlocking objects, (9) a suggestion of dynamic motion, and (10) a sense of spontaneity. By contrast, photogenic quality is diminished when: (1) the subjects appear to be posing, (2) the shot appears to be contrived, and (3) the shot is framed from a distance.

Basic Compositional Guidelines. Gregg Berryman (1979) relies directly upon Gestalt psychology for guidelines for graphic design. He maintains that while the *parts* of a visual image may be seen as distinct components, the *whole* image, being different from the mere sum of its parts, should be analyzed and evaluated as a gestalt. He identifies seven gestalt factors which influence design:

1. *Figure/ground.* The contrast provided between the positive elements (figure) and the negative space (ground) allows visual images to be recognized.
2. *Equilibrium.* Berryman claims that: "Every psychological field tends toward order, balance, and maximum efficiency. Natural phenomena gives [sic] expected shapes to things." Thus, soap bubbles become perfect spheres.
3. *Isomorphic correspondence.* "Experiences of people, both physical and psychological, are recalled and triggered by specific visual images." For example, the image of a sizzling steak elicits memory of its taste and aroma.
4. *Closure.* Since "closed" shapes tend to be more stable, we tend to close images that are left open. For instance, letters printed with damaged or broken type are typically seen as perfect or whole.
5. *Proximity.* The eye tends to be attracted to groups or clusters rather than to isolates; thus, five coins would be noticed more readily if they were in close proximity than if they were widely separated.

Table 5.1

Scale of Photogenic Quality

	Simplicity (Order, Clarity)	
Very complex	1 2 3 4 5 6 7	Very simple
	Contrast	
Low	1 2 3 4 5 6 7	High
	Detail	
Dull	1 2 3 4 5 6 7	Sharp
	Texture	
Lifeless	1 2 3 4 5 6 7	Life-giving surface
	Form	
Weak	1 2 3 4 5 6 7	Bold
	Outline	
Ill-defined	1 2 3 4 5 6 7	Crisp
	Pattern	
No repetition	1 2 3 4 5 6 7	Repetition of related forms
	Depth	
Flat	1 2 3 4 5 6 7	Receding lines or interlocking objects
	Motion	
Static suggestion	1 2 3 4 5 6 7	Dynamic suggestion
	Spontaneity	
Little	1 2 3 4 5 6 7	Much

- -

	Posed	
Much	1 2 3 4 5 6 7	None
	Contrived	
Much	1 2 3 4 5 6 7	None
	Shot Distance	
Distant	1 2 3 4 5 6 7	Close

6. *Continuation.* Straight or curved lines tend to lead the eye along, and even beyond, the line. A finger pointed at something leads your eye to it.

7. *Similarity.* Similar objects, as defined by shape, size, color, and direction, are seen together in groups; consequently, one black sheep in a flock tends to be noticed.

In a similar kind of listing, Kemp (1980) itemizes four "principles" and five "tools" of visual design:

Principles of Design

1. *Simplicity.* Simpler designs tend to be better designs.

2. *Unity.* A pleasing design possesses unity.

3. *Emphasis.* Better designs emphasize a single element.

4. *Balance.* Formal, symmetrical balance is appropriate for creating static feelings, and informal, asymmetrical balance is useful for a dynamic, attention-getting design. Whichever form of balance is employed, "good" visuals are balanced.

Tools of Design

1. *Line.* A line (not necessarily the shortest distance between two points, but more as a path or a trail) can not only connect visual objects, but can lead the eye as well.

2. *Shape.* An easily perceived shape, which differs from the usual, can lead special interest and attractiveness to an image.

3. *Space.* People generally feel more comfortable with images that have open space around the visual elements. The space tends to prevent a crowded feeling.

4. *Texture.* Visual texture serves to substitute for the tactile sense. It can provide diversity, engagement, emphasis, etc.

5. *Color.* Color in general provides emphasis, mood, and realism. Harmonious colors are perceived as pleasant; complementary colors tend to be perceived with some annoyance.

In addition to the guidelines suggested by Berryman and by Kemp, there are three which deal with framing, spacing, and size.

1. *Framing.* An image can be "framed" by placing it into a visual context by showing elements of the foreground at the edges of the graphic. By contrast, an image can be "unframed" (it can defy the confines of the physical limits of the graphic) by "bleeding" the image off the edges. That is, show the image in such close-up range that the entire image cannot be contained on the graphic.
2. *Spacing.* Spacing, particularly in regard to lettered text, can create varying degrees of comfort or discomfort in the viewer. The spacing of text can be controlled through letter spacing, word spacing, and line spacing. These variables can generate several different combinations available to the designer.
3. *Size.* Large visuals have not been found to be more effective in producing comprehension than small ones, provided that the small ones are not so small that perception is uncomfortable or disrupted. However, audiences tend to prefer larger images and type than smaller, and they may tend to avoid that which is uncomfortable for them. A good rule-of-thumb for type or lettering size is that one-inch type can be read comfortably at 50 feet by most people. Double the size when you double the viewing distance, and halve the size when . . . . Somewhat related to type size is type style: (1) when text is printed in "all caps," it slows reading speed by about 15 percent; (2) Gothic type (plain-cut without serifs), such as "Helvetica," is more readable than the more ornate Roman, script, or text types.

I must offer a word of caution regarding these sets of guidelines. There has been a common tendency among graphic and photographic artists to define rules for producing "good" artwork. "Goodness" is most frequently defined by the single dimension of pleasantness. When we regard the graphics as a means of achieving desired message complexity levels, however, the "artistic" criteria often seem inappropriate. Your complexity prescription may call for increasing tension and aloofness, maximizing diversity, and increasing erudition. In filling this prescription (which is appropriate to the audience and situation at hand), it would be necessary to violate several of the prescriptive guidelines. It appears much more desirable to regard these "guidelines" as topics or variables under your command or control, to be used as your communication situation requires. Regard them as descriptive rather than as prescriptive.

Rules-of-Thumb for Supporting Graphics. Probably Dwyer (1972) has conducted the most extensive empirical research in the area of instructional graphics. Even so, his conclusions do not go unchallenged (Travers, 1970). It seems plausible that apparently contradictory conclusions result from efforts to explain appropriate usage of graphic material in unidimensional rather than in more complex, systemic relationships. For instance, it seems plausible that both highly defined, "realistic" visual support and graphics that reduce reality to its most essential components and relationships could be effective in accomplishing learning. The differences in their relative effectiveness might well be the function of differences in readiness, sophistication, and the nature of the cognitive or perceptual task. Be that as it may, my students and I have found the following algorithm, which I have abstracted from Dwyer, to be a useful guide over the past decade. Since it appears self-explanatory, no elaboration is offered; see Table 5.2.

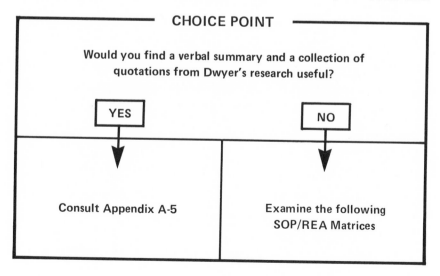

Table 5.2

Rules-of-Thumb for Selecting Visual Supports

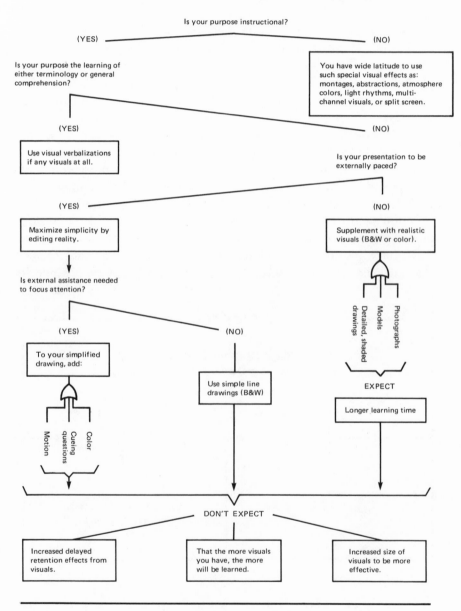

Graphics Choices Based Upon Sophistication/Readiness Levels.
The use of a matrix enables us to avoid the problem of confusion
resulting from a unidimensional focus suggested above. The matrix
inherently introduces two variables: sophistication and readiness.
Yet, there are several graphics features which are influenced by
sophistication and readiness levels. We can best grasp these
complex relationships by first examining an over-simplified matrix
for making basic graphics decisions, then we can add finer
distinctions. Figure 5.4 displays the Basic Graphics Matrix.

The categories used in the Basic Graphics Matrix synthesize
several features. Assignment to a category is determined by a
preponderance of features present rather than requiring all of
them. We must remember that matrices are "convenient fictions,"
and assignment to a single cell is sometimes not possible. Be
reminded that interpolation between cells is more appropriate
than attempting to force-fit an item into a single cell. Figure 5.5
analyzes the basic matrix into its rows and columns and lists the
more salient defining features of each. Since these categories are
synthetic and somewhat cryptic, slight elaboration of each appears
to be appropriate.

Representational reality is created by visual materials which are
realistic, objective, concrete, and commonplace. Photography
provides the best means of capturing representational reality,
especially when shot with a normal lens in normally lighted
situations.

Interpreted or distorted reality represents an object subjectively
as it might be seen through the unique goggles of an interpreter;
for example, a photograph shot from an unusual angle, under
special lighting effects, with a distorting lens tends to filter
objective reality through the interpreter's nervous system to
provide a symbolic or analogic rendering of the object. In a similar
way, a cartoonist or caricature artist interprets reality by
distorting it. Verbal accompaniment is more appropriate at this
level than at the representational level where the graphic tends to
speak for itself.

Abstracted reality is created by extracting the essential qualities
of something and emphasizing them in order to minimize the

SOPHISTICATION

	H	M	L
H	ELITE (Expert) Abstracted Reality Low Definition	PROFESSIONAL (Responsible) Interpreted or Distorted Reality Low Definition	OVER-ACHIEVER (Dedicated) Representational Reality Low Definition
M	DISPLACED EXPERT (Quick Starter) Abstracted Reality Moderate Definition	MODAL (Competent) Interpreted or Distorted Reality Moderate Definition	LAY AUDIENCE (Popular) Representational Reality Moderate Definition
L	UNDER-ACHIEVER (Slow Starter) Abstracted Reality High Definition	RANK and FILE (Adult Workforce) Interpreted or Distorted Reality High Definition	MASS AUDIENCE (Common Denominator) Representational Reality High Definition

(Vertical axis label: READINESS)

Figure 5.4. Basic Graphics Matrix for Decisions Based upon Receiver-Imposed Constraints.

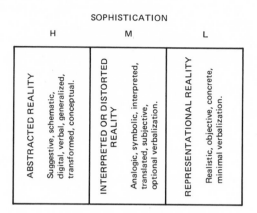

A. The matrix *columns* define "reality" differently according to sophistication level. A predominance of features places a given graphic in a column; presence of all features is not required.

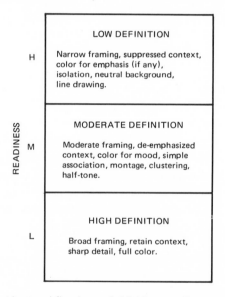

B. The matrix *rows* define degree of definition according to readiness level. The row which most fully describes a given graphic determines its classification.

Figure 5.5. Analysis of Basic Graphics Matrix.

uniqueness of the object and emphasize its generality or universality. Because it results from analysis, it tends to be more digital than analogic. It is symbolic and suggestive—often more subtle than interpreted reality. It represents a transformation from species to genus and thus is more compatible with conceptual interpretations.

High definition in graphics is achieved in part by framing the object in a large enough frame to capture the context without destroying it. Grainy or half-toned photographs tend to reduce definition without destroying the subtlety or texture.

Moderate definition accommodates montage and comparison/contrast nicely. Color is used to establish mood or emotional response.

Low definition, which is suitable for high readiness, isolates the figure and often suppresses the context. Mounting the isolated figure on a light gray background is a common way of suppressing the context or background. Simple black and white line drawings (with color added only for emphasis), especially when framed narrowly, generate a kind of stark isolation that minimizes distraction.

It is difficult to represent all of these features in the cells of a single matrix. Figure 5.6 is a reasonably good attempt to illustrate the general matrix more concretely. A good exercise to test your understanding of the general matrix is to study Figure 5.6 in an effort to find ways of making it comply more closely with the theoretical matrix. For example, this matrix is presented without color; where would you add color and for what purpose to this matrix to make it more in keeping with the basic matrix?

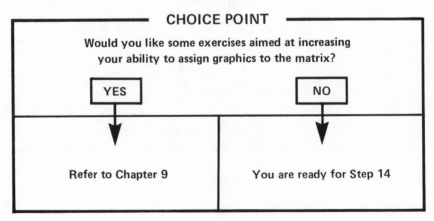

CHOICE POINT

Would you like some exercises aimed at increasing your ability to assign graphics to the matrix?

| YES | NO |

Refer to Chapter 9   **You are ready for Step 14**

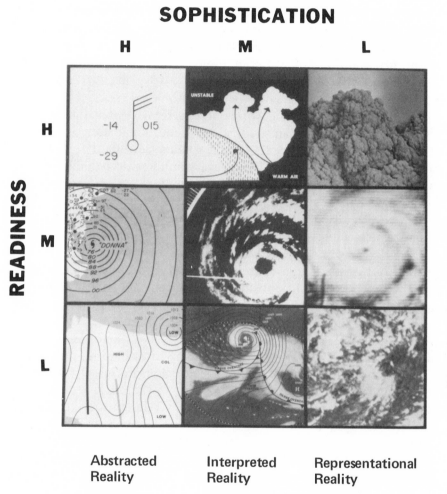

Figure 5.6. Basic Graphics Matrix Illustrated.

Step 14. Select the Appropriate Language Style

Even though a single picture may be worth a thousand words, the power of the word should not be underestimated. The ability to use language is, after all, one of the most distinguishing human traits. Language not only allows us to solve problems in the absence of the problem's environment, but also it allows us to record our solutions and to communicate them with our contemporaries and with posterity. Thus, we can create societies, cultures, and civilizations. But language is not only a necessary condition for thought, it can also govern our emotional states. The right combination of words can modify one's emotional state as surely as can a hypodermic needle which injects personality-changing drugs into the bloodstream. Language stimuli can evoke responses in our smooth muscles as well as in stripped, skeleton-controlling muscles. When the smooth muscles activate the endocrine system, our blood chemistry is changed—just as if we had changed it with a hypodermic needle.

Using language to generate emotional states is not a special trick we pull out of our bag for rare and important occasions. Emotion and thought are not at opposite ends of a continuum, nor do they make up a dichotomy. We are always in some emotional state, even when it might be described as "blah." The point of this is that a message designer will influence a receiver's emotional state whenever he or she presents a message, and it seems appropriate, therefore, to generate the kind of emotional environment that will facilitate the source's purpose. This step in the process calls our attention to the need for and the ability to design the message's language in such a way that it is consistent with the source's purpose and the receivers' levels of sophistication and readiness. Let us first consider some ancient advice for selecting the type of style that is appropriate to our strategy.

Cicero (H. Rackham trans., 1942) recognized three types of style associated with distinctive strategies: (1) the grand (or elevated) style, which is appropriate for *moving the passions*; (2) the plain style (the counterpart of the grand style), which is useful for *instruction*; and (3) the middle style (midway between plain and grand), which best serves wording an argument in an attempt *to prove* a case.

Demetrius (W. Rhys Roberts' edition, 1902) drew a distinction within the middle-style classification, thus specifying four style types: plain, elegant, forcible, and elevated. In an earlier book, I have synthesized and summarized these style types, and I find it instructive to include those descriptions here (Marsh, 1967). The stylistic figures (some of which are a bit esoteric) are defined and illustrated in the original work. I will not provide that elaboration here. Two clarifications are needed, however, to understand these descriptions at the level of our immediate interest: "diction," as used by rhetoricians, means the selection of words; "composition" means the combination of those words into sentences (or "periods").

The Plain Style. Plainness is unconcerned with embellishment and impressiveness; its sole function is to express ideas clearly to achieve maximum comprehension. Because it is not ornate, it is appropriately applied to familiar subjects, common objects, everyday experiences, and ordinary people. Rudolf Flesch (1946) has particularized several of the classical interpretations of plainness to make them more useable.

By combining the contributions of Flesch and Demetrius, we discover that the simple style's diction normally includes (1) a preponderance of Anglo-Saxon words; (2) frequent, personal references rather than formal, impersonal ones; (3) concrete words; (4) active words; and (5) some degree of phonetic symbolism.

Both writers likewise add to the features that contribute to simple composition. In general, plainness requires that the units be clearly connected with transitions, that ideas be amplified and repeated, that sentences be short and simple—using the subject-verb-object order, and that figures and references be concrete, vivid, and familiar. Narration is particularly useful as are examples and illustrations. One precaution that should be taken when developing the plain style is to avoid the obvious when using the familiar.

* * *

The Elegant Style. Elegance strives for grace and charm in an attempt to disarm one's listeners. Any subject can be handled tastefully with wit and pleasantry, although the elegant style is especially useful in refutation.

Diction, in the elegant style, is almost completely suppressed by the composition. The compositional devices that contribute greatly to the achievement of dignified and noble grace include (1) compressed expression with a light and rapid touch—often with two ideas in the same sentence; (2) unexpected and veiled meanings; (3) repeated references to previous remarks; (4) courteous and well-mannered conducts; (5) light talk in which all subjects are treated frivolously; and (6) the following specific stylistic figures: climax, epanophora, correction, aposiopesis, paralipsis, and proverbs. Charm results from the addition of fables, similes, hyperbole, and relating of unfounded fears. Charm relies on wit rather than on humor: It finds pleasantness in things not meant for laughter, whereas humor deliberately provokes laughter; it uses ornamental words, whereas humor uses common words: wit is charming, whereas humor is funny.

* * *

The Forcible Style. The creation of feelings of power, determination, and excitement is the function of the forcible style. It is normally used to express strong convictions, accusations, defenses, and calls for action; thus, it is often found in forensic and deliberative speeches. Forcefulness, unlike elevation and elegance, is incompatible with artistry and subtlety. When one is moved by excitation, there is neither the time nor the control required for ornate or witty composition. The forcible style has been described as a dog that seems ready to bite you even when it yawns.

The style will be forcible when the diction evokes no poetic images and uses vigorous and picturesque words, and when the composition appears spontaneous. More specifically, the compositional factors of forcefulness are (1) the use of slogans; (2) sarcasm; (3) cacophony (opposite of euphony); (4) slight obscurity; and (5) uninterrupted series. Antithesis and exact parallelism should be avoided. Stylistic figures that tend to intensify forcefulness include paralipsis, aposiopesis, personification, epanophora, asyndeton, homoeteleuton, and innuendo.

* * *

The Elevated Style. The elevated, or grand, style strives for eloquence and dignity. It attempts to inspire or move the listeners. Elevation is best applied to great subjects, noble and heroic. It normally is used at dignified and formal ceremonies, such as funerals, inaugurations, and commencements, where epideictic speaking is appropriate.

The diction of elevation will be grandiose, elaborate, and distinctive. These qualities are achieved in part by using (1) compound words (law-givers rather than legislators); (2) onomatopoeia; (3) new words for freshness, (4) occasional similarity and obvious harshness of words; (5) highly connotative words; (6) a touch of poetic diction; (7) rugged words (shrieking for crying); and (8) phonetic symbolism.

The composition of elevation requires artistic balance, and therefore, it makes ample use of certain stylistic figures. Elevation is generally achieved when the periodic structure is used, especially when the members are long, and when they open and close with strong words. The following figures are particularly applicable: asyndeton, conjunction, disjunction, adjunction, epanophora, antistrophe, interlacement, transplacement, reduplication, synonomy, hiatus, assonance, alliteration, homoeteleuton, metaphors, and allegories.

Language Choices Based upon Interest and Difficulty Levels. Rudolf Flesch's (1949) widely recognized formula for calculating the readability of written language involves two main concepts: "reading ease" and "human interest." I have generated a language matrix defined by sophistication and readiness in which the cells prescribe appropriate levels of both difficulty and interest. Flesch's definitions and parameters have guided my efforts in this construction. Figure 5.7 displays the matrix, but the abbreviated phrases require identification and definition before it is useable.

Flesch defines "human interest" as a function of the percentage of *personal words* and the percentage of *personal sentences:*

"Personal words" are:

(a) All first-, second-, and third-person pronouns except the neuter pronouns *it, its, itself,* and *they, them, their, theirs, themselves,* if referring to things rather than people.

(b) All words that have masculine or feminine natural gender, e.g., *John Jones, Mary,* father, sister, iceman, actress. Do not count common-gender words like *teacher, doctor, employee, assistant, spouse.* Count singular and plural forms.

(c) The group words *people* (with the plural verb) and *folks.*

* * *

"Personal sentences" are:

(a) Spoken sentences, marked by quotation marks or otherwise, often including speech tags like "he said," set off by commas. . .

(b) Questions, commands, requests, and other sentences directly addressed to the reader. . . . But do not count sentences that are indirectly or vaguely addressed to the reader . . . (e.g., . . . *You never can tell.*)

(c) Exclamations. . .

(d) Grammatically incomplete sentences whose full meaning has to be inferred from the context. . .

If a sentence fits two or more of these definitions, count it only once.

The other concept, "reading ease" (and its counterpart "difficulty"), is a function of the number of syllables per 100 words and the average number of words per sentence. Given these definitions, you should be able to examine a written text and place it on the matrix. Remember that $>$ means more than and $<$ means fewer than.

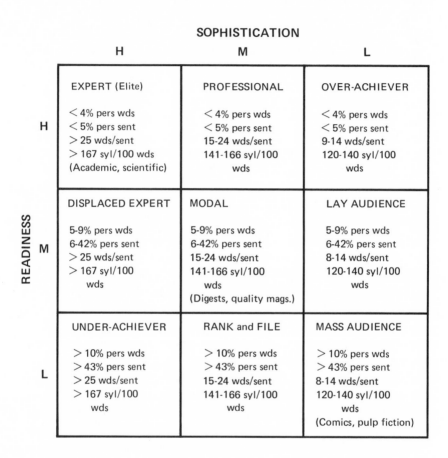

Figure 5.7. Language Matrix (Interest and Difficulty Levels).

Let's try an example. Look back to the previous section, entitled "The Elevated Style." Count off 100 words and analyze the sample as described above. I found an average of about 19 words per sentence and 183 syllables in that 100-word sample. The number of words per sentence places the style in the "professional" cell, and the number of syllables places it in the "expert" cell. This piece of prose properly lies between those cells in regard to difficulty.

In searching that sample for personal words, I found none ("law-givers" and "legislators" are excluded because they are common-gender words). Neither were there any personal sentences. This passage is therefore devoid of "human interest" value, and is most appropriate for an expert audience. It is in a style category that includes academic and scientific literature—and so it was intended.

To become proficient in adapting language styles to any given audience, you will need to sharpen your awareness of potential uses of language by classifying style types and analyzing their properties. The goal of this discipline, of course, is to internalize or integrate these skills to the point that you can function independently from the matrix. Here are some suggestions that will promote that kind of independence.

Collect a wide variety of discarded magazines from friends. Sample the writing styles in each and, based upon your intuition, assign each to one of the nine matrix cells. Continue until all cells are filled. Then analyze a randomly selected 100-word passage from each and see whetherʾ your intuitions match the matrix prescriptions.

Now, use the same magazines and classify the style by type (plain, elegant, forcible, and elevated). When you find a good example of each, copy a passage of a few hundred words from each example. As over-simplified as this task might sound, my students report that it increases their sensitivity to the nuances of style. Incidentally, this kind of drill was practiced by many great orators of antiquity.

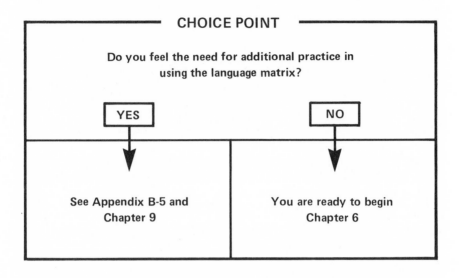

Chapter 6

INFORMATION LOAD AND BODY STRUCTURE	SUPPORT TACTICS AND OBSCURITY INDEX	PURPOSE STATEMENT

CONTEXTUAL ATMOSPHERE	ORGANISMIC CONSTRAINTS	RESPONSE STYLES

Central Idea

You can increase the chances of eliciting desired responses from your receivers by translating selected styles into "aloofness" and "tension" values and then designing those values into the message.

Step 15. Translate desired response styles into an aloofness/tension profile. Consider *music* as a means of achieving the desired response style. Consider *color* as a means of achieving the desired response style. Consider *visual composition* as a means of achieving the desired response style.

Objectives

1. To assign a list of response styles to the appropriate cells on an ALO/TEN matrix.
2. To scale aloofness and tension reliably.
3. To select musical effects according to their ALO/TEN qualities.
4. To select color effects according to their ALO/TEN qualities.
5. To select visual-composition effects according to their ALO/TEN qualities.

Chapter 6

Achieving Desired Response Styles

The 1960's spotlighted and popularized knowledge that social and physiological scientists have possessed for some decades. Two influences from the sixties are particularly worthy of our momentary attention. I refer to Marshall McLuhan's writings and to the Aquarian movement, which McLuhan attempted to explain and probably to some extent unintentionally influenced.

McLuhan (1964) relabeled and amplified the older Apollonian/Dionysian and classic/romantic dichotomies. The contemporary version of these dichotomies he called "hot/cool." The chief dimension of the hot/cool dichotomy is defined by its extremes of "aloofness" and "engagement." In other words, something—a dance, for instance—is "hot" (classic or Apollonian), when it is highly structured, specialized, and formal. The impact of these qualities on the viewer of the dance is to increase the gap between the performer and the spectator. The spectator becomes a passive witness; the spectator is excluded from the action. A ballet dancer remains *aloof* from the audience. By contrast, a "cool" (i.e., romantic or Dionysian) dance, such as disco, invites audience participation. It is innovative, improvisational, informal, and *engaging*.

This dimension, aloofness/engagement, plays a central role in defining and predicting response styles in the complexity model. The other main dimension which defines the response-style matrices has its roots in a practice the Aquarian movement calls bio-feedback. It is the recognition that muscular tension both influences and is influenced by emotional states. By monitoring indexes of one's muscular tension, a person can willfully alter

141

one's emotional state and general state of consciousness. To the extent that stimuli influence muscular responses, varying types and degrees of response styles can be generated by controlling the tension-provoking factors within a message. Thus, "response-style" matrices will be defined in the complexity model by aloofness (ALO) and tension (TEN).

The Basic Response-Style Matrices

Behavioral responses are described on two matrices defined by aloofness and tension: the first one defines *spontaneous* responses and the second defines *compulsive* responses. A spontaneous response is one made by a confident, unthreatened person who can react freely to the environment as viewed objectively. A compulsive response, produced habitually and often fearfully, may be difficult to explain in terms of the objective aspects of the environment; it must be seen in terms of subjective schemata if it is not to be interpreted as inappropriate or perhaps absurd behavior.

When an audience is relatively uninhibited by fears and defenses, its response styles can be anticipated reasonably well through Figure 6.1. When dealing with receivers whose behavior is relatively dominated by fear or habit, Figure 6.2 provides a more appropriate matrix.

Before examining the individual cells of these matrices, it will be appropriate to discuss the dimensions defining them.

The Aloofness Scale

Let us examine the working definition of aloofness:

> Aloofness is the opposite of "engagement." But when estimates of engagement (which is easier to conceptualize perhaps) are added to the other elements of message complexity, complexity is reduced rather than increased. Aloofness and tension together make up the "response-style" segment of the message model. By controlling these variables, a designer can increase the probability of eliciting the desired response from the receivers. To generate aloofness, one would withhold reward and prevent involvement while increasing frustration. An impersonal lecture in

Figure 6.1. Basic Response-Style Matrix: Spontaneous.

ALOOFNESS

	H	M	L
H	AGGRESSIVE/ SUBMISSIVE	HOSTILE	MANIC
M	WITHDRAWN	DEFENSIVE	VIGILANT
L	DEPRESSED	INGRATIATING	SOLIPSISTIC

TENSION (vertical axis label)

Figure 6.2. Basic Response-Style Matrix: Compulsive.

a crowded auditorium with an intermittent public address system would probably generate a strong sense of aloofness.

Reward. Reward is the positive reinforcement provided by the message which satisfies some felt need of the receiver and functions to promote *approach* rather than avoidance of the reinforcing agent. The classic example from behavior-modification theory is the food pellet received by the hungry rat following its pressing the bar. A rewarded response tends to become a learned response.

Involvement. Involvement is essentially what Wiener and Mehrabian (1968) have defined as "immediacy." They would identify a message as possessing high immediacy when: (1) there is an indication of physical or psychological closeness, (2) references to the present predominate, (3) a person or object is seen as a unity, (4) individuality is recognized, (5) source and receiver engage in activities jointly, (6) behavior is expressed freely rather than under compulsion or influence, and (7) qualifying and modifying remarks are omitted. An example of immediacy (involvement) ranging from engaging to aloof is contained in this series of remarks: "Our daughter-to-be," "our son's fiance," "our son's lady-friend," "that woman."

Frustration. When you are prevented or detained from accomplishing something you have set out to do, you are likely to become frustrated or irritated. The frustration tends to concentrate your attention on the source of the frustration and results in greater engagement. Television commercial designers have long recognized that a certain degree of irritation in their messages increases their effectiveness.

When reward, involvement, and frustration values are averaged from the following scales, we have a working estimate of the message's aloofness level:

ALOOFNESS   1 2 3 4 5 6 7

Reward	High _ _ _ _ _ _ _ Low
Involvement	High _ _ _ _ _ _ _ Low
Frustration	High _ _ _ _ _ _ _ Low

The Tension Scale

Again, a working definition will serve to put this scale into perspective:

> Tension, the other element in the response-style set, is a measure of the degree of "up-tightness" produced by the message. The actual muscular responses to message stimuli occur in both smooth and stripped muscles so that the blood chemistry is influenced as well as posture, movement, and facial expression. The indexes selected for estimating tension levels are shock, suspense, and conflict (although other variables such as novelty, noxity, etc., can influence tension responses also). Two common experiences illustrate the tension element in a message: the buildup and release of tension in a plot line and a story-line joke that quickly releases mounting tensions.

Shock. Shock is generated when something unexpected is observed. If you were to hear a gunshot while sitting in the quiet sanctity of your home, you would likely be shocked and would respond with a startle reflex. The same shot observed on a firing range would not elicit that response. In a message, shock can be produced through any number of language, structural, visual, musical, etc., effects.

Suspense. Suspense is the counterpart of shock; it occurs when the expected is *not* observed. For instance, a speaker might announce that he or she is going to develop four points and then appear to be concluding after having only developed three. Or, a narration can build gradually to a climax, delaying the critical insight into the plot. Even a sentence can be constructed in such a way as to withhold the "key" until the last word is reached.

Conflict. When two forces oppose each other in such a way that each becomes an obstacle to the course of the other, tension-provoking conflict is created. It can be a conflict between attitudes, beliefs, values, ideas, facts, etc. Or, it can be a clash of colors, styles, or personalities. It can be produced by pitting person against person, person against nature, person against institutions, etc. Conflict creates tension because an imbalance is created in a cognitive system that strives for stability. The strain toward resolution is manifested in muscular tension.

Although there are many ways of building tension levels, these three probably account for the most common ones, and they serve as good indexes for estimating the tension level of a given message. The following scale is useful, when averaged, in establishing a message's tension level:

TENSION		1 2 3 4 5 6 7	
Shock	Low	_ _ _ _ _ _ _	High
Suspense	Low	_ _ _ _ _ _ _	High
Conflict	Low	_ _ _ _ _ _ _	High

The Tension Hierarchy

Tension, in either the smooth or stripped muscles, caused by shock, suspense, conflict, and other conditions, tends to build up in a hierarchical pattern. In general, tension takes longer to build and requires longer to release, the higher it is found on the hierarchy.

The First Stage. Simple, muscular tensions caused directly by a stimulus build and disappear quickly. The common trembling hand, shaking knees, quick breathing, quivering voice, flushing or paling symptoms, and sweating are typical of this stage. If prolonged tension occurs at this stage, dark circles under the eyes, headaches, and cold hands and feet may be observed. The skeleton and the circulatory system are principally involved here.

The Second Stage. When first-stage tensions mount and cannot be relieved by environmental changes, the hypothalamus begins to elicit defenses in preparation for resisting the perceived threat, either physical or psychological. The changes are largely metabolic, and the symptoms are noticed in the form of upset or cramped stomach, elimination problems, or dizziness.

The Third Stage. When the second-stage defenses are ineffective in combating the perceived threat, the lymbic system, which controls emotional states, adds new defenses. These defensive emotional states also tend to be ordered in a hierarchy: (1) The earliest to occur is a feeling of *urgency*; everything seems to require immediate attention. (2) The urgency soon evolves into *irritability* if the tensions persist and mount. (3) Next, *apprehen-*

sion dominates; this fear is typically focused on specific outcomes. (5) Apprehension becomes more generalized to produce a state of *general anxiety*; when the source of the fear is undetectable, solutions cannot be discovered, and the tension becomes chronic and intense. (6) If the chronic, debilitating tension cannot be controlled or reduced, the body resorts to its ultimate emotional defense—*depression*. Depression serves as a circuit-breaker and forces the body to give up its efforts to cope.

Knowledge of this hierarchy allows the message designer to monitor receivers for the purposes of either: (1) analyzing them, (2) influencing or changing them, or (3) interpreting their responses.

Cell Descriptors for the Response-Style Matrices

Now that we have defined the complexity factors which govern response style, we can re-examine the matrices (Figures 6.1 and 6.2) and describe the styles assigned to each cell. Both the spontaneous and the compulsive response styles will be described for each cell identified.

High ALO/High TEN. Spontaneous behavior: REGIMENTED style is intense and impersonal as one might expect to find exemplified in a surgeon in an operating room or in an air traffic controller during a crisis. *Compulsive behavior*: A person may exhibit predominantly AGGRESSIVE style, or predominantly SUBMISSIVE style, or may display both styles as in the case of the rather complex "authoritarian personality." Both traits result in aloof behavior, and both are functions of fear-induced tensions, although the fears are of different types. An aggressive person has high confidence in self but fears being overthrown by incompetent others. By contrast, the submissive person has greater confidence in others than in self and fears that if others discover his or her incompetence, they will avoid him or her. The submissive relies upon the support of the "more-competent others." An authoritarian perceives society as a highly structured hierarchy. He or she responds submissively to those on higher status levels and aggressively toward those below his or her own status.

Moderate ALO/High TEN. Spontaneous behavior: HEURISTIC

style, although systematic, involves discovering for one's self. It is therefore moderate in aloofness. At the same time, it involves an intense, serious probe into the unknown; hence it is high in tension. Another connotation is often assigned to the word "heuristic" also; it suggests the use of a pragmatic or practical manner rather than one that is exhaustive. In other words, a heuristic approach to solving a problem would concentrate efforts on the few most promising possible solutions, rather than requiring a meticulous examination of each possibility. *Compulsive behavior:* The defensive emotional counterpart of heuristic behavior is HOSTILE style. Although the hostility may be somewhat suppressed, the barbed, hostile meaning or attitude is often present under conditions of moderate aloofness and high tension. Hostility implies opposition, competitiveness, antagonism, and adversity.

Low ALO/High TEN. Spontaneous behavior: EMOTIONAL style entails both intensity and an openness of expression about one's feelings. The feelings are strong, and they may be from any direction. That is, they could be loving or hateful. They could involve pity, fear, contempt, benevolence, etc. In this state, intuition tends to dominate. Reason need not be absent, but the premises upon which one's logic is based are likely to be subjective preferences rather than empirically-founded generalizations. *Compulsive behavior:* Compulsively-driven behavior of high intensity and high engagement often is manifested in the MANIC style. In general, "mania" suggests great excitement or enthusiasm, or even craze. Psychiatrically, it means, ". . . a form of insanity characterized by great excitement, with or without delusions, and in its acute stage by great violence" (Barnhart, 1963).

High ALO/Medium TEN. Spontaneous behavior: The PROVOCATIVE style is characterized by its incisive, penetrating, stimulating manner. It may be regarded as irritating or even vexing. It instigates, incites, stirs up, and arouses feelings and actions. The provocative style reflects its aloofness in an air of formality and structure. *Compulsive behavior:* When provocative behavior loses its spontaneity, it becomes WITHDRAWN. Withdrawn style reflects greater confidence in self than in others, but not enough self-confidence to be openly aggressive. The result of this orientation is a tendency toward physical avoidance from the situation, but when that is not possible, psychological avoidance or withdrawal suffices. Such a person relies excessively upon rules and formulas; things must be done "by the numbers"; behavior often becomes ritualistic.

Medium ALO/Medium TEN. Spontaneous behavior: The CAL-CULATING style occupies the least extreme cell on the matrix; it is modal in a definitional if not in a statistical sense. It is characterized by its anticipation of consequences and its designing of courses of action in response to them. The estimates and plans are often based upon common sense rather than upon mathematical probability or scientific observation. They are frequently founded upon self-interests. *Compulsive behavior:* The DEFEN-SIVE style pushes calculation to an extreme position that becomes selfishly scheming, shrewd, and cautious. Such a person manipulates others, but having anticipated detection, has defenses prepared in advance. He or she always has an answer for any criticism.

Low ALO/Medium TEN. Spontaneous behavior: The CONTEM-PLATIVE style is one of thoughtful observation, consideration, reflection, or meditation. It may suggest purpose, intention, or expectation. It substitutes mental for physical activity. *Compulsive behavior:* The excessive form of the contemplative style is a VIGILANT style. When one is vigilant, he or she is keenly attentive to detect signs of danger, alert, watchful. Compulsive vigilance entails distrust of others' motives. The pathological form of this wakefulness is insomnia.

High ALO/Low TEN. Spontaneous behavior: The LETHARGIC style is a function of under-stimulation, perhaps sensory deprivation. It is manifested in signs of boredom, drowsiness, and sluggishness. A person in a lethargic state is both inattentive, apathetic, and forgetful. *Compulsive behavior:* Lethargy's mirror image is the DEPRESSED style. While the cause of depression (as we discussed under "The Tension Hierarchy" above) is excessive and unrelieved tension, the onset of depression signals an involuntary abandonment of that tension. Psychiatrically, depression is: ". . . a morbid condition of emotional dejection and withdrawal; sadness greater and more prolonged than that warranted by any objective reason" (Barnhart, 1963).

Medium ALO/Low TEN. Spontaneous behavior: The PRODUCTIVE style is manifested by what Erich Fromm (1947) has called the "dynamic" character type. A dynamic (or productive) person is one who acquires and assimilates (integrates) both things and information parsimoniously; relates to others and to self through recognition of an individual's dignity; and lives life courageously in pursuit of valued goals. In this person's relaxed state (low tension), he or she has respect for both subjective and objective reality and thus avoids excessive aloofness and engagement. *Compulsive behavior:* The INGRATIATING style, on the surface, appears submissive because of a somewhat inferior self-assessment. But rather than *fearing* the "superior others," he or she wishes to *emulate* them and compulsively attempts to establish himself or herself in the favor or good graces of them. This style often displays signs of false modesty and flattery.

Low ALO/Low TEN. Spontaneous behavior: The CREATIVE style thrives in a relaxed environment in which a confident, unthreatened person engages freely and knowingly in "looking at one thing and seeing another." In other words, objective reality becomes the stimulus for analyzing, altering, and re-integrating something in such a way that something new, original, and unique results. The word "genius" is often used in conjunction with a creative person, but being a genius is not a necessary condition for creativity. An old adage states: "a gifted person *possesses* talent, but a genius *is possessed by* talent." This suggests that some degree of compulsion is characteristic of a genius. Another common misinterpretation of a creative person is that he or she is particularly receptive to visits from the "muse" and that the muse is the source of the creativity. The creative style I am describing, while influenced by sudden insights, enables one to pursue actively, even systematically, creative experiences. Anyone, given the necessary conditions to create, can do so. *Compulsive behavior:* Another adage—"A creative person builds air castles; a psychotic attempts to establish residence in them." When one compulsively dwells in the realm of subjectivity, to the extent of ignoring objective reality, he or she exemplifies the SOLIPSISTIC style. Solipsism holds that the self is the only source of verifiable knowledge and that whatever one creates is reality.

Step 15. Translate Desired Response Styles into an Aloofness/Tension Profile

To use these matrices in designing a message, you should first review the performance objectives from your purpose statement. Then determine which of the cell descriptors best describe the kinds of responses that are compatible with your objectives. These decisions can then be translated into ALO/TEN profiles to complete the overall message complexity profile. You may have to modify (compromise) some of the complexity profile values at this point in order to keep the total value at the level you have determined is appropriate for your receivers.

Figure 6.3 illustrates the ALO/TEN profile in the context of the completed message complexity profile. Given an instructional message for a college sophomore audience from which the source desires a *comtemplative response,* this complexity profile appears appropriate. The average complexity for this profile is 3.83. If you had determined *a priori* that your receivers would do best at a complexity level of 4.1, you would need to adjust some value(s) upward. Two obvious choices for compromise would be: (1) Raise the density level to 4, thus changing the contextual atmosphere from "exciting" to "compelling"; or (2) raise the aloofness level to 4, thus changing the response style from "contemplative" to "calculating." The choice should be made on the basis of your relative desires.

When you are satisfied with your ALO/TEN profile, you may use the matrices that follow as means of creating the conditions in your message that will facilitate the style(s) you have selected. Three matrices have been developed to serve this purpose; they include: one for the selection of music, one for color selections, and one to guide your choice of visual vantage points.

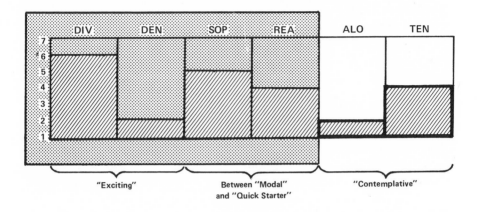

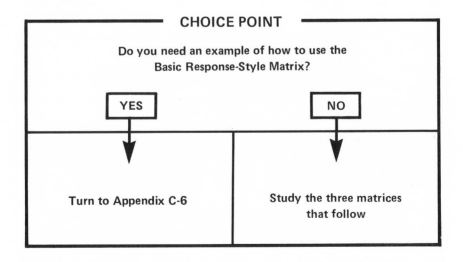

Figure 6.3. Response-Style Matrix Relative to the Complete Complexity Profile.

Step 15a. Consider Music as a Means of Achieving the Desired Response Style

It is, of course, impossible to classify all music (with its infinite possible variations and combinations) into the nine cells of a matrix. However, some broad, general guidelines can enable you to eliminate about 89 percent (i.e., 8/9) of the available possibilities. Once within a category, your choices will have to be more subjective. But, given this qualifier, let us enumerate some of the functions music can serve to enrich or augment a message.

Message Functions of Music

Framing

Music can "frame" a message just as a picture frame *frames* a painting or a theater stage *frames* an action. Framing, you will recall, is one of the dimensions of *readiness,* and musical framing should be used with readiness in mind. In the broadest sense, theme songs for radio and television shows "set the stage" and "open and close the curtain."

Transitions

These structural elements, discussed in Chapter 5 under the heading of "Dispositional Patterns," serve to lead or guide the receiver's attention from one point to another. An appropriate segment of music (usually very brief) can signal the end of one point and the beginning of the other. It can also signal the passage of time or the changing of place. Musical transitions help receivers "bridge gaps" and "shift gears."

Mood Control

Since the subject matter of pure music is mood rather than thought, music provides one of the quickest and surest ways of controlling the moods of its listeners. Just a few bars of "Mood Indigo," "Pomp and Circumstance," "Stars and Stripes Forever," or "Beethoven's Fifth," can alter the mood of a whole audience.

I once had an opportunity to study the way music was used to prepare an audience of several thousand people to receive President John F. Kennedy. After the Coliseum had been sealed off by the Secret Service, there was a delay of over an hour before the President's party arrived. To pass the time, musical entertainment was provided. At first it was simply orchestral background music over which we could carry on conversations. Later, folk singers were staged, and conversation ceased. The songs became more spirited as time passed, and the audience began to clap in rhythm with the music. This mild involvement was intensified when the folk singers were replaced by a pep band and cheerleaders. By the time the band and orchestra played, "Hail to the Chief," every person was standing and applauding. This enthusiastic reception continued for almost five minutes after President Kennedy had positioned himself behind the podium. This planned mood change from passive curiosity to wild enthusiasm was created almost entirely by the impact of music.

Punctuation

Musical punctuation can serve a similar function to grammatical punctuation. It can indicate continuation of thought or termination; it can provide emphasis, parenthetical statements, separation, or coherence; it can mock, question, exclaim, or interrupt. On a larger scale, music punctuates the onset of danger, the climax, and the denouement. What melodrama fan does not recognize the power of music to punctuate?

Theme Recognition

Various pieces of music have assumed semantic qualities—they become symbols for particular referents. Ballads and tone poems are especially rich in this kind of association. What musical symbols come to your mind when you think of the Grand Canyon, or the sea, or going to a baseball game, or walking in the rain? The semantic nature of some music is so well established as to serve as emblems: "Anchors Aweigh," for instance. Others, which possess even deeper meanings and feelings, function as anthems. Also, the semantic association with historic periods allows us to specify different eras by playing either a minuet or a Charleston rhythm.

The question sometimes is not what music to select, but rather *whether* to use music at all. Your design decisions involving *diversity* often help to answer this question. But assume that your design calls for music, how do you select appropriate pieces? The matrix that follows provides some useful guidelines.

Response-Style Matrix for Music

Figure 6.4 displays the matrix for music which is defined by aloofness and tension. From your response-style matrix, you can determine the appropriate ALO/TEN profile. Given that profile, you can now select one of nine musical categories that can augment your message to help you achieve your desired response. A description of each cell follows.

Unsettling (Avant Garde)

Much of the music on the forefront attempts to elicit feelings commonly experienced in our complex, depersonalized, frustrating, unstable culture. Much of it issues musical editorial statements about corruption, filth, and futility. It is not music to be enjoyed; it is about understanding. Such music tends to be loud, suspenseful, shocking, discordant, methodical, deliberate, heavily textured, and it possesses a marked rhythm. An example of this category can be found in the overture to "Jesus Christ Superstar."

Exciting (Rock, Fusion)

The music in this category is less aloof, but equally tension-provoking. It tends toward fast tempo, fast attack, and sophisticated rhythms. It is pointed and sharp and produces sounds of short duration. Crescendo and repetition are common characteristics. An example of this category is the Mahavishnu orchestra.

Passionate (Romantic)

The Romantic Movement, which romanticized and glorified individualism, liberty, and nature, is characterized by the music of Beethoven, Liszt, Wagner, Berlioz, Brahms, Tchaikovsky, etc. The engaging, soul-lifting, passion of this music can be attributed in part to its use of: graduated dynamics (crescendo and decrescendo), extremes in both pitch range and volume, de-emphasized form (as compared with its classic predecessor), and thick texture.

	ALOOFNESS		
	H	M	L
H	UNSETTLING (Avant Garde)	EXCITING (Rock, Fusion)	PASSIONATE (Romantic)
M	PROVOCATIVE (Classic)	EVOCATIVE (Impressionistic)	INVIGORATING (Traditional Jazz)
L	LETHARGIC (Primal)	NOSTALGIC (Mood)	INNOVATIVE (Novel)

TENSION (vertical axis label)

Figure 6.4. Response-Style Matrix: Music.

Romantic music also employs climax and retreat, often in series to build to ever higher tension peaks. It welcomes virtuosity, and incorporates unusual instrumentation (unusual to the classic orchestras, that is) as well as using classic instruments unusually. This emotional music appeals to the qualities often associated with right-brain activity.

Provocative (Classic)

The music of Mozart and Hayden is essentially different (almost the counterpart) of that of the romantic composers. It is Apollonian (left-brain) music. It is much more aloof and less tension-provoking than the romantic. It is structurally elegant. It generates rich, full, complex, bold, grand, and noble music within rather precisely defined constraints. It is open, pure, sometimes spacious, and it enjoys equally major and minor keys. Classic music employs only traditional instrumentation played traditionally. Harps, pianos, and chimes—not to mention any kind of electric amplification—immediately remove a selection from the classic orchestral category.

Evocative (Impressionistic)

Music that evokes mental pictures—tone poems—enjoys a wide variety of styles, forms, and instruments. Its sounds and dynamics are descriptive. Since it is moderate in both aloofness and tension, it represents the most common source of musical augmentation for film and television productions. A good test of this music is to see if receivers of the message are unable to recall whether music was used in the message. Its best use is to add richness and subtle flavoring without calling attention to itself. Provide your own examples by listening for the "everyday work-horse" music employed during an evening's television viewing.

Invigorating (Traditional Jazz)

The up-beat quality of traditional jazz and "swing" tends to generate an effervescence that heightens engagement but does not overkill on tension responses. It compels attention, but does not overwhelm. Music in the invigorating category is typically syncopated, brittle, light, clean, in a major key, and marked by the fast decay of tones.

Lethargic (Primal)

Keep a Gregorian Chant or other medieval church music in mind as you attempt to conceptualize "primal" or "lethargic" music. Most notable are the soft dynamics originating from instruments without sophisticated resonance or amplification features. The instrumentation of primal music also limits the pitch variation to a moderate range. It is generally mellow, avoids excesses, employs simple and obvious form, and employs simple, voice-like instruments if not the voice itself as an instrument.

Nostalgic (Mood)

This sentimental mood-music category is only moderately engaging; it is reminiscent and nostalgic, but not compelling. It is usually gentle, soft, casual, and sometimes sad. Its slow attack, long tone duration, and use of diminuendo contribute to its overall effect. Often reed instruments and the darker strings (e.g., cello) create the somber mood.

Innovative (Novel)

Some music is created by careful editing of recorded sounds from the environment. And some music attempts to create such sounds instrumentally. Also, our electronic technology has introduced countless new possibilities for creating artistically engineered sounds which we are coming to regard as music. For such music to fit into this matrix cell, it must be limited to engaging, but low tension, selections. Such music is soft, harmonious, continuous, and employs long, smooth tones. Any kind of instrument is appropriate so long as it is used within these constraints. It should be light in texture with expressive variations, and the form should be de-emphasized. Improvisation is characteristic.

Some of my students have found these cell descriptors useful; others have not. The important consideration is not the category labels but the defining dimensions. Select your music according to the degree of tension and aloofness it generates. If you cannot use a panel of judges to rate various musical selections for you on these two scales, then trust your own judgment. The chances favor your selection made with these variables in mind over selections made only at the intuitive level.

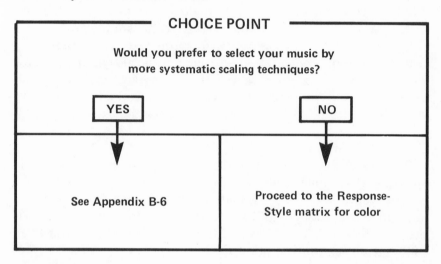

CHOICE POINT

Would you prefer to select your music by more systematic scaling techniques?

YES   NO

See Appendix B-6   Proceed to the Response-Style matrix for color

Step 15b. Consider Color as a Means of Achieving the Desired Response Style

We discovered in the "Analysis of Basic Graphics Matrix" (Figure 5.5) that color, used according to readiness level, influences the degree of graphic definition. Our choice to use full color, mood color, or color for emphasis is influenced by how "ready" we estimate our receivers to be. In considering the receiver-imposed constraints on our design, we were concerned with *whether* and *how* to use color. But now as we consider ways of achieving desired response styles, our concern must be with *which* colors to employ.

A synthesis of several sources on color theory—with heavy emphasis given to Luscher (1969)—led me to assign selected colors to the ALO/TEN matrix according to Figure 6.5a, but an attempt to test this construct against empirical data raised serious doubts regarding its validity. Figure 6.5b represents the findings of a pilot

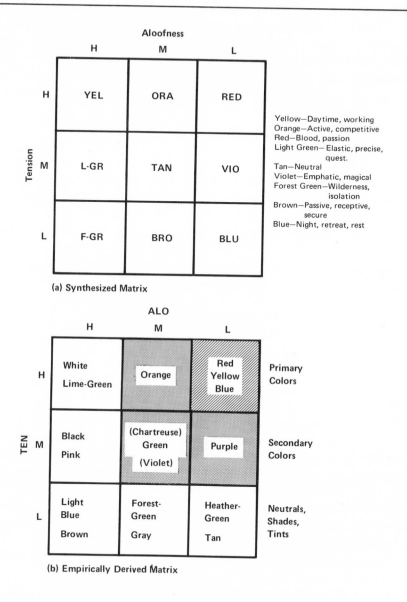

(a) Synthesized Matrix

Yellow—Daytime, working
Orange—Active, competitive
Red—Blood, passion
Light Green—Elastic, precise, quest.
Tan—Neutral
Violet—Emphatic, magical
Forest Green—Wilderness, isolation
Brown—Passive, receptive, secure
Blue—Night, retreat, rest

(b) Empirically Derived Matrix

Figure 6.5. Response-Style Matrix: Color.

study in which subjects were asked to rate a number of color chips on scales of aloofness and tension. Close comparison of these matrices reveals some significant disagreement. Although the pilot test should be replicated under tighter controls and with a larger sample of judges, I must place greater confidence in the empirical data than in those conclusions drawn largely from analogy and analytic interpretations.

I theorize that the colors in the matrix contribute to the generation of behavioral responses associated with related cells. For example, white and lime-green singly or together will generate regimented responses if the behavior is spontaneous, or aggressive/submissive responses if one is responding compulsively. Similarly, purple (low ALO/moderate TEN) will generate contemplative responses (or vigilant responses under compulsion). These predictions assume the control of all other variables; by themselves the colors may not be sufficient to produce the expected responses, but addition of a selected color to a related visual composition and a related musical selection should interact to generate noticeable signs of the predicted response.

The matrix is self-explanatory in terms of which cells relate in which ways to aloofness and tension variables, but some less obvious generalizations may be drawn from the matrix. Perhaps the most obvious (and most surprising) generalization relates to the primary colors. Rather than being relegated to three corners of the matrix, they are united in the high tension/low aloofness cell. This suggests that the primal quality (perhaps primitive) is a stronger factor than the hue in generating various response styles. Primary red, yellow, and blue elicit tension, and they are highly engaging. The secondary colors of orange, green, and purple elicit responses either lower in tension, or lower in engagement, or lower in both. Appropriately, they make up a secondary ring around the primary nucleus.

The third band of color radiating from the nucleus, while generally consistent with expectations, is a bit more complex. Both black and white (which technically are not colors at all) not only generate their own impact, but also, when mixed together, produce neutral gray and when mixed separately with colors, produce tints (color plus white) or shades (color plus black). Thus, the outer ring is characterized by black, white, neutral colors, and tints. Black, white, and tints appear to be associated with high aloofness; neutral and shades seem to be related to low tension.

These generalizations seem to be in keeping with traditional practice: formal attire (noted for its aloofness) is traditionally black and white, and neutral and muted colors are customarily used for reducing tension. Similarly, it should not be surprising that black and white television is less engaging than color television. Nor should it be surprising that television viewing (whether black and white or color) is less relaxing than dining by candlelight.

Tension can be controlled further according to the color combinations used. "Harmonious" colors are ones that are adjacent on the color wheel. They tend to reduce tension. But "complementary" colors (opposites on the color wheel) increase tension. Thus, yellow and green or yellow and orange are harmonious, but yellow and violet or red and green are complementary.

But tan, being neutral, is neither harmonious nor complementary. It provides a kind of *tabula rasa* (a blank tablet) that clears the mind for creating or for retreating into solipsistic self-sufficiency. Gray and other neutral and muted colors share tan's chameleon-like quality that blends with and supports mental activity without being noticed. Selective use of these colors can reduce tension.

Step 15c. Consider Visual Composition as a
Means of Achieving the Desired Response Style

What are some of the special trade secrets that enable a film director to intensify the drama in a "cliff-hanger" or a "horror movie"? And how can he or she capture the lyrical quality of an Irish countryside in spring? Once again, the secret lies in the designer-director's ability to control tension and aloofness. There are several compositional devices for creating visual images with differing impacts. Figure 6.6 offers abbreviated prescriptions for each matrix cell, and Figure 6.7 illustrates the extreme cells found

ALOOFNESS

		H	M	L
TENSION	**H**	Long shot Low angle Off-balance Objective viewpoint Zoom or dolly-out High contrast Dark background Deep field	Medium shot Low angle Off-balance Mixed viewpoint Jump-cut in and out High contrast Dark background Moderate field	Close-up Low angle Off-balance Subjective viewpoint Zoom or dolly-in High contrast Dark background Shallow field
	M	Long shot Eye-level Unfixed (balanced) Objective viewpoint Zoom or dolly-out Detail in shadows Deep field	Medium shot Eye-level Unfixed (balanced) Mixed viewpoint Jump-cut in and out Detail in shadows Moderate field	Close-up Eye-level Unfixed (balanced) Subjective viewpoint Zoom or dolly-in Detail in shadows Shallow field
	L	Long shot High angle Stable (secure) Objective viewpoint Zoom or dolly-out No shadow (light back- ground) Deep field	Medium shot High angle Stable (secure) Mixed viewpoint Jump-cut in and out No shadows Light background Moderate field	Close-up High angle Stable (secure) Subjective viewpoint Zoom or dolly-in No shadows Light background Shallow field

Figure 6.6. Response-Style Matrix: Visual Composition.

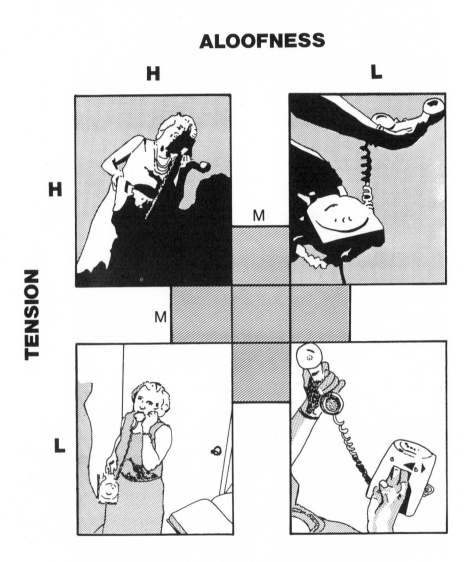

Figure 6.7. Response-Style Matrix: Visual Composition Examples.

in the four corners of the matrix. It should suffice to define these devices and to assign them to cells in different combinations. Amplification and illustration of each cell would be needlessly redundant.

Shot Distance

The shot distance is a way of controlling how much of a visual frame will be occupied by the central figure or subject. For example, in a *close-up* of a person, the face will fill the full frame; in a *medium shot,* the upper body will fill the frame; and in a *long shot*, the full body will be framed by the background. All three distances can be photographed with a 50mm lens, for instance, but extreme long- or close-shots can be photographed with wide-angle and telephoto lenses, respectively. In general, the longer the shot, the more aloof is the connotation.

Shot Angle

A visual composition may be shot from below the subject— looking up. This *low-angle* shot tends to increase tension; it makes the subject larger than life. A visual composed at *eye-level* corresponds to our normal perception of things; it normally suggests moderate tension. Finally, a shot taken from above the subject (*high angle*) tends to minimize any threat it may impose. A high-angle shot, therefore, tends to minimize tension.

Balance

To achieve visual balance, you should: (1) center the subject or counterbalance subjects according to size and distance, (2) frame for symmetry, (3) establish a wide and secure base, and (4) anchor or brace unstable objects. Stability is a concept closely related to balance; to illustrate stability, visualize: (1) a marble resting on top of a basketball (unstable), (2) a marble lying on a flat surface (neutral stability), and (3) a marble in the apex of an ice-cream cone (positive stability). Instability and imbalance tend to increase tension responses.

Viewpoint

When you view a scene as a spectator—from the grandstand so

to speak—the viewpoint is *objective.* An objective viewpoint promotes aloofness. But when you view a scene from the point of view of the subject of that scene, the viewpoint is *subjective.* Some movie scenes, for instance, are shot as if the camera were the eye of the actor; the spectator sees everything just as if he or she were doing the acting; you see your hand reaching for the door knob, but you do not see your face. Subjective shots promote engagement—low aloofness. Moderate aloofness is achieved by mixing objective and subjective points of view.

Movement In/Out

Video and movie cameras can capture the movement toward or away from the subject. A close-up shot can change smoothly to a distant shot or *vice versa.* This movement "in" or "out" from the subject can be accomplished either by moving the camera toward or from the subject (dolly shot), or by changing the focal distance of the lens (zoom shot). "Zooming- or dollying-in" (moving from a distant to a close shot) increases engagement, and the reverse increases aloofness. A *jump-shot,* a series of still shots toward or from a subject produces moderate aloofness or engagement depending upon whether the movement is in or out.

Contrast

A *high contrast* image consists only of light and dark areas. A person's face photographed in very bright sunlight produces black shadow areas and white lighted areas. High contrast shots (favorites of horror movie makers) increase tension. *Moderate contrast* shots show detail in shadowed areas, while *low contrast* shots are devoid of shadows and are comprised of only gray tones.

Background Tone

The tone of the background can be used not only to control contrast between figure and ground, but it can also lighten or darken the total impact. Generally, darker backgrounds destroy contextual information and thus produce tension-arousing uncertainty.

Depth-of-Field

Depth-of-field could affect tension in the same way background tone does by presenting or withholding information about the context. However, the stronger effect of depth-of-field seems to be associated with the aloofness factor. A shallow depth-of-field emphasizes the subject and renders both foreground and background less clear. This "zeroing-in" on the subject forces attention and thus engagement. By contrast, a deep field sometimes invites distraction and thus generates aloofness.

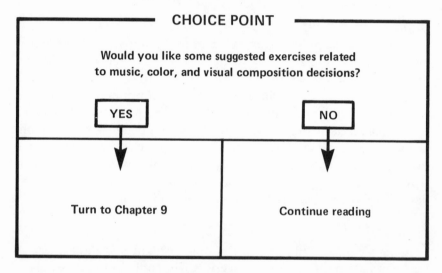

Now that you have determined how to elicit the desired response styles by controlling aloofness and tension through music, color, and visual composition, you should understand the total concept of "message complexity" well enough to finalize your fundamental design decisions. It remains only to synthesize these decisions into a time-coordinated visual pattern which can be translated into a production-ready script. Then the message can take its final form and can be submitted to the ultimate test: Does it work? Does it meet the sources' objectives? If not, how can it be revised to do so? These matters are the focus of Part III.

PART III

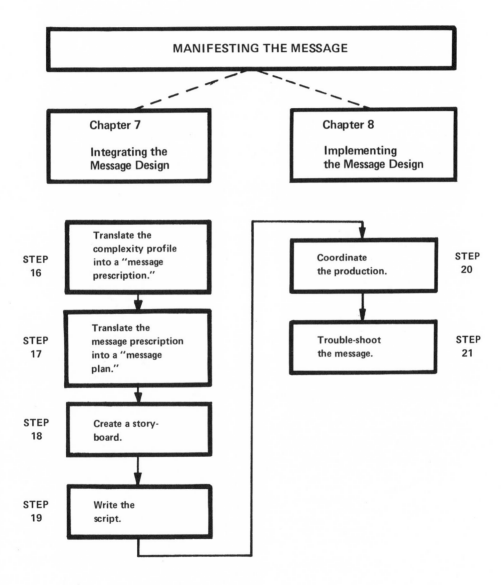

MANIFESTING THE MESSAGE

Chapter 7

Integrating the
Message Design

Chapter 8

Implementing
the Message Design

STEP
16
Translate the
complexity profile
into a "message
prescription."

STEP
17
Translate the
message prescription
into a "message
plan."

STEP
18
Create a story-
board.

STEP
19
Write the
script.

STEP
20
Coordinate
the production.

STEP
21
Trouble-shoot
the message.

169

Part III

Manifesting the Message

Part III provides the payoff for all of the investments of time and energy made in Parts I and II. Having worked through the intricacies of information and complexity control, we now have at our command the key elements of the model. Given the information-load commitments (in the form of an outline) and message-complexity commitments (symbolized by the complexity profile), we can now determine the appropriate duration of the message. Then, by laying the outline and the complexity patterns out visually, coordinated along a time line, we will generate a "blueprint" of the whole message. This "message plan" not only enables us to determine at any moment what is needed to make the message work, but also it allows us to view the whole message in the mind's eye.

This is where the whole message comes together! It is probably the most exciting and rewarding part of the entire process. Marshall McLuhan has noted that clients often enjoy the production at the "storyboard" stage more than they do at the finished-production stage, because they are intimately involved with the image's creation, as their imaginations are prompted by the sketches and descriptions.

The schematic model for Part III, unlike the one for Part II, is inherently sequential—each step must follow the preceding one if the process is to be meaningful. Chapter 7, "Integrating the Message Design," develops four steps: Step 16 involves translating the complete message profile into verbal descriptions of how the complexity levels are to be achieved. Step 17 translates these verbal *prescriptions* into a visual, time-coordinated *message plan* or "blueprint." Step 18 transforms each moment of the message plan into a page on the storyboard. And, finally, Step 19 delivers a storyboard-coordinated production script.

Chapter 8, "Implementing the Message Design," develops the final two steps in the process model. Bear in mind that a message designer's function is analogous to that of an architect. Each takes on the responsibility of creating a design that works to serve the client's needs. Neither is inherently responsible for producing the design. While an architect is not charged with building the edifice, he or she is usually expected to oversee (or at least be available for consultation during) its building. Similarly, a message designer can provide great service as a coordinator of production without actually becoming involved with the technicalities of production. Step 20 defines the tasks of coordinating production.

In Step 21, the designer examines the responses to the produced message in light of the source's purpose. He or she evaluates the message by the criteria established in the performance objectives. If the responses match the objectives, the designer's job is finished; if not, it is "back to the drawing board" in an effort to trouble-shoot and revise the message.

"We could ... [use a complexity profile] as a critical tool. As an archaeologist might, we could regard ... [any given message] as an artifact and attempt to infer the motives of the people who created it. Or, we could offer predictions about its probable impact. ...

"But our main interest at this point is to use the profile to generate a message prescription for a message we might wish to design. ..."

Chapter 7

PROFILE

MESSAGE
PRESCRIPTION

MESSAGE PLAN

STORYBOARD

SCRIPT

Central Idea

You can integrate your information-control and complexity-control design decisions into a unified message by: (1) translating the complexity profile into a message prescription, (2) translating the message prescription into a message plan, (3) creating a storyboard, and (4) writing the script.

Steps

16. Translate the complexity profile into a "message prescription."
17. Translate the message prescription into a "message plan."
18. Create a storyboard.
19. Write the script.

Objectives

1. To list means of achieving any given level for each of the six complexity elements.
2. To assign time values to the entire message and to each informational/structural component.
3. To coordinate variations in message complexity with the informational/structural components within a given complexity level.
4. To generate storyboard pages from given message complexity values specified by the message plan.
5. To write a production script which reflects all of the previous design decisions.

174

Chapter 7

Integrating the Message Design

A summary of the ways to select a complexity profile mentioned previously will provide an appropriate focal point. The method that is probably foremost in your mind is to build up a profile from the various matrices according to the qualities you anticipate or desire in the given communication situation. Another method is to determine first (by means of empirically derived "U-curves") (Marsh, 1973) the optimal or preferred complexity level for a given audience, and then to assign profile values within that constraint. A third way to select a profile is to find a "model message" you would like to emulate and scale it on each of the complexity scale items. The derived values provide the data for the profile.

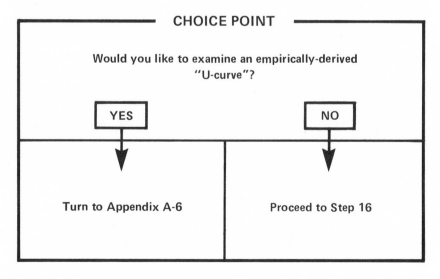

CHOICE POINT

Would you like to examine an empirically-derived "U-curve"?

YES

NO

Turn to Appendix A-6

Proceed to Step 16

**Step 16. Translate the Complexity Profile
into a "Message Prescription"**

To illustrate Step 16, I will use a complexity profile generated by analysis of a model message. I asked 13 trained judges to scale a short film on each of the six complexity elements. The selected film is entitled: "Is It Always Right to Be Right?" Translating the averaged ratings into a graphic display, I identified the profile shown in Figure 7.1.

We could, at this point, use this profile as a critical tool. As an archaeologist might, we could regard that film as an artifact and attempt to infer the motives of the people who created it. Or, we could offer predictions about its probable impact. Given that the average complexity value is almost perfectly at the scale's midpoint, we might infer that it was intended to reach a broad, literate audience who could get the message with little strain. The diversity value (the highest) suggests that the designer wanted the audience to like or enjoy the presentation of this "average weight" message. The contextual atmosphere was generally "routine"—appropriate for allowing the viewers to recognize the film's position, and appropriate to be viewed in an assembly of viewers. Its general style would likely be "elegant/subtle," given its SOP/REA values. And it was probably designed to elicit a "calculating" response style—characterized by its anticipation of consequences and its designing of courses of action.

As a matter of interest, this brief sketch rather accurately describes this film. If we were to pursue this critical challenge through all of the matrices, we would discover even greater correspondence between the profile-generated predictions and the actual film. But our main interest at this point is to use the profile to generate a message prescription for a message we might wish to design—not to play critic or anthropologist more than is necessary to illustrate this opportunity.

The message prescription typically is organized according to the six complexity elements displayed in the complexity profile:

Diversity
The film contained about 20 identifiable elements of diversity,

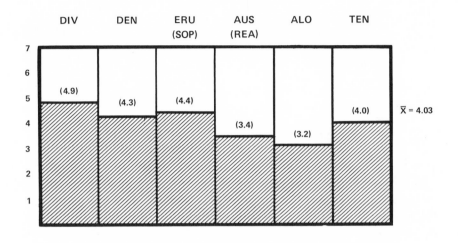

Figure 7.1. Complexity Profile: "Is It Always Right to Be Right?"

and that provides a good guideline to employ in this prescription. We can vary visual, audible, or structural qualities any way we prefer so long as we select about 20. For our illustrative prescription, I will specify the following: Not only must there be color, but it must be used at times to distort reality for the sake of shock, emphasis, and mood. The medium must accommodate motion at variable speeds. Visual presentations must include normal and distorted photography, animated character art, and verbal displays. Special effects, such as double-exposures, fades, wipes, and stop-frames, are to be employed. A wide range of voices heard singly and in choral reading is to be augmented by music of various styles and sound effects. The sound effects are to be used both to describe and to punctuate. A variety of camera angles and viewpoints is required. The structural patterns will include: strong overall framing, narration, problem-solution development, comparison-contrast, and montage.

Density

By assigning the following values to the three dimensions of density, I can retain the average density value of this profile:

Rate of change	6
Redundancy	3.4
Structural depth	3.5

$$12.9/3 = 4.3$$

In order to achieve this definitely high level of rate of change, this message must suppress transitions and conjunctions, provide several and disparate supports, suppress pauses, and employ a rapid speaking rate. Also, several cut-in and cut-out shots as well as various angles should be employed in developing single supports. Plan enough shots to change every three to five seconds. Greater than average redundancy can be achieved by preview, development, and summary treatment; numerous supports for each terminal point, comparison-contrast structure; parallelism, repetition, and paraphrasing in scripting style; and repetition of sound and musical effects. Structural depth will achieve the appropriate level by dividing the central idea into a few (three or four) main points and then subdividing two or three of those. Thus, some information chunks will be created by supporting main points directly, and others will be created by supporting first-level subpoints.

Erudition (Sophistication)

I have elected to distribute the erudition dimensions in the following way to achieve the profile's average of 4.4.

Abstraction	5
Implicitness	5
Precision	3.2

$$13.2/3 = 4.4$$

Thus, the points should be cast at a "general rule" level so that their generality allows them to be applied to a wide range of circumstances. Also, to preserve this level of abstraction, select supports with a universal recognition-value and avoid identifying any specific referent. The implicitness will be achieved by subtle suggestion, characterization, and self-stimulating association. In particular, the use of montage and synecdoche as stylistic devices, as well as incomplete thoughts and fragmented quotations, is advised. Precision must be lower than average. The temptation to document claims with evidence and to qualify claims to limit their generality must be resisted.

Austerity (Readiness)

Since we anticipate an audience that is slightly below average in readiness, our message must be less austere than normal. In other words, the framing, relevance, and memory aids must be some-what pronounced. The framing will be promoted by the overall introduction, body, and conclusion structure but should be reinforced with a brief expository background and a division step immediately following the statement of the central idea. Rele-vance of the topic for the audience should be explicit, especially in relation to the nature of the problem and the benefits of the solution. Care must be exercised, while stressing relevance, not to offset the overall implicitness level prescribed for erudition. Apply obvious association methods to the action requested in the peroration in order to fix the desired response in the memory. Use association, repetition, rhyme, and rhythm to strengthen memory.

The visual materials best suited to this sophistication/readiness interaction level should center around images of moderate definition which either interpret or distort objective reality. The language should be elegant and forcible alternately and should approach the style of popular digest and quality household magazines.

Aloofness

Aloofness on this profile is clearly (although slightly) below normal; thus, the engagement properties of this message must be enhanced somewhat. To accomplish higher than normal engagement, we see that reward, involvement, and frustration should be intensified by roughly equal degrees. A strong opportunity for reward will present itself at the solution stage where the benefits of the proposal can be stressed. Similarly, frustration can be aroused emphatically as the problem is described in terms of failing present efforts. The chief ways of gaining greater involvement should be through personalized language style, invitations to complete thought sequences and provide one's own further examples, and through imaginatively filling-in definition and closure on the visual aspects.

Tension

The function of tension at an "average" level (4.0) is to strike a balance between a state of attention and that of relaxation. Tension responses should be subtle, but not absent. I have elected to play down shock (level 3.0) because of its blatant nature. Slight shock will be created by unexpected visual composition (especially montage) and unexpected musical and verbal effects. Suspense, above average in this message (5.0), will be created primarily by announcing what is to come and then delaying its immediate treatment. This structural suspense can be intensified by sentence composition which withholds the active verb until the end of the sentence is reached. In general, anything that can prevent prediction will intensify suspense. An average amount of conflict should be employed. Care should be taken to prevent a conflict between the source's values and those of the receiver. The conflict should be aimed at a clash between desired goals and the present policy and between our solution and alternative solutions.

When we consider the ALO/TEN interaction, we can prescribe music that alternates from evocative (impressionistic) and invigorating (traditional jazz). The predominant colors should be tan (especially for background) and violet. To intensify the tension at selected points, use violet with yellow. Reduce tension by combining violet and blue. Finally, the visual composition should be shot primarily from a medium distance and secondarily at close-up range. Maintain eye-level on most shots. Strive for a precarious balance (balanced, but not anchored), or an alternation between predominantly balanced shots with an occasionally unbalanced one. Use several subjective-viewpoint shots. Employ jump-cuts, zooms, and dolly shots in and out. Retain detail in shadows and vary the depth of field from normal to close.

Step 17. Translate the Message Prescription into a "Message Plan"

A message plan, you will recall, coordinates the informational content with the message complexity factors along a time line. It allows for simultaneous comparisons of information and development at any moment in the message. It represents a further refinement in the distribution of complexity characteristics.

The first item to consider in the development of a message plan is the *time line.* Begin planning the time line by determining the message's length. While the duration of a message is often set by outside considerations, there are some general norms for given message types. For instance: television commercials range from ten to 90 seconds, college lectures tend to range from 30 to 120 minutes, and instructional films range from four to 75 minutes. Perhaps the best way to determine the range for any given message type is to sample many messages in that category and to develop a statistical profile.

Table 7.1 represents my findings and scaling efforts involving a large sample of instructional films drawn from a college film catalog. (Notice that the intervals above the mean are not equal to the intervals below the mean because the distribution was not normal.)

Given such an empirically-derived time scale and the following matrix (Figure 7.2), you can determine for any time value (in the cells) what the appropriate message complexity and information load are. Actually, given any two values, you can determine the third. For example, if you are designing an instructional film with an average complexity of 4 and an information load of 3, your time value should be 3. When that scale value is translated to minutes in Table 7.1, we learn that your film should range between 18.8 and 28.1 minutes. Unless you have a reason to do otherwise, your best decision would be to set your message length at the midpoint on that range. Your message should, therefore, be set at a duration of 23.4 minutes.

Table 7.1

Time Scale for Instructional Films.

Scale Value	Range (in minutes)	
1	0 - 9.3	
2	9.4 - 18.7	
3	18.8 - 28.1	
4	28.2 - 43.8	$\overline{X} = 32.9$
5	43.9 - 54.9	
6	55.0 - 66.0	
7	66.1 and above	

With the message duration established, you must now assign times to each information chunk so that they total to that time. These time assignments are somewhat arbitrary, but a good guideline is to make their times proportional to their obscurity indexes. Notice that on the "message plan" worksheet (Figure 7.3), there is a row for "unit time" (U/T) and one for "cumulative time (C/T). Unit time measures the duration of any given structural unit (e.g., information chunk, introduction, transition, etc.), and cumulative time carries a running total so that at any point in the message, you know how much time has been accounted for.

At this point, you transfer your box-outline onto the message plan according to the time you wish to allot to each structural unit. Notice in Figure 7.3 how the complete outline is laid out above the time line. This example has been foreshortened, but

7				1	2	3	4
6			1	2	3	4	5
5		1	2	3	4	5	6
4	1	2	3	4	5	6	7
3	2	3	4	5	6	7	
2	3	4	5	6	7		
1	4	5	6	7			
	1	2	3	4	5	6	7

Message Complexity (vertical axis label)

Information Load

Cell values represent the time scale. Time scale values are determined empirically by sampling the duration of messages in a given population of messages.

Figure 7.2. Time/Information/Complexity Matrix.

enough is presented to illustrate how the outline is transferred onto the message plan.

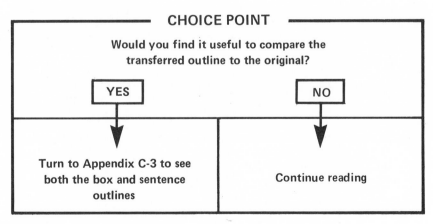

CHOICE POINT

Would you find it useful to compare the transferred outline to the original?

YES

NO

Turn to Appendix C-3 to see both the box and sentence outlines

Continue reading

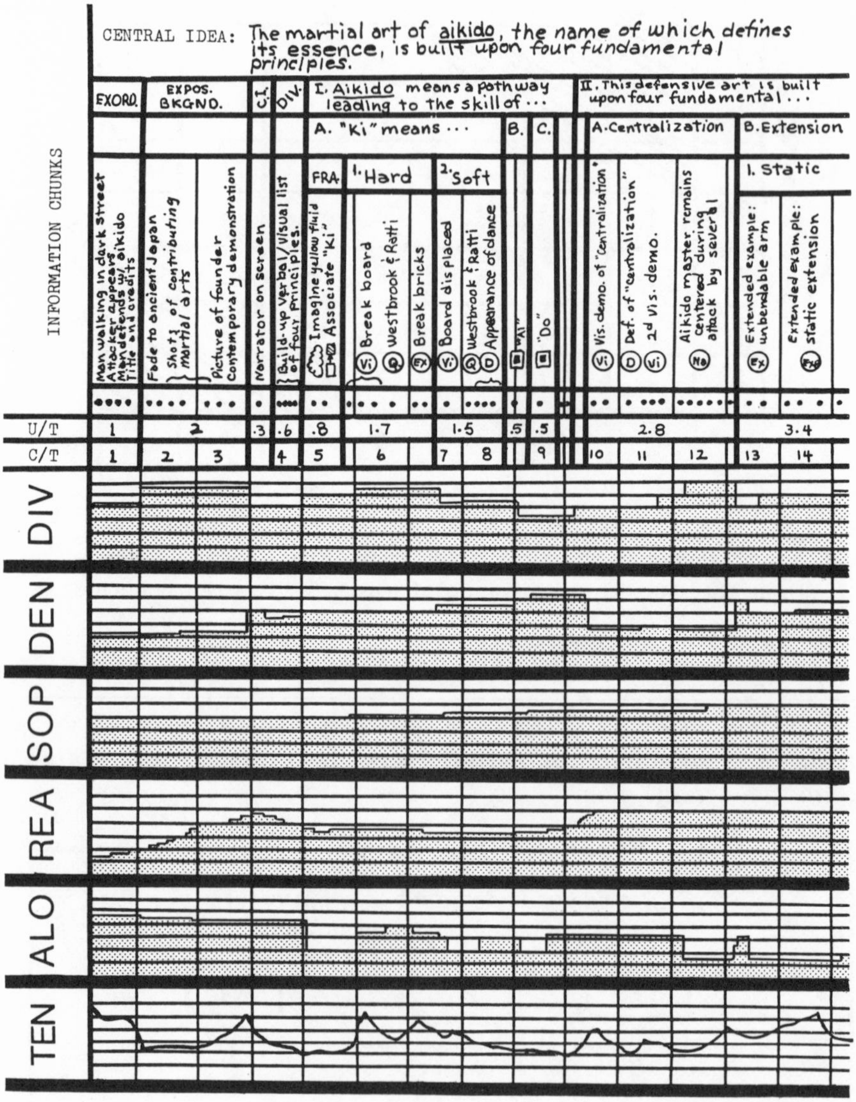

CENTRAL IDEA: The martial art of aikido, the name of which defines its essence, is built upon four fundamental principles.

	EXORD.	EXPOS. BKGND.		C.I.	DIV.	I. Aikido means a pathway leading to the skill of ···							B.	C.	II. This defensive art is built upon four fundamental ···				
						A. "Ki" means ···									A. Centralization			B. Extension		
							FRA	1. Hard			2. Soft								1. Static	

INFORMATION CHUNKS

Man walking in dark street / Attacker appears / Man wards off aikido / Title and credits

Fade to ancient Japan

Shots of contributing martial arts

Picture of founder / Contemporary demonstration

Narrator on screen

Build-up verbal/visual list of four principles

Imagine yellow fluid / Associate "Ki"

(V.) Break board
(a) Westbrook & Ratti
(V.) Break bricks
(V.) Board dis placed
(a) Westbrook & Ratti
(V.) Appearance of dance

"Ki"
"Do"

(V.) Vis. demo. of "centralization"
(D) Def. of "centralization"
(V.) 2nd vis. demo.
(N) Aikido master remains centered during attack by several

(V.) Extended example: unbendable arm
(V.) Extended example: static extension

U/T	1	2		.3	.6	.8	1.7			1.5			.5	.5		2.8			3.4
C/T	1	2	3	4		5	6			7	8		9		10	11	12	13	14

DIV

DEN

SOP

REA

ALO

TEN

Figure 7.3. Message Plan.

Look for the small dots just above the unit-time row. Each dot represents one page on the storyboard. These dots not only indicate how many storyboard pages you will need (and each page translates into a slide if you are doing a slide show), but also the visual pattern of the dots provides a sense of movement and pace.

When the outline has been correlated with the time line, you may direct your attention to the assignment of complexity elements to the message plan. Remember that each element must average out to the value specified by the complexity profile. In other words, if you employ more tension at one point than the prescribed profile value, you must use less at another point in order to maintain an averaged-out value. I begin by drawing a light line straight across the scale at the prescribed level. (In our current example, diversity is established at 4.9.) Then, as I work through each unit of the message, I determine where the greater diversity is required and where I can compensate for having exceeded the average. So it continues through the other complexity scales. I should point out that sophistication tends to remain flat. In this example, however, I designed in a slight increase as time progresses because latent ability to handle abstraction and precision might be released owing to the special nature of the subject matter. Also, notice that I expect readiness to vary at different times in the message.

The tension line is probably better depicted by more pointed peaks and valleys than is appropriate for the other elements. Tension can peak and fall away, or build gradually and decay in such a variety of ways that I find it useful to capture both the desired and the anticipated tension levels in much the same way that bio-feedback instruments do on their graphs.

It is generally advisable, when you have completed your message plan, to lay it aside for awhile. When you return to it a few hours later, or perhaps the next day, attempt to visualize the message just as you have specified it. If it seems to need some adjustment, do it, but remember to trade off any complexity values you change. This is a good time to consult with your client or others whose reactions you need to monitor. Given this message plan, you can communicate rather fully what the message will be like. It is much easier to change it now than it will be later. If you wait for approval until after you have completed the storyboard, any change represents a waste of time and energy. But changes can be incorporated rather specifically and reasonably in the message plan without damaging the integrity of the design—SO LONG AS YOUR COMPLEXITY VALUES CONTINUE TO AVERAGE OUT TO YOUR PROFILE VALUES.

Step 18. Create a Storyboard

The storyboard integrates all of your design decisions into the message's first manifested form. With a storyboard in hand, you can share rather precisely the product of your design efforts. This pre-production peek at the message allows you to invite feedback once again before the costly production gets under way. Some designers have reported to me that as they complete a segment of their storyboards, they seclude themselves, relax, close their eyes, and run that segment of the message in their private, internalized "editing studio." If something does not work the way it should, they just blink their eyes and rerun the edited version. With a little practice, most people can learn to visualize and edit in their heads from a storyboard. It is both a cost-effective and enjoyable editing process.

Storyboard techniques vary widely: some use 3 x 5 cards which they can lay out on a table top; others use prepared sheets which they bind into a booklet; some prefer small frames; still others prefer large ones; and some merely write verbal descriptions in lieu of sketches. Actually, artistic talent is not required for creating storyboards. What *is* required is the ability to visualize a shot and to communicate your desires to production specialists. One exception to this statement is worthy of note: If your project requires approval from a client or a committee, etc., it may be advisable to prepare a "finished" storyboard. Otherwise, it seems needlessly costly to render your storyboard with "perfection."

I have selected two storyboard pages from the message plan for illustrative purposes. Thirteen minutes into the message, at point II.B.1, I am to support the point related to "static extension" with a 1.5 minute example. The four dots below the support symbol indicate that four storyboard pages will be required to develop this example. I will select the first two for my purposes. Refer to Figures 7.4 and 7.5.

I prefer the practice of writing that portion of the script on the back of the previous storyboard page so that I can read the script as I look at the frame. This script material is written to prescription also. In the case of these two pages, the scripted portions take this form:

(Frame 47)

MUSIC: Under (invigorating Japanese selection).

ANN: Notice the defender's relaxed arm. Actually, his whole body is relaxed because he is centered.

MUSIC: Up three seconds, then under voice.

DEF: I am thinking that my power is extending through my arms to my fingertips. I am concentrating on my conviction that my power is constantly going out into the distance and that my arm is unbendable.

ANN: Even though the attacker is applying his full strength, the defender's arm is relaxed enough that he can move his hand from side-to-side.

MUSIC: Up.

(Frame 48)

MUSIC: Under voice.

DEF: In Aikido we feel that our power must be constantly extended because if it were not, it would stop short. If that happens, we lose control over the attacker's power, or "ki." If I stop believing for one second that my power is flowing through my arm, it will bend.

MUSIC: Up three seconds, then under.

Try visualizing this portion of the "aikido" message. Close your eyes. Relax. Ask someone to read the script within the times prescribed. (Or, better still, tape record the script and play it.) Do not try to force your images—let them come up as they will. After three or four runs through the imagined production, check the prescription to see how close your working image is to what is needed. Make one or two alterations at a time and continue re-running it. Try different approaches to achieving the same end. By experiencing the message in this manner, you will acquire tacitly many details of which you are not consciously aware. So, equipped with expectations based upon your mental "ideal," you will be better able to direct the production of your message and to know when it has reached the desired state.

Figure 7.4. Storyboard Page (Example 1).

Figure 7.5. Storyboard Page (Example 2).

It is at this point that your creativity can breathe life into your creation. The subtle nuances of your uniqueness will leave their marks on your message. This kind of disciplined creativity—creativity within situation-imposed constraints—is the mark of a professional. It captures the essence of a Shakespeare or a Beethoven creating brilliantly within the constraints imposed by the sonnet or the sonata format. *Artistry requires both freedom and constraint.* The message-design model provides the constraints; you can provide the freedom. Freedom is related to the number of options you have available. The more variations you can generate within your prescription, the greater your number of choices, and the greater your freedom and your artistry.

When you reach the point that you can command this kind of private performance of your own message, and when you are satisfied with what you experience, you are ready to capture that experience in the form of a production script.

Step 19. Write the Script

The script, in essence, should be written by the time your storyboard is complete. It remains only to put it into a format that communicates your decisions to others and facilitates its production.

There are a few format conventions that make scripts easier to use both for the talent and the director:

First, leave a wide margin on the left side of the page (two or three inches on an 8½ x 11-inch sheet). This margin serves two purposes: it makes lines shorter so that it is easier for the reader to keep his or her place while recording, and it provides space for coordinating visual and technical information with the audio track.

Second, always *type* the script, and further, always type the portions to be spoken in "ALL CAPS." It is often better for both vocal projection and microphone technique to hold the script at an arm's length from the face. The script typed in all capital letters is simply more easily seen at that distance.

Third, double- or triple-space the typing of the spoken portions. This practice, like typing in all caps, makes the text easier to see, and it also allows space for writing corrections or substantive changes in the script. Additionally, some readers like to mark their scripts for pauses, emphasis, and pronunciations. Triple-spacing leaves enough space to mark the script without interfering with legibility.

Fourth, be consistent in the manner of presenting the marginal notes. Some directors/producers prefer a miniature sketch or image from the storyboard to accompany the spoken texts. Others are satisfied with either a frame number or a number and a brief verbal description of the shot. Select the format that meets the requirements of your situation, but use it *consistently*. The production booth can get pretty busy at times, so finding information at a glance can make the difference between a smooth, professional production and one that falls short. For the same reason, be consistent in the order of presentation. Typically, the visual frame reference is the first item needed. Then special camera or lighting instructions, and finally, audio instructions, such as music or sound effects cues.

Fifth, be specific regarding the timing of special effects. Indicate when the music goes under the voice and when it terminates. Pinpoint the sound effects. Detail when the colored light goes on and for how long.

Sixth, remember to number the pages. Numbered pages make it easier for the director/producer and the talent to communicate, and sometimes script pages get jumbled during reading. It is embarrassing during a second take for a reader to discover that page five follows where he or she left page three mid-sentence. Incidentally, it is a wise practice to avoid ending a page of script mid-sentence.

Here are two examples of how a production script may take different forms:

Example 1

Frame 47.
(Unbendable arm)
Cam. From L/S zoom-in
to subj. C/U.
Mus. Cut #7 under ANN,
then up for 3 sec.
Mus. Under DEF.

ANN: NOTICE THE DEFENDER'S RE-
LAXED ARM. ACTUALLY, HIS
WHOLE BODY IS RELAXED BE-
CAUSE HE IS CENTERED.

DEF: I AM THINKING THAT MY POW-
ER IS EXTENDING THROUGH MY
ARMS TO MY FINGERTIPS. I AM

Mus. Up after "side." Hold
until Frame #48.

CONCENTRATING ON MY CON-
VICTION THAT MY POWER IS
CONSTANTLY GOING OUT INTO
THE DISTANCE AND THAT MY
ARM IS UNBENDABLE.

ANN: EVEN THOUGH THE ATTACKER
IS APPLYING HIS FULL
STRENGTH, THE DEFENDER'S
ARM IS RELAXED ENOUGH
THAT HE CAN MOVE HIS HAND
FROM SIDE-TO-SIDE.

Example 2
Frame 47.

CAM: F R O M   L / S
Z O O M - I N   T O
SUBJ. C/U.
MUS: CUT #7 UNDER
ANN, UP 3 SEC.,
T H E N   U N D E R
DEF.

ANN: NOTICE THE DEFENDER'S RE-
LAXED ARM. ACTUALLY, HIS
WHOLE BODY IS RELAXED BE-
CAUSE HE IS CENTERED.

DEF: I AM THINKING THAT MY POW-
ER IS EXTENDING THROUGH MY
ARMS TO MY . . . .

One final note of caution should be offered regarding script writing. Most writers write so that their material will be seen rather than heard. The result is that what is intended to sound like talk turns out to sound, as the late Professor Brigance observed, like "an essay on its hind legs." Writing assumes a history of visual reference and thus can refer to the "example cited above." When spoken rather than seen, such phrases sound stilted.

One excellent way of "writing for the ear" is to tape record extemporaneous comments spoken from an outline. When transcribed, the undesired repetitions, non-fluencies, and inaccuracies can be edited out and still retain the desired spoken quality. Some scriptwriters always strive to write in a conversational style, but such a general rule ignores differences both in receivers' needs and appropriate response styles. A better general rule would be: while you need not always write scripts conversationally, you should always write them for the ear. Becoming aware of the differences between reading and speaking styles, augmented by some practice, will lead to more effective scriptwriting.

Chapter 8

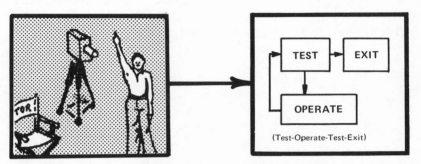

COORDINATE THE PRODUCTION　　　**TROUBLE-SHOOT THE MESSAGE**

Central Idea

Implementing the design message involves both coordinating the production and trouble-shooting the produced message in order to make needed revisions.

Steps

20. Coordinate the production.
21. Trouble-shoot the message.

Objectives

1. To recognize basic production-related logistic techniques.
2. To recognize basic production-related economic concepts.
3. To recognize basic legal precautions associated with production.
4. To discriminate professional from amateur productions.
5. To recognize the director/producer's responsibilities for:
   a.　Selecting and directing talent.
   b.　Managing the visual production.
6. To recognize the appropriate relationship between a designer and a director/producer.
7. To diagnose the causes for message failure.
8. To recommend modifications in produced messages required to achieve the unobtained objectives.

194

Chapter 8

Implementing the Message Design

This book is about *designing* messages; it is *not* about directing and producing them. The parallel between the roles of an architect and a building contractor is a useful one for understanding the relationship between a message designer and a director/producer. While it is necessary for the architect to understand the capabilities, limitations, and responsibilities of the contractor, it is not necessary for the architect to be able to build the structures he or she designs. Similarly, the message designer must know what is technically possible, feasible, and acceptable to be produced, but it is not essential for the designer to be able to direct and produce the physical product.

Nor is it mandatory that the designer and the director/producer roles be executed by different individuals. Indeed, many professionals have worked up through production specialties to become designers. Certainly, they are capable of both designing and producing a media message. And, similarly, many designers have gone on to acquire the training and experience in production after they have been established as designers. In smaller operations, the luxury of following an original design through to its final production stages is feasible and certainly rewarding. But in larger-scale operations, it is generally more "comparatively advantageous" economically for each person to specialize in the thing he or she does best. A corollary to this general principle is that the more one narrows the scope of his or her activities, the more highly discriminating (and thus more valuable) that person becomes. Therefore, role separation is usual in larger operations, yet it is imperative that the functions be coordinated if efficiency and effectiveness are to be realized. In this chapter, we will consider what the designer should know about directing and producing in order to design messages better. Ultimately, the constraints imposed upon production must be considered by the designer. The practical world seldom supports the "fountainhead" ideal.

Step 20. Coordinate the Production

Designer Responsibilities During Production

When you are ready to take your production script and storyboard to a production house, you should also be prepared to experience pressure to agree to a "state-of-the-art" production. The professional producers are generally aware of the latest technical advances, and they have refined their discrimination abilities to detect the slightest technical imperfection. Naturally, their jobs are more interesting when they are challenged to their capacity. It is more rewarding for them to strive for the best possible production, and it is more profitable. Yet, the decisions regarding production quality probably ought to be based upon an economic trade-off between quality and cost rather than upon considerations of quality alone. The mathematical curve that approaches the "state-of-the-art" condition is exponential rather than linear. That is, your stereo set may produce a 90 percent noise-free signal, and it cost you $500. If you wanted to up-grade to a set that produced a 95 percent noise-free signal, it would cost you perhaps $1,000. Every step closer you get to "state-of-the-art" production, the more your costs accelerate. Often you can get a very acceptable production at half the cost of the "top-of-the-line" product.

I take the position that the quality of the production is situation-relative and that the decision should be made on the basis of design principles rather than on aesthetic grounds. An examination of some basic economic concepts will help clarify this aspect of the designer's responsibilities for the production.

Make Basic Economic Decisions
Allocating Resources Between Design and Production. Duna-

than (1979) holds that the distribution of resources between design and production should be made on the basis of the receiver's need for the message:

> Only when the need for the proposed instruction is known can the developer make a rational decision appropriating resources to design and production.
>
> . . . the point of view should be that design values are an absolute; instruction works or it does not work. . . . There can be no compromising on design and its related components of task analysis, pretesting, field testing, and so forth. . . .
>
> Production, on the other hand, is not an absolute. . . . Other things being equal, resources can be given to or taken from the cost of production value without handicapping the design.
>
> . . . If the audience need is high, production value can be safely reduced. If the audience need is low, more resources need to be allocated to production, keeping in mind that the resources added to production must not come from the resources available for design.
>
> . . . When need is low or unknown, the ratio of design to production cost is 1:1. If need is moderate, production costs should be approximately half of design costs. When need is high, the cost ratio of design to production could be as high as the developer feels is safe without jeopardizing first adaptations.
>
> . . . Design value is constant; once its costs are determined, adding more money is not frosting the cake; it is frosting the frosting, and it results in overdesign (pp. 17-18, 59).

Figure 8.1 illustrates Dunathan's model abstracted above.

Product Transformation Curve. Another basic economic concept of which the designer should be aware is the "product transformation curve," illustrated in Figure 8.2. This curve says in essence that if you produce more of one product, you must do it at the expense of another. In other words, the more of Product A you produce, the less of Product B you will be able to produce. It is a fundamental principle of "trade-offs." Here are a couple of examples:

(1) Given that your total resources are fixed and all others are committed except the amount in question, your task is to decide what the trade-off should be between quality of talent and quality of technical production. If you spend enough to get star-quality talent, you will not have enough money left to pay for adequate

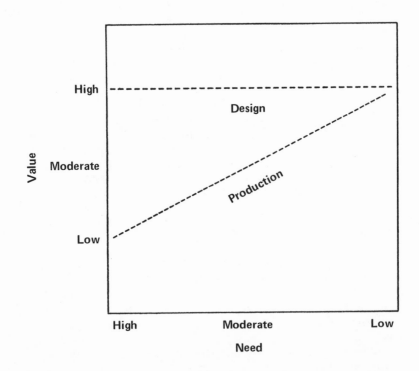

*Figure 8.1. Relationship of Design and Production Value to Need.
(Reproduced by permission.)*

technical production. The reverse is also true; if you use
state-of-the-art technical production, your talent will have to be
amateurs. Of course, these are extreme cases. You should choose
the point on the curve that represents the balance to which you
are willing to be committed.

(2) Within a given time limit, you wish both to persuade and to
instruct. Persuasion and instruction are your products, and since
both require different methods of development, you must decide
what the appropriate trade-off should be.

In Figure 8.2, point X is unattainable and point Y is less

Figure 8.2. Product Transformation Curve (after Mansfield, 1977).

desirable than the points on the curve. Sometimes inefficiency or unforeseen circumstances force an operation to point Y. Yet, technical advancement may result in greater cost-effectiveness so that the whole curve may shift upward, thus raising the original limits. For example, if you were to seek out a production house that uses a new editing console, which increases editing efficiency, the resulting savings could be distributed between talent and production at your desired trade-off ratio. Such efficiency has the same impact that increased resources would offer.

Equilibrium Price Curve. Another economic constraint that affects the limits within which a designer must produce is the total cost of the product and a part of that cost is the price the designer must set on his or her services. Establishing the price of services is related to two variables: supply and demand. Let us consider briefly these interrelated variables, as illustrated in Figure 8.3.

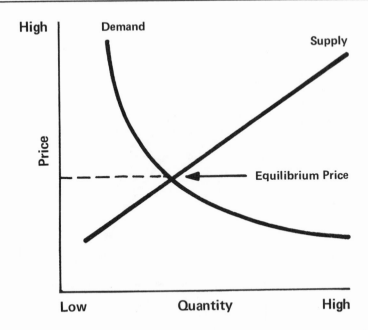

Figure 8.3. Equilibrium Price Curve (after Mansfield, 1977).

First, the smaller the quantity demanded, the higher the price. Certain "economies of scale" permit the price to be reduced as more product is required. For instance, the second hundred copies of printed matter may cost half as much as the first hundred because the cost of "set-up" is not involved in the second hundred. Notice also that the demand curve falls off as the supply curve rises. It falls off more sharply at first and then begins to level out. (There will be an enduring minimal demand regardless of supply.) But as the demand decreases, the price comes down. As long as there is high demand for your training film, it will command a good price, but as competition decreases the demand for your film, you will have to lower your price if you wish to sell it.

Now notice how supply is related to demand. When high demand commands a high price, the competition, wishing to take advantage of this favorable market, rushes into production and thus increases the supply of films to meet that demand. But since the demand is decreased as the supply is increased, the price will also drop. Then either you or your competition would have to stop production because the price cannot pay the costs. The decreased supply then increases both the demand and the price. This cycle could continue indefinitely. One way to combat this kind of destructive cycle is not to charge all that the traffic will bear in the first instance. It would be better in the long run to set an "equilibrium price" for your film. Since an equilibrium price matches the quantity supplied with the demand, it is the price which will not attract undue competition, which pays a fair return, and which can be maintained for a long time.

Even though these economic concepts are quite basic and very general in application, they do describe methods for dealing with the economic realities that ultimately influence design decisions. Perhaps the best single bit of economic advice for a designer is to abandon the idealistic position that "this message deserves the very best of everything, and if I can't do it *right,* I won't do it at all." Great design is nearly always done within constraints. It is the business of economics to provide guidelines for distributing your resources wisely within the constraints of your unique situation.

Make Basic Logistic Decisions

Logistics is the art of having the right thing at the right place at the right time. Unless the designer is also the director/producer, it is not necessary for him or her to coordinate every light, camera, microphone, etc., directly; but it is important to plan, on an overall scale, what must be done, when it must be done, and who is responsible for getting it done. Four basic logistic techniques are described below. When they are used wisely, they not only increase the chances for a successful production, but they also minimize the "worry factors" that can divert your energies from more productive pursuits.

The Gantt Chart. A Gantt chart is a simple time line which represents visually *when* each essential activity begins and *how much time* it requires. The example provided in Figure 8.4 is

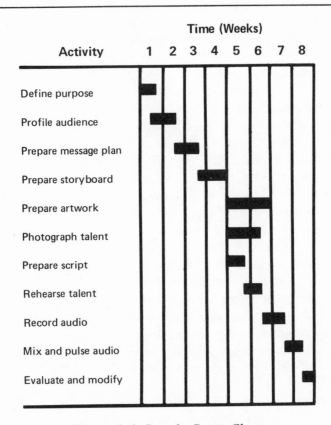

Figure 8.4. Simple Gantt Chart.

self-explanatory. Although the example is a very simple one, this technique can be applied to projects involving many activities, and it can be coded in any unit of time. This kind of visual display allows one to determine which activities can be conducted simultaneously and which ones must be conducted sequentially. It provides a convenient way of determining when work-load peaks will occur and who will be involved when. For instance, rather than keeping a graphic artist on retainer for the entire project period, you can schedule him or her for only the one and a half weeks required. This costs you less and frees the artist to accept other commitments without jeopardizing your project.

The PERT Chart. PERT (Program Evaluation and Review Technique) was developed by the U.S. Navy for the purpose of coordinating massive naval operations. It allows a planner to: (1) determine the order in which events occur, (2) estimate the completion time for each event and the entire project as well, (3) identify the "critical path" (the one that should be most closely monitored), and (4) calculate the probability of completing the project on schedule. It is beyond our scope to develop each of these capabilities here. Banghart (1969) and Riemer (1968) have treated this tool more definitively. For our immediate purposes, it will be sufficient to consider the very simple case illustrated in Figure 8.5.

It is important to distinguish two terms at the outset: event and activity. An *event* is a dimensionless point in time; it is represented by a circle; and it is stated as having already been accomplished. An *activity* takes place in the time period between two events. Activities can be measured in time units.

Construction of a PERT chart begins with the final (or terminal) event. The next step is to determine which event (or events) must *immediately* precede the terminal event. When that (those) event(s) is(are) identified, the same determination is made in regard to the newly identified event(s). So it goes until the point of origin is reached. The result is that each event (except for the first and the last) has at least one event preceding and following it to create a chain of events. It is possible for several chains to branch from a single event, as for instance with event 4 in our example. The single chain leading to event 4 must proceed sequentially (event 3 cannot begin until event 2 has been completed). But the chains leading from event 4 may occur simultaneously, thus requiring less time to get to event 14 than if the chains had to be connected sequentially.

When the chart is completed, the planner estimates the time of each activity. For example, once the purpose is defined, we might estimate that it will take three days to profile the audience. These time estimates are educated guesses which take into consideration both the *optimistic time* (the time required if everything goes perfectly) and the *pessimistic time* (the amount required if everything that *could* go wrong *does* go wrong—"Murphy's Law").

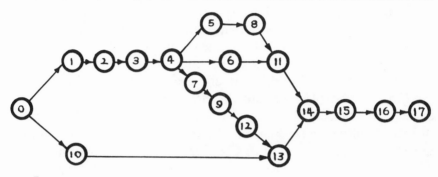

Events

0. Commitment to project mode
1. Purpose defined
2. Audience profiled
3. Message plan completed
4. Storyboard completed
5. Artwork completed
6. Live photography shot
7. Script prepared
8. Copywork shot

9. Talent selected
10. Recording facilities reserved
11. Slides developed
12. Talent rehearsed
13. Audio-recording completed
14. Message pulsed and packaged
15. Message evaluated
16. Message modified
17. Message delivered

Figure 8.5. Simplified PERT Chart.

With certain formulas and some patience, the best estimate of completion time can be made, and the estimated "slack time" for each pathway can also be calculated. The pathway that has the smallest amount of slack time is called the "critical path." It is the one that must be kept on schedule if the deadline is to be met. In order to keep the critical path on schedule, it may be necessary to add resources. For instance, one might have to hire more help, or subcontract for a part of the work, or invest in more efficient equipment. In some ventures, PERT is essential—we could not have gone to the moon without it. But even where it is not essential, it provides greater control over the operation and it lends economic and professional integrity to it.

Fault-Tree Analysis. Fault-tree analysis derives its name from the tree-like structure that is generated when necessary and/or sufficient conditions are plotted to arrive at a given output. By analyzing such a structure, you can discover where the system is breaking down; thus the term "fault-tree analysis." This convenient planning tool identifies both the requirements and the options operating within a process. Its two principal devices are: (1) the "and-gate" (where all inputs must be present before an output is emitted), and (2) the "or-gate" (where any one of the inputs is sufficient to emit the output). Beyond its management applications, this tool is useful both in computer programming and in electronic circuit designing. It is a form of symbolic logic.

Figure 8.6 illustrates a simple application of this tool for planning purposes. Begin with the output or goal simply for the sake of clarity. In order to produce our completed slide-show message, we must have both a visual *and* an audio component. Notice that those components feed into an and-gate. But the visual component may consist of either direct photographic slides *or* copywork slides. On the other hand, the audio component requires talent *and* facilities, but the talent may be either professional *or* amateur.

The chief advantages of this tool for planning purposes are that it lays out clearly what one's options and requirements are, and it allows one to generate an exhaustive set of alternative designs. Some of the most promising options might be overlooked in a complex situation when this technique is not employed.

The "Single-Unit Analysis" Method. If you were responsible for meeting the physical needs of a large group of people over an extended time period (setting up a refugee camp, for instance), your best planning tactic would be to determine first all of the needs for just one person. How much sheltered space at what temperature is required for health and comfort? How much food, water, clothing, bedding, medical supplies, etc., must be provided for that one person? Next, you must determine how many people will be involved. Then consider how many people will be required

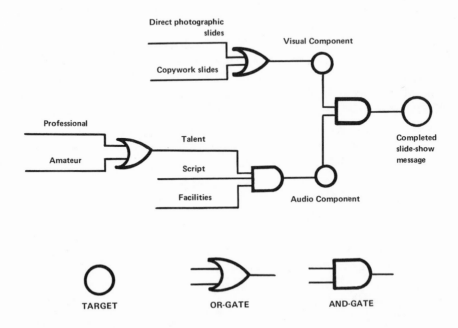

Figure 8.6. Simple Fault-Tree Analysis Layout.

to distribute goods and to coordinate the clients. Now, you must estimate what equipment, supplies, and services are required to satisfy the needs of the staff. By proceeding in this manner, you would ultimately be able to design living quarters, supply warehouses, administrative offices, plumbing systems, etc., sufficient to meet the need without being wasteful.

Closer to your circumstances as a designer, you might ask: "What services, supplies, equipment, permissions, etc., are involved in shooting a single scene for a film? Talent? cameras? photographers? assistants? scenery? lights, scripts, etc., etc., etc." Then:

"How many scenes are there, and how many can be shot by one 'outfit'?" "How many outfits will be required?" "How much coordination between outfits is needed?" "What are the special requirements of the coordinators?" When you have exhaustively anticipated these requirements, you will be in a position to translate time, space, personnel, equipment, and supplies into actual costs. These costs determine your budget, and your design is constrained by your budget. Whether you serve as producer in addition to your designer function or not, your ability to make accurate budgetary estimates and decisions (and your ability to monitor others who do so) can enable you to design within realistic economic constraints.

Take Basic Legal Precautions

All communication is *social* in nature, and mass media-rooted communication is especially so. These simple definitions illustrate this truism:

Dialogue:	Free and reciprocal information exchange between two persons.
Tutorial:	Information exchange from a more to a less informed person.
Public Address: (Lecture)	Communication from one person to many people.
Mass-Media Communication:	Messages prepared and transmitted by many people for presentation to many people.

We should also note that all social interaction is rooted in *agreement.* In the simplist of cases, members of a society must agree upon certain values and procedures that define the rights of membership in that society. A legal system is merely a formalization of the privileges and limitations that a society grants to or imposes upon its members. The methodology of a legal system is to make those *social agreements* explicit.

Now, since any media message is inherently affected by legal considerations, it is prudent for a designer to understand the freedoms and restrictions under which he or she must operate.

Certain legal instruments are especially relevant to designers' activities.

Contracts. A contract is a legal instrument which formalizes an agreement between two parties. It is generally advisable to execute a contract whenever you accept a design assignment from a client. It is also often advisable to formalize agreements in writing with production houses, talent, assistants, subcontractors, suppliers, location and facility owners, etc. Entering into a contract serves to work out misunderstandings and disagreements in advance and to provide legal protection in case either party defaults. For contracts which involve large and costly commitments, it may be safest to have them drawn by an attorney. You can, however, write your own contracts that are perfectly legal, provided that all of the "elements" are properly included.

Hamilton (1978) provides explanations, models, and advice for writing your own contracts. He lists five essentials and two optional components of a contract:

1. Name of the document.
2. Introductory remarks.
3. Recitals.
4. Operative provisions.
5. Closing.
6. (optional) Witnesses.
7. (optional) Acknowledgments.

The *introductory remarks* must state that the document is an agreement; it must be dated; and it must specify the parties to the agreement. The *recitals* establish the basis for the agreement—often listing clauses beginning with "Whereas. . ." The *operative provisions* state the substance of the agreement. The *closing* includes dated signatures of all parties. Some contracts require *witnesses* to sign and some require *acknowledgments* by a notary public.

Specific requirements for contracts may vary from state to state. It would be a wise precaution to write a contract you need in your consulting and then to have an attorney review it. When it is perfected, use it as a model for future contracts.

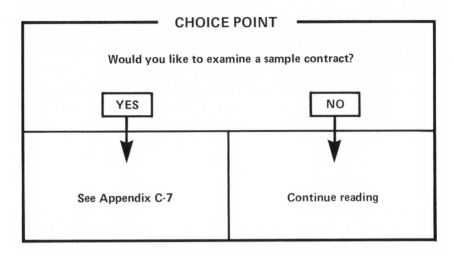

Releases. A person can grant permission or give up a legal right or claim by signing a release. Three kinds of releases are advisable for a designer to secure: A *photographic release* is protection against subsequent legal action which allows you to use photographs of people in your message. It should include the date, a statement of permission to use the photograph for any legitimate purpose, a signature, and the complete address of the person photographed. A minor child's release must be granted by a parent or legal guardian. A *satisfaction release* testifies that a product or service has been satisfactorily delivered and that no further claim is warranted. Some designers seek such releases so that a project can be legally terminated. A *copyright* release grants you permission to use copyrighted material (print, photographs, music, etc.) for prescribed purposes. Whenever you make more than one copy, or when you use that copy for a purpose other than for direct instructional use in the classroom, you should secure a release from the copyright holder.

Incidentally, to protect your own material, you might consider the practice of placing a circled ©, followed by your full name and date, on the first page of any material you have reproduced. The law states that within a reasonable length of time following its first publication, material with that note on it will be protected, until it can be formally copyrighted (filed with the Library of Congress on special forms). Since the law does not define a "reasonable length of time," it seems in practice to be fairly lengthy.

Discriminate Professional from Amateur Production

As we have stressed above, the designer *per se* need not be able to produce what he or she designs, but it is important for the designer to distinguish and design for professional quality. Basically, a professional is one who analyzes a situation thoroughly, thus perceiving it with fine discrimination, and then controls it through established methods and procedures. Even a lay person or an amateur can generally sense the polished overall quality of a professionally produced product, but he or she cannot usually specify why it is a quality product or how the quality is achieved. The designer ought to be able to make the same kinds of quality discriminations that the professional producer makes, but need not know all of the technicalities required to produce it. For example, a designer ought to recognize at a glance that a color photograph was improperly lighted, but it is not necessary for him or her to understand the properties of the lights, the film, and the development that went into its production.

One of the best ways for acquiring this ability to discriminate is to study sets of "examples" and "non-examples." For instance, if you were to set up two slide projectors to show on the screen at the same time, you could compare a professionally-shot slide with one shot by an amateur. If the professionally-shot slide in each pair is randomly assigned to the projectors by someone else who could prepare an "answer key" for you, you could practice making the discriminations. Having the correct answer after each selection will facilitate your ability to discriminate. It is not necessary for you to be able to tell *why* you selected the professional slide; it is enough that you be able to do it consistently. The first sets of pairs should be fairly easily discriminated. Later ones should match professional photographers' shots with those of advanced amateurs. At this latter stage, it might be helpful to list the differing attributes of the pairs you fail to discriminate. There is some advantage to doing this exercise in a group so that discussion from various points-of-view may refine the discriminations.

Monitor the Production

Even though someone else assumes the responsibilities of the director/producer, it is advisable, whenever possible, for the designer to be present at critical stages of the production. The designer's role in this situation is not to compete with the director, but to communicate with him or her. Expensive productions are often rendered useless because of some fundamental misinterpretation of the designer's intent. By being present during rehearsals, the designer can monitor the director's interpretation of the script and make necessary corrections before they are solidified in the production. In my own experience, otherwise brilliant productions have been marred by the mispronunciation of key concepts and by textual interpretations that reversed the intended meaning.

To be most useful at the production stage, the designer should have completely visualized his or her message from the storyboard. During a pre-production conference with the director, the designer should attempt to communicate fully that visualization. He or she should be prepared to accept reasonable modifications required by technical considerations, clarity, economy, etc., but to resist any change that fundamentally alters the integrated design.

The relationship between designer and director is essentially the same as that of a musical composer and a performing artist, or a poet and an oral interpreter. Both are essential to creation of the manifested work—the end-product. The director must be allowed to bring something from himself or herself to the production—to *interpret* the script through his or her own set of perceptual "goggles"—to leave a unique mark of style on the production. But, if the source's purpose is sacrificed for the sake of the director's aesthetic fulfillment or ego-gratification, the production loses its reason for being. It is the designer's responsibility to prevent this from happening.

Director/Producer Responsibilities During Production

This set of guidelines is intended to serve the designer who elects to assume the additional roles of director/producer. The items discussed here will be commonplace to the trained or experienced director/producer.

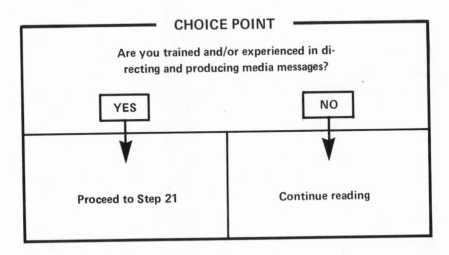

In addition to the responsibilities discussed above, when you serve as director/producer as well as designer, you must be prepared to undertake the following responsibilities. Considering the purpose and scope of this book, this section must be limited to a checklist of responsibilities, some guidelines, and a few rules-of-thumb. These basic aids and suggestions should be augmented (in each category) through reading, formal training, or consultation or tutorial with a professional.

Select and Direct Talent
Casting. The production budget is often the controlling factor in casting: given a small budget, you must use people who are available. Sometimes, however, directors wear blinders that limit their vision of who is available for little or no direct cost. In a community of any size at all, there are high school or college broadcasting and theater students; there are voice and drama coaches; there are modeling agencies and community theaters; there are trained talent who are building credentials and will work for the experience and credit. On the other hand, if your budget allows it, go directly to a casting agency.

Once you have clearly defined your talent needs, publicize your tryouts through appropriate media to attract your target population, and begin screening the applicants. Avoid miscasting because of pressures from friends.

Linder (1976) states: "It is better to use a non-actor whose looks and behavior fit a part than an experienced, even talented, actor whose appearance and manner are not quite right." His reason for this position is that in media productions, as opposed to theatrical productions, it is necessary to establish quickly the *presence* of the character.*

Coaching. Having selected your talent for a production, you should assess each person according to role requirements. If he or she is to be seen and heard, you should evaluate his or her appearance, voice, movement, and talent in order to emphasize the strengths and to improve upon abnormalities or weaknesses.

Coaching to overcome deficiencies is a much narrower task than training. In coaching you are equipping the performer to execute one particular role, not to develop fundamental skills. At times the director will serve as coach; at other times the coaching can be handled by someone else (perhaps at the performer's own expense). In the latter case, the director's responsibility is to specify the objectives of the coaching.

Rehearsing. The director is responsible for conducting three kinds of rehearsals: technical rehearsals (for determining camera, microphone, lighting positions, etc.); talent rehearsals (for blocking action and interpreting roles); and complete rehearsals (for putting it all together).

Hawes (1978) suggests the following responsibilities of the director regarding rehearsals.

1. Post an advance schedule, including time, place, and expectations.
2. Give concise and courteous direction.
3. Allow the performer as much freedom to develop the role as circumstances permit.
4. Be available for private consultation with talent.
5. Facilitate cast/crew cooperation.
6. Maintain a reasonably quiet and orderly atmosphere.

7. Provide notes and/or comments throughout the rehearsal period.
8. Share whatever praise or criticism received.

Directing the Visual Production

Aside from the compositional aspects of the visual production, there are some basic technical matters with which the designer/director/producer must be aware. It is convenient to consider graphic art and photography separately.

Graphic Art. The easy (and expensive) way to acquire the graphic art required for your production is to deliver your storyboard to a professional graphic artist and keep yourself busy with other aspects of production. But, more realistically, you may have to rely upon a willing and reliable non-artist to do your artwork. With a little direction from you, even a novice can produce quite acceptable graphics. Nor do you have to be an artist to direct your assistant. What you do need is a basic knowledge of some available graphic techniques. Minor and Frye (1977) provide detailed, illustrated instructions for several techniques appropriate for media usage. I will merely list and define briefly some of these methods and aids.

1. *Visual transfer.* By using carbon paper, chalk, and other devices, images are traced onto tracing paper and transferred to the graphic surface.

2. *Acetate transparencies.* You can capture an image on clear acetate sheets either with ink, adhesive material, or thermal processing. The basic black and white transparency can be painted on the back side to provide appropriate color rendering. Then, by placing the cell-colored transparency over a background sheet (colored or patterned), you create a camera-ready graphic.

3. *Projection drawing.* A slide projector (or other projection device) can be used to project an image to various sizes onto an art paper where it can then be traced, inked, and colored.

4. *Grid drawing.* By superimposing a grid over the original and by drawing onto a grid of a different scale or projection, you can enlarge, reduce, or distort the original by coordinating points on the grid and then connecting them with lines.

5. *Photosketching.* By inking contours, shadows, and details on a glossy photographic enlargement, you can capture the essence of a photograph to serve your purposes. Be sure to use permanent India ink. When the ink is dry, immerse the whole photograph in an iodine solution, rub gently, and watch the photographic image disappear leaving only the inked lines. All that remains is to wash the photograph, fix it in photographic hypo, and wash it again. Your photosketch will have captured the perspective and scale of the original, and you can add color or detail as you wish.

6. *Clip- or paste-up-art.* Any kind of printed material (magazines, newspapers, posters, etc.) provides usable images for clip-art. You simply clip the images that serve your purposes and paste them on to whatever kind of framed sheet serves your purposes. Clip-art can be photographed to produce slides or can be used directly.

7. *Dry transfer.* Art stores stock hundreds of dry transfer sheets of various type styles and sizes as well as borders, textures, and common figures and symbols. The sheets are transparent plastic with transferable printing on them. By placing the dull side on your art paper and rubbing the shiny side with a blunt instrument, the printed item adheres to the art paper when the plastic sheet is removed. With a little patience and even less practice, a novice can produce professional looking layouts.

8. *Spray techniques.* Either with aerosol-can colors or airbrushes, you can stencil or profile letters, shapes, and objects. For instance, if you were to place a maple leaf on an art pad and spray it lightly and then remove the leaf, you would have produced a perfect leaf image. The same thing can be done with a cardboard silhouette of any identifiable object or symbol.

9. *Freehand drawing.* Mugnaini (1974) demystifies drawing of the human body. For instance, if you can draw a beer can, he can show you how to draw a human torso. Since low-definition drawings are often appropriate for media graphics, this option should not be overlooked—it beats stick figures!

Besides these techniques, there are two other aspects of graphic art that can make your artwork look more professional. Both have to do with the lettering used in your graphics:

Lettering size. If printed material has letter height that is below the appropriate viewing distance/letter height ratio, it will be illegible to the viewers. There are several rules-of-thumb available: Young (1980) submits these formulas along with the rule-of-thumb that says: ". . . one inch of letter height for each ten feet of viewing distance."

(1) Viewing Distance/Ratio Number = Letter Height.

(2) Ratio Number x Letter Height = Viewing Distance.

(3) Viewing Distance/Letter Height = Ratio Number.

Minor and Frye (1977) plot a line on a graph between ½-inch @ 14.5 feet and 2-½ inches @ 73 feet. Kemp (1980) recommends a maximum viewing distance of projected material to be eight times the vertical height of the screen; he recommends as a maximum for non-projected material, a one-inch letter height for a viewing distance of 32 feet. A final rule-of-thumb from the public domain is that if you can read the print on a 35mm slide at normal reading distance, it will project legibly at any viewing distance.

Letter spacing. Kemp (1980) advises allowing one and one-half letter widths for space between words; three letter widths between sentences; and optical spacing between letters within words. Avoid equal spacing between letters because an "i" cannot balance an "m." A good rule-of-thumb for spacing between lines is to separate lines by one and one-half lower-case letter size.

Directing the Photographic Productions

The technical details of photography should be left to the discretion of the photographer; but by understanding some basic concepts, the director can communicate his or her compositional needs more accurately and concisely.

Lenses. The most important thing for the director to understand about lens selection is the effects of different focal lengths. Table 8.1 shows how the focal length of a lens (the distance from the lens to the film, measured in millimeters) is directly related to the angle of view. Notice in Figure 8.7 that the shorter the focal length, the wider the viewing angle will be; and note that because of the wide viewing angle, the image will be smaller on the film.

The most obvious uses for wide- and narrow-angle lenses are to get more into the picture and to photograph objects at a distance,

Table 8.1

Relationship of Focal Length to Angle of View

Focal Length	Angle of View	Focal Length	Angle of view	Focal Length	Angle of view
8mm	180°	35mm	63°	200mm	12°
16mm	180°	50mm	47°	300mm	8°
18mm	100°	85mm	29°	400mm	6°
21mm	92°	100mm	24°	600mm	4°
24mm	84°	135mm	18°	1000mm	2.5°
28mm	75°	180mm	14°		

The 50mm lens most closely approximates what the human eye sees.

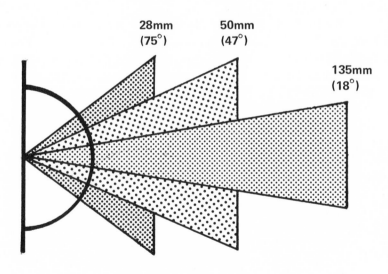

Figure 8.7. Angles of View for Various Lenses.

respectively. But the more subtle uses, which the designer should understand, are to control *perspective* and *depth of field.* A wide-angle lens exaggerates the perspective and provides a greater depth of field while a narrow-angle lens minimizes (and sometimes eliminates) perspective and shortens the depth of field.

Lighting. There are countless ways a professional can light any given scene, and only through thousands of experiences does the professional learn his or her craft. Yet, there are a few basic concepts and terms which can help a director discriminate more closely and communicate his or her desires.

Figure 8.8 illustrates the most common "key" lighting techniques. These images represent the effects of a single main light. The "pancake" or "frontal" lighting requires the light to be directly in front of the subject at camera level. The absence of shadows creates a flat look ("flat as a pancake") that is associated with shots taken with a flash attachment on the camera. By lowering the frontal light to cast shadows upward, you produce an unnatural, "grotesque" effect.

By moving the light 45° to either side and raising it, we can light for "45°" or "triangle" lighting. The key to lighting a face with this technique is to leave a small lighted triangle under the eye on the shaded side of the face. Also, the nose shadow should just touch the upper lip.

When we place the light at 90° to the camera, we create "hatchet" lighting. The light should be at camera level for hatchet lighting.

Move the light to 135° from the camera and raise it again and you will discover the famous and dramatic "Rembrandt" technique. It highlights the rim and the top and allows some light to spill over into the frontal, shaded areas. Lower the light in that position to create a "line" or "rim" lighting effect.

Finally, place the light slightly behind the subject (180° from the camera) and raise it quite high. This is called "glamor" or "butterfly" lighting. When properly executed, there should be a small butterfly-shaped shadow under the nose. Now, lower the light and move it farther behind the subject to produce a "backlighted" or "silhouette" lighting.

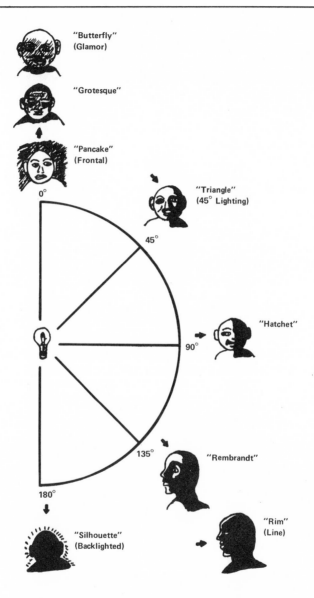

Figure 8.8. Basic "Key" Lighting Techniques.

The "key" light thus provides the basic modeling effect, but its overbearing intensity often creates undesirable shadows. To eliminate the unwanted shadows behind the subject, shine a background light directly on them. Rather than completely eliminating the shadows on the subject cast by the key light, you may prefer merely to soften them so that some detail may be seen in the shaded areas. The "fill" light serves this purpose, and to prevent removing the key light shadows altogether, it should not be as intense as the key. A ratio of 1:3 or 1:4 is generally appropriate. The fill light's intensity can be controlled by reducing the wattage or by moving it farther away from the subject.

Figure 8.9 illustrates a basic lighting setup using the "key," the "background," and the "fill" lights.

Filters. A filter's function is to modify the light before it enters the camera. There are several reasons for using filters, but the most common are: (1) to correct for the diffusion effects of the atmosphere on the sunlight which tends to produce a disproportionate amount of blue light; (2) to select certain colors from the light in order to control tone and contrast of the photograph; (3) to adapt the light to film that was not intended to be used in that light; (4) to create special lighting effects such as sparkles, multiple images, rainbow effects, etc.; and (5) to reduce the intensity of light for exposure purposes.

Understanding how filters work takes much of the mystery out of how to use them. Shipman (1979) explains filters this way:

> If you hold a color filter between your eye and white light, you see the colors which are *transmitted* or passed through the filter. The effect of a filter on film is often more easily predicted by thinking about the color the filter *stops* rather than those that get through.
>
> If a filter blocks red, then it transmits both blue and green. To the eye, light coming through the filter appears bluish-green—a color photographers call *cyan.* We say cyan is the *complementary* color to red because you get cyan if you block red but transmit blue and green. Each of the three primary colors has a complement, according to this table.

Some find verbal descriptions of filter effects to be confusing. If you require a visual demonstration in order to understand it, consult a photographic reference book that displays filtered photographs in comparison with a full-color original.

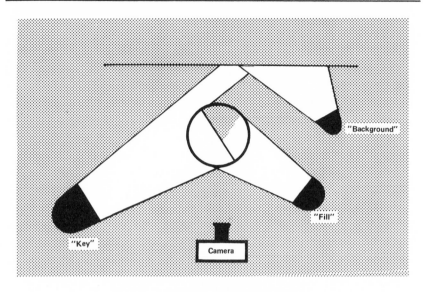

Figure 8.9. Basic Lighting Setup.

PRIMARY COLORS	COMPLEMENTARY COLORS
Red	Cyan (Blue + Green)
Green	Magenta (Blue + Red)
Blue	Yellow (Red + Green)

Editing. The main functions of editing are to select and arrange images for the purposes of controlling the continuity, emphasis, and mood of the message. There are two fundamentally different approaches to editing: a *discursive* (linear, explicit, McLuhan "hot") *approach* and a *juxtaposition* (simultaneous, montage, poetic, McLuhan "cool") *approach.* The discursive approach is more appropriate for exhaustive, technical, accurate, detailed, representative productions such as documentaries. The juxtaposi-

tion approach is better suited to engaging, inspirational, provocative, suggestive, and fantastic productions. Intent, of course,
dictates the appropriate editing approach.

Smooth-flowing continuity matches the message to the high
expectations and low-readiness needs of the receivers and thus
reduces tension. To achieve continuity through editing, care must
be taken to *match the action* from shot to shot. This is especially
important when changing shot angles and distances so that there is
no break in the action being emphasized. Often the pace or
rhythm of the action can be accentuated by editing to change
angles as the action varies. One obvious, but easily overlooked,
interruption in continuity results from changing the direction of
action from shot-to-shot. You can surely recall a western in which
the sheriff's posse would be in a dead heat from left to right one
second, and the next second they would be riding just as hard
from right to left across the screen. For a moment, the viewer is
confused as to whether they are continuing in "hot pursuit" or
whether they are "beating a retreat."

There are times when the editor only has available two such
pieces of footage, but instead of creating such an abrupt "jump
cut," he or she could either "cut-in" to a close-up or "cut-out" to
a distant shot between the reversals in *screen direction* in order to
minimize the abruptness of the change. An alert director will
anticipate the possibilities of needing this kind of flexibility and
will shoot a number of "protection shots" at the time the main
action shots are being photographed.

Another effective means of establishing continuity through
editing is to employ systematically planned *transitions.* Some
common techniques for creating transitions include: fade-outs,
fade-ins, dissolves, wipes, jump-cuts, split screens, and any number
of special effects that can be generated electronically.

As we mentioned, the counterpart of continuity is abrupt
juxtaposition. The principal device for creating this effect is the
"montage," made famous by Sergei Eisenstein (1947, 1949). By
placing two seemingly unrelated images side-by-side (or even
within the same scene), the editor can stimulate the viewer to
search his or her own mind for a meaningful linkage between

them. Thus, the viewer becomes intimately engaged in creating the meaning. Such personal meanings are nearly always saturated with private connotations and emotional triggers. The montage is an extremely effective editing device, but the director trades off his or her control of the line-of-thought for this engaging, emotional reaction.

An editor can provide emphasis as well as continuity. By moving from an establishing shot, which places an action or object into perspective, a zoom-in or cut-in can lend emphasis to that action or object. In general, the closer the vantage point, the greater the emphasis also. But one of the best ways of providing emphasis is through the control of time. Not only is the duration of a shot related to emphasis but the unity or disunity with natural time is as well. By "freeze-framing," and slow-motion, and lapse photography, the editor can upset routine sequences in ways that demand attention and thus create emphasis.

Directing the Audio Production

State-of-the-art sound recording is a highly technical and costly process. The services of an audio engineer are essential to achieve such quality. Acceptable, working-grade quality can be achieved by sub-professionals when they are attentive to certain requirements and precautions. The director, without being sophisticated technically, can enhance the quality of audio production by attending to certain basic conditions.

Minimize Number of Recording Generations. The director should plan the sound recording operations not only to ensure the best quality on the "master" recording that is possible under given conditions, but also to conserve the quality of the master by employing as few dubbings as possible. When a recording is made from a recording, some quality is lost. Each new "generation" retains the imperfections of the previous recording and adds its own to it.

Insist upon the Use of Proper Microphones. The two main considerations in microphone selection are the *mode of transducing* acoustic energy into electrical energy and the *sensitivity pattern.* Consider first the modes: (1) Crystal or ceramic microphones are rugged and inexpensive, but are very limited in sensitivity on both ends of the sound spectrum. (2) Dynamic microphones are more expensive, can stand abuse, and provide moderately good fidelity. (3) Condenser microphones are also durable, but more expensive, and they provide high fidelity even though they can be quite small and inconspicuous.

The sensitivity of microphones is another basis for classification: (1) *Non-directional* microphones are sensitive in all directions. The advantage is that voices from anywhere in the studio can be picked up, but this is also its disadvantage. Unwanted voices and accidental or unobserved sounds are picked up also. (2) *Cardioid* microphones are sensitive in a heart-shape on one side of the microphone; they are essentially uni-directional. (3) *Bi-directional* microphones allow a person on each side to be heard, but noises from other directions are suppressed. (4) A *shotgun* microphone does for sound reception what a telephoto lens does for photography; it can pinpoint one sound in the environment from a distance and transduce it with fidelity.

Insure Proper Recording Levels. A good rule-of-thumb for adjusting recording volume is to set the "pot" (potentiometer) so that during most of the modulation, the needle falls just below the red area on the "VU" meter. Some sounds will "peak" into the red without distorting the overall effect. If the recording volume is set so low that only the peaks reach the red, the quality will be good, but playback volume may be limited. Generally, it is better to suffer a bit of distortion than to get too weak a signal recorded.

Balance the Acoustics of the Recording Environment. If you record in a room with hard, bare, flat surfaces, the sound will resonate or reverberate off of those surfaces to produce "too live" a sound. It is the sound you have heard when moving into an empty house. The other extreme is "too dead" a sound that sounds as if you recorded under the blankets in a bed. A delicate balance lies somewhere between these extremes which will suit your purposes. Usually the solution is to hang towels, drapes, carpets, acoustic board, etc., near the recording area to enrich by deadening the sound. A director can do two things to insure better recording quality: (1) train his or her ear to discriminate between too live and too dead a sound, and (2) test the recording environment carefully before full recording by recording "test takes."

Minimize Noise Factors. Noise is the unintended or unwanted sounds picked up on a recording. The human ear habituates to many sounds to which the microphone is sensitive. Air conditioners, fans, airplanes, distant traffic, etc., are cases in point. Even the wind blowing over a microphone or a brush of skin or clothing over it, or an unnoticed kick of the microphone stand, or a rustle of the script can mar an otherwise satisfactory recording. The designer should be on constant alert during recording to prevent having to "re-take" because of noise.

Index and Edit Tapes. To facilitate sound tape editing, keep, or insist upon having kept, a log of footage index numbers. The original "takes" can be easily reviewed and selected for retention on the master recording by referring to the index numbers. It is generally easier and more economical to edit the log book than to edit tape, so much of the decision-making can be done with paper and pencil.

There are two basic methods of implementing the log-book editing decisions: electronic editing and physical editing. Electronic editing requires two high quality recorders (either reel-to-reel or cassette) which can be stopped and started quickly and silently. By stopping the master recorder precisely on cue, the input recorder can be rewound or advanced to the next "take." Then the master can be started (by releasing the pause control) to accomplish a clean splice. Physical editing entails cutting the tape to remove the unwanted portions and splicing the desired "takes" together with a piece of adhesive tape. This method can be extremely precise, but must be done on a quality reel-to-reel recorder.

Mix and Synchronize Sounds. Once the narration track(s) has(have) been edited, music and sound effects can be added by inputting two or more live and/or recorded selections into an electronic mixer. The mixer allows each input to be varied in volume from none to full, and it allows for master controlling the output volume. The balanced output is fed into the master recorder for storage.

There is no problem with synchronizing the sound-track with the image when they are recorded simultaneously as in the case of sound film. But in the case of filmstrip or slide displays, the images must be changed at the appropriate instant according to cues on the sound-track. The most common and convenient method of synchronization is electronic. A low-frequency signal which activates the slide changer is recorded directly onto the tape at the appropriate point. The signal may be recorded either on the sound-track or on a stereo-track reserved for this purpose. When synchronization has been completed, the designed and produced message is ready for evaluation.

Step 21. Trouble-Shoot the Message

There are different approaches to the evaluation of messages: Some critics hold that if a message complies with theoretical standards of excellence, it should be judged as excellent. Others evaluate a message solely on the basis of their personal reactions to it. But this model for designing messages is committed to communicating a source's message to particular receivers in an effort to generate responses that are consistent with the source's purpose. Thus, evaluation must be centered around the issue of whether the source's objectives have been met.

To resolve this issue, objective data must be collected from a sample of receivers that is representative of the whole population of receivers for whom the message was designed.

After presenting the message to such a trial audience, the designer should administer some sort of test instrument derived from the performance objectives stated in the purpose statement. The test format may range from an objective paper-and-pencil test to a structured interview or an actual performance according to the nature of the original objectives. But enough objective data must be collected to answer the question of whether the performance objectives have been met.

Hsia (1971) defines two kinds of distortion which may occur during a receiver's processing of a message: "Equivocation," which tends to result from information overload, is the "leveling" or loss of information contained in the message. The receiver just does not process the information that is available. "Error," which results from under-stimulation or interference by strong emotional or attitudinal associations, is the "sharpening" of some parts of the message so that the receiver adds information or content that was not present in the message.

Garner (1974) identifies two causes for a message's failure to achieve its objectives: "State limitations," which in our terms is related to the receiver's reduced state of readiness, is best dealt with by presenting the entire complex message to the receiver for additional viewings. "Process limitations," on the other hand, identify flaws in the message itself and require redesigning troublesome parts of the message. Process limitations are likely to be a result of inadequate adaptation to or appraisal of the receiver's level of sophistication. Garner suggests three remedies for message failure of this origin: (1) translate the ineffective passages into a different set of verbal or visual symbols; (2) restructure the message (with particular attention to order of presentation); and (3) divide the message into major divisions and repeat each division sequentially over a period of time.

Modifying the message on the basis of receivers' reports of dissatisfaction with it should be approached with caution. For one thing, receivers are not always clear about the source's purpose: many expect to be entertained even though the source's strategy may be to inform or to persuade. Koegel and Marsh (1979) found a near-zero correlation between "liking" and "learning." It must be granted that none of the material presented in their study was extremely disliked, but given variation in affective ratings for 20 instructional messages, the correlation with objective test scores over the content was practically non-existent. It can be argued, of course, that if receivers are distracted by unfavored messages, they will not listen and view it efficiently. In extreme cases, that may be so, but successful television commercials frequently have notable irritation factors designed into them, and further, such an argument fails to take into account the optimal overall complexity level (including the tension dimension). Given the systemic balance considerations of the complexity model, it is dangerous to place too much stock in popular general rules commonly employed by message receivers as they regard message effectiveness.

The following algorithm should be useful in isolating the source of the problem for messages that do not achieve their objectives. Start at the beginning and follow the branching dictated by your answers. The terminal boxes contain the recommended modification or action. After incorporating the changes into the message, conduct another field test and evaluate it in the previously described manner.

Algorithm for Trouble-Shooting Messages

Did the response match the behavioral objectives?

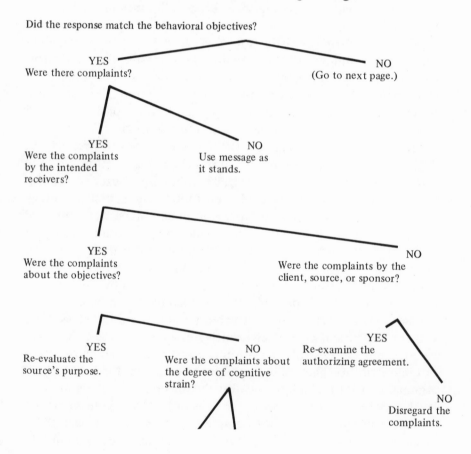

YES   NO
Were there complaints?   (Go to next page.)

YES   NO
Were the complaints   Use message as
by the intended   it stands.
receivers?

YES   NO
Were the complaints   Were the complaints by the
about the objectives?   client, source, or sponsor?

YES   NO   YES
Re-evaluate the   Were the complaints about   Re-examine the
source's purpose.   the degree of cognitive   authorizing agreement.
                     strain?
                                                                      NO
                                                               Disregard the
                                                               complaints.

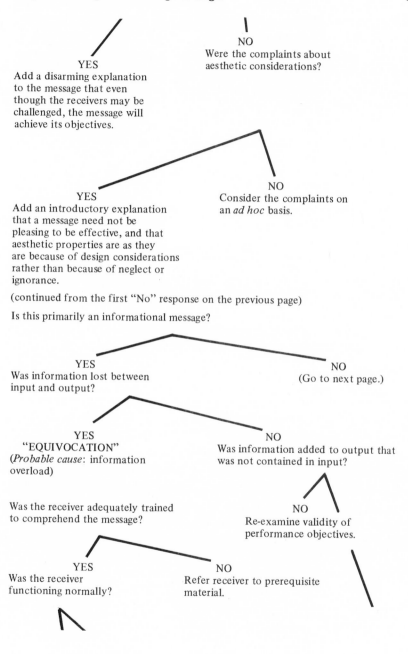

YES
Add a disarming explanation
to the message that even
though the receivers may be
challenged, the message will
achieve its objectives.

NO
Were the complaints about
aesthetic considerations?

YES
Add an introductory explanation
that a message need not be
pleasing to be effective, and that
aesthetic properties are as they
are because of design considerations
rather than because of neglect or
ignorance.

NO
Consider the complaints on
an *ad hoc* basis.

(continued from the first "No" response on the previous page)

Is this primarily an informational message?

YES
Was information lost between
input and output?

NO
(Go to next page.)

YES
"EQUIVOCATION"
(*Probable cause*: information
overload)

NO
Was information added to output that
was not contained in input?

Was the receiver adequately trained
to comprehend the message?

NO
Re-examine validity of
performance objectives.

YES
Was the receiver
functioning normally?

NO
Refer receiver to prerequisite
material.

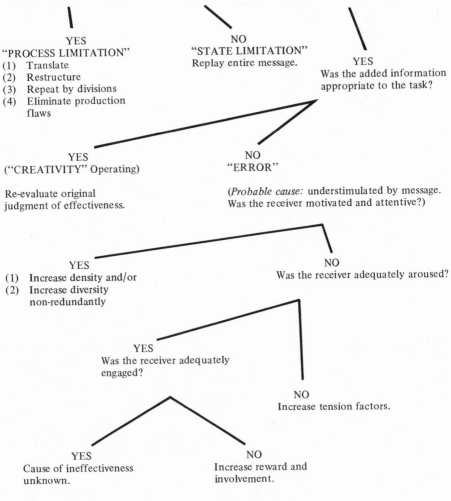

YES
"PROCESS LIMITATION"
(1) Translate
(2) Restructure
(3) Repeat by divisions
(4) Eliminate production
      flaws

NO
"STATE LIMITATION"
Replay entire message.

YES
Was the added information
appropriate to the task?

YES
("CREATIVITY" Operating)

Re-evaluate original
judgment of effectiveness.

NO
"ERROR"

(*Probable cause:* understimulated by message.
Was the receiver motivated and attentive?)

YES
(1) Increase density and/or
(2) Increase diversity
      non-redundantly

NO
Was the receiver adequately aroused?

YES
Was the receiver adequately
engaged?

NO
Increase tension factors.

YES
Cause of ineffectiveness
unknown.

NO
Increase reward and
involvement.

(continued from the undeveloped "No" response on the previous page)

Is the message primarily propositional?

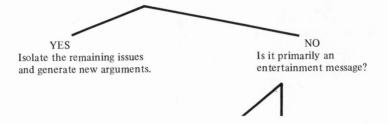

YES
Isolate the remaining issues
and generate new arguments.

NO
Is it primarily an
entertainment message?

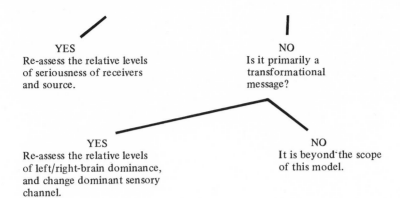

YES
Re-assess the relative levels
of seriousness of receivers
and source.

NO
Is it primarily a
transformational
message?

YES
Re-assess the relative levels
of left/right-brain dominance,
and change dominant sensory
channel.

NO
It is beyond the scope
of this model.

PART IV

APPLICATIONS OF THE DESIGN PROCESS

CHAPTER 9

APPLICATIONS OF THE
DESIGN PROCESS: SOME
EXERCISES FOR
INTERNALIZING THE PROCESS

CHAPTER 10

APPLICATIONS IN RESEARCH:
A FORMAL THEORETICAL
STATEMENT

Chapter 9

ACQUISITION

$$n(\mathstrut^{(}S^{)} \cdot R \longrightarrow S_r)$$

(B. F. Skinner)

(Learning is a function of repeated reinforcement of an organism's responses.)

Central Idea

With guided practice, the 21 steps of this message-design process can be mastered; and after designing a few messages, the entire process can be internalized so that you may design with professional competency.

Exercise Categories

1. Conceptual review.
    A. The 21-step process.
    B. Summary of central ideas.
2. Skill-development exercises by chapter.
3. Exercises in basic creativity processes.
4. Suggested major design projects.

Objectives

1. To recognize or recall the major processes, matrices, and instruments developed in this book.
2. To acquire the skills required to apply this design process.
3. To integrate and internalize the process so that you may become independent of this book.
4. To acquire professional-level competence.

Chapter 9

Applications of the Design Process:
Some Exercises for Internalizing the Process

Conceptual Review

The 21 Steps in Summary
1. Select the strategy.
2. Profile the receivers.
3. Determine the central idea.
4. Establish performance objectives.
5. Expand the central idea into a "box-outline."
6. Identify the appropriate tactics.
7. Calculate the "obscurity index."
8. Estimate the information load.
9. Select the message-body organizational pattern.
10. Check the outline for structural weaknesses.
11. Identify the appropriate diversity/density profile.
12. Select the appropriate dispositional patterns.
13. Select the appropriate graphics.
14. Select the appropriate language style.
15. Translate desired response styles into an aloofness/tension profile.
16. Translate the complexity profile into a "message prescription."
17. Translate the message prescription into a "message plan."
18. Create a storyboard.
19. Write the script.
20. Coordinate the production.
21. Trouble-shoot the message.

Chapter Central Ideas in Summary

1. By committing yourself to a purpose statement, you eliminate thousands of ways you could develop your message, thus providing direction and focus in your design; failure to make this commitment almost guarantees reduced message effectiveness.

2. With the information provided in your purpose statement and the appropriate matrix, you can expand your central idea into a "box-outline," identify the appropriate tactics for developing the outline, and calculate the "obscurity index," which will be useful later in determining the appropriate information load.

3. Given the tactical choice and the obscurity index for each terminal point, you can: first, estimate (and modify, if desirable) the message's information load; then, select an appropriate organizational pattern for the message body; and, finally, complete the information control phase of the process by inspecting the body for structural weaknesses.

4. The structured content of your message, achieved through the information-control process, can be placed into the desired "contextual atmosphere" created by the selection of appropriate levels of diversity and density.

5. Your assessment of your receivers' levels of sophistication and readiness can guide your choice of dispositional patterns, graphics, and language style for the further refinement of your message.

6. You can increase the chances of eliciting desired responses from your receivers by translating selected styles into "aloofness" and "tension" values and then designing those values into the message.

7. You can integrate your information-control and complexity-control design decisions into a unified message by: (1) translating the complexity profile into a message prescription; (2) translating the message prescription into a message plan; (3) creating a storyboard; and (4) writing the script.

8. Implementing the designed message involves both coordinating the production and trouble-shooting the produced message in order to make needed revisions.

9. With guided practice, the 21 steps of this message-design process can be mastered; and, after designing a few messages, the

entire process can be internalized so that you may design with professional competency.

10. This axiomatic theory identifies and organizes axioms, postulates, propositions, and hypotheses derived from the basic model in such a way as to generate research which will either validate the theory or indicate required modifications in theory.

Chapter 1 Exercise

Exercise 1. Matching Strategies with Definitions

Importance and Purpose of the Exercise
One of the greatest causes for message failure is the source's failure to select the appropriate strategy. Since the way the message should be is dependent upon the strategy selected, the wrong choice at the first stage insures reduced effectiveness. The purpose of this exercise is to insure that you can identify the critically different attributes of each of the strategies.

Instructions
Match the correct definition, cue, or example in the right-hand column with the strategies in the left-hand column. Do this by writing the letter of the cue in the blank preceding the strategy. More than one cue may be assigned to a strategy.

Strategies	*Cues*
....1. To inform	a. To elevate direct experience to explicit thought.
....2. To stimulate	b. To reduce the gap between the desired and the actual state of affairs.
....3. To interpret (educe)	c. To recognize intuitive knowledge.
....4. To instruct	d. To test a case's adequacy.
....5. To solve	e. To recall or demonstrate knowledge, attitudes, or skills.
....6. To persuade (promote)	f. To hold, divert, or amuse.
....7. To argue	g. To form associations, classifications, or patterns.
....8. To entertain	
....9. To transform	h. To recognize new information.

i. To reframe perceptions fundamentally.
j. Is measured by an attitude scale.
k. To change selected beliefs, attitudes, or values.
l. Is measured by an open-ended question.
m. To retrieve tacit knowledge.
n. Is measured by a multiple-choice test.
o. Is adapted according to level of seriousness.

Evaluation of Your Efforts

Review Steps 1 and 6 to discover the correct answers, or compare your answers with classmates. After you have discovered the correct answers, wait at least 24 hours and repeat the exercise. Continue this exercise until you have reached a criterion of perfection.

Chapter 1 Exercise

Exercise 2. Defining the Audience

Importance and Purpose of the Exercise

Messages work best when they are tailored to fit the intended receivers as closely as possible. To serve this end, you must know who your audience is and how they process information. The purpose of this exercise is to provide experience with three different techniques of profiling receivers.

A. Sophistication/Readiness Profile

Instructions

Visit three or four different types of audiences and profile them for sophistication and readiness. Use the six dimensions from the "complexity scale" for your ratings; average the three for sophistication and the three for readiness.

SOPHISTICATION

Abstraction	Low _ _ _ _ _ _ _	High
Implicitness	Low _ _ _ _ _ _ _	High
Precision	Low _ _ _ _ _ _ _	High

READINESS

Framing Required	High _ _ _ _ _ _ _	Low
Relevance Required	High _ _ _ _ _ _ _	Low
Mnemonics Required	High _ _ _ _ _ _ _	Low

Evaluation of Your Efforts

Compare your ratings with those of other observers and discuss your differences and the reasons for them.

B. Questionnaire

Instructions

Consult the "Useful Instruments for Profiling" section in Chapter 1, and design a questionnaire for a specified audience on a topic and strategy of your interest. Administer the questionnaire and profile your findings.

Evaluation of Your Efforts

Have one or more members of the audience study your profile and report their impressions of its accuracy.

C. Token/Field Profile

Instructions

Study Figure 1.2 and design a similar token/field instrument. Then question an informant, using this instrument, about an audience for whom you might consider designing a message.

Evaluation of Your Efforts

Ask another informant to evaluate the profile.

Chapter 1 Exercise

Exercise 3. Imaging the Audience

Importance and Purpose of the Exercise

The more valid your inferences and the more vivid your images of your receivers, the greater is the probability that you can design an effective message for them. The purpose of this exercise is to develop these two skills.

A. Inference Drawing

Instructions

Select one item at random from each column listed below thus creating a demographic profile. Then list all of the inferences you can draw from this profile regarding how a message of your choice should be designed for their needs. Do several profiles, and when possible, compare your inferences with those of a classmate.

Age	Sex	Occupation	Education	Socioeconomic
15-19	100% M	Students	High School	upper-lower
20-30	100% F	Teachers	High School Grad.	lower-middle
30-40	20% F/80% M	Clericals	Some College	upper-middle
50-65	80% F/20% M	Professionals	College Grad.	lower-upper
65	50% F/50% M	Administrators	Graduate Degree	upper-upper

Evaluation of Your Efforts

Ask an impartial person to examine your profile and identify the kinds of unwarranted prejudices he or she sees underpinning your inferences. Reflect upon those observations and see if you agree that the assumptions were unwarranted.

B. Imaging an Audience

Instructions

Select one of the profiles above and collect pictures from old magazines or newspapers that approximate your interpretation of the profile. Cut and paste those pictures to form an audience. Study that collage in detail for five to ten minutes; then close your eyes, relax, and reconstruct the image in as much detail as you can. When you have a clear image, let them become animated. Hear them talk and watch them move and interact. Listen to their responses to your message to them.

Evaluation of Your Efforts

Either you got an image or you did not. If you did, what you got is all right. If you did not, try this exercise again later.

Chapter 1 Exercise

Exercise 4. Identifying and Analyzing Central Ideas

Importance and Purpose of the Exercise

The central idea of a message summarizes and condenses the essence of the content. Messages built upon faulty central ideas bear inherent weaknesses. A message designer must know how to *identify, create, evaluate,* and *analyze* central ideas. The purpose of this exercise is to guide your experience in acquiring these four skills.

A. Identifying Central Ideas

Instructions

Select two of these messages: (1) letters to the editor; (2) chapters in books; (3) magazine articles; (4) full-page advertisements; and (5) newspaper editorials. For each of your selections, write a central idea according to the specifications in Chapter 1.

Evaluation of Your Efforts

In class or with a study partner, have someone check your central ideas both for form and fidelity to the original content.

B. Creating Central Ideas

Instructions

List several topics on which you feel authoritative. Write a central idea for a short message for each of these topics.

Evaluation of Your Efforts

Check each central idea against the requirements in Chapter 1. Have your instructor or study partner evaluate them for you.

C. Evaluating Central Ideas

Instructions

Exchange papers with a study partner for "A" and "B" above and: (1) classify each alleged central idea as "acceptable" or "not acceptable," and (2) if not acceptable, specify why it fails.

Evaluation of Your Efforts

Where there is disagreement between you and your study partner, consult either your instructor or Chapter 1 in an effort to resolve the issue.

D. Analyzing Central Ideas

Instructions

For each of the legitimate central ideas in "A" and "B" above, list the main points (if any) that inhere in it.

Evaluation of Your Efforts

Check to see whether your list of main points (expressed in complete sentences) exhausts the scope of the central idea. Check to see whether any of your points are outside the scope of the central idea (and therefore irrelevant). If a central idea cannot be divided into main points, describe how it might be supported directly.

Chapter 1 Exercise

Exercise 5. Identifying and Classifying Performance Objectives

Importance and Purpose of the Exercise

All messages aim to elicit some kind of response from the receiver. When those aims can be identified in terms of observable responses, you know better how to achieve them, and you have an objective basis for evaluating the impact of your message. The purpose of this exercise is to provide practice which will enable you to identify properly-stated performance objectives and to classify them according to the Mager model or the Kibler model.

Instructions

For each of the items below, indicate in the blanks: (1) whether the item is a properly-stated performance objective; (2) if so, does it take the form of the Mager (M) model or the Kibler (K) model?; and (3) if it is not properly stated, tell why it is not.

(1) (2)

.... 1. Given eight alleged performance objectives, write "yes" if it is legitimate and "M" if it is in the form of Mager's recommendation. You are expected to have no more than one error according to the key at the bottom of the page.

.... 2. Given a box of oranges, isolate those defined as "ripe" with 100 percent accuracy according to the judgment of a certified fruit grader.

.... 3. Applicants will write a 200-word statement following the interview which paraphrases each of the company's major goals.

.... 4. To persuade each member of the audience to contribute $5.00 within two days.

.... 5. The purpose of this lecture is to enlist your support on this project.

.... 6. Without referring to your notes, write the first ten steps of the process in order and *verbatim*.

.... 7. Given the conditions necessary for flight, an airplane will rise naturally from the ground.

.... 8. Given an opportunity to speak to the audience, I will trace the concept back to its philosophical roots according to Aristotle's criteria.

Evaluation of Your Efforts

Use this key to determine how well you did on this exercise.

Answer Key

(1) Yes, M. (2) Yes, M. (3) Yes, K. (4) No; this is confused with a strategy statement. (5) No; this statement describes what the source will do rather than what the receiver will do. (6) Yes, M. (7) No; this is more like a central idea than a performance objective. (8) No; again, this states the sender's intent rather than the desired performance by the receiver.

Chapter 2 Exercise

Exercise 1. Creating and Evaluating Box-Outlines

Importance and Purpose of the Exercise

The human mind must classify and categorize in order to function. To the extent that a message designer can organize a message in the manner in which the mind operates, the message is likely to work better. The box-outline, which is essentially a categorization device, is the intervening step between the central idea and the information chunks which determine the message's appropriate scope. The purposes of this exercise are to show you how to superimpose outlines on anything you see and how to detect faulty attempts to outline.

A. Creating Box-Outlines

Instructions

Look at the room you are in, or at the scene out of your window, or at your desk top, or at a picture in a magazine (anything will do). Let the whole scene be represented by a big empty box drawn at the top of your paper. Now divide the scene into natural clusters, groups, segments, etc. (For example, a distant scene can be seen in divisions of foreground, middle ground, and background.) Write a descriptive word for each cluster or division in a separate box drawn under the big box. Draw lines from each smaller box to the bottom of the big one. Now do the same thing for each of the smaller boxes that you did for the larger one—attach smaller boxes under it representing the items in that group or division. Continue this until everything has its own separate box. Repeat this exercise until you can automatically see a box-outline superimposed upon anything you look at.

Evaluation of Your Efforts

Make sure that no box has only one box under it. These "boxes" are *points* and a point must *divide*.

B.   Evaluating Box-Outlines

Instructions

Have a study partner join you in this game. Each of you, independently, is to create a faulty box-outline by incorporating as many "incorrect" patterns from Table 3.2 as you can into your outline. Do not worry about content in this exercise; just draw an extensive, abstracted pattern. Then exchange outlines and without reference to the text, identify as many of the faults as you can.

Evaluation of Your Efforts

Each of you should identify your intended "faults" after the other has exhausted his or her efforts to discover them.

Chapter 2 Exercise

Exercise 2. Mastering the Tactical Matrices

Importance and Purpose of the Exercise

While it is not important to memorize the tactical matrices (as long as you have the book handy for reference), it is important to know how to interpret them quickly and to begin to think in terms of the tactics. With a little practice, you will automatically begin to recall sequences, thus freeing you from the book. The purpose of this exercise is to engage you in a game that will take the tedium out of studying the matrices. Play it alone or with a partner. You may wish to devise a system of rewards or scoring.

Instructions

By some random means (e.g., the toss of a die), select one of the following tactical matrices: inform/stimulate/interpret, instruct, persuade, or entertain. Then by random means, select a cell from the matrix. This cell is your entry point. Begin there and describe the tactics or the sequence of tactics required to develop the strategy for that particular audience. You may wish to generate examples of each tactic. Use this matrix for assigning cells:

1	2	3
4	5	6
7	8	9

Example

I have randomly been assigned cell 3 on the persuasion matrix. The appropriate tactical development for this issue with my audience would be first to appeal to the emotions, then to offer a rationale with the use of enthymemes and examples, and finally, to stress our sharing of common ground (that is, to acknowledge our basis of agreement).

Evaluation of Your Efforts

Check your prescription against the appropriate matrix and rely upon your partner for refinement or correction of your efforts.

Chapter 2 Exercise

Exercise 3. Finding the Obscurity Level

Importance and Purpose of the Exercise
Determining a message's information load requires more than a knowledge of the number of information chunks in that message. The quantity of information interacts with the receiver's degree of familiarity or acceptance of the information. The "obscurity index" is an estimate of how salient/obscure the information is for the receiver. Consequently, your ability to determine the average obscurity level of a message is critical to discovering the appropriate information load. The purpose of this exercise is to enable you to estimate the average obscurity level of any given message reliably.

Instructions
A. Examine the box-outline and note that: (1) the numbers in parentheses correspond to the numbers in parentheses found in the *cell of entry* in the tactical matrices; (2) the numbers in parentheses (i.e., the "obscurity indexes") are associated only with the points or subpoints that define the "information chunks" (i.e., the terminal points); and (3) the "average obscurity index," required for determining the "information load," is the sum of those numbers in parentheses divided by the number of them indicated on the box-outline.
B. Note that obscurity indexes are assigned to the initial point structure (before tactics are added) that resulted from the analysis of the central idea. When tactics are added to the outline according to the estimated obscurity level, additional division of some points may be required. But, the added subpoints are not assigned obscurity

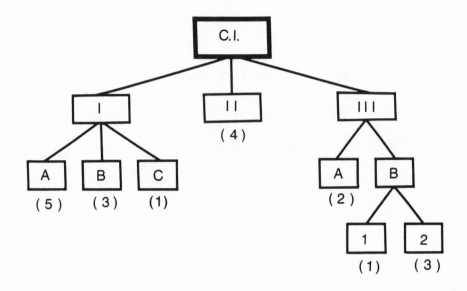

indexes. The division changes the number of information chunks, but it does not change the average obscurity index.

C. Select one of your own box-outlines and assign obscurity indexes in the manner described above, then calculate the average obscurity index. You may also wish to diagram the appropriate tactical development under each of your terminal points.

Evaluation of Your Efforts

With your box-outline and obscurity index estimate in hand, re-read this exercise and check your effort for compliance at each step.

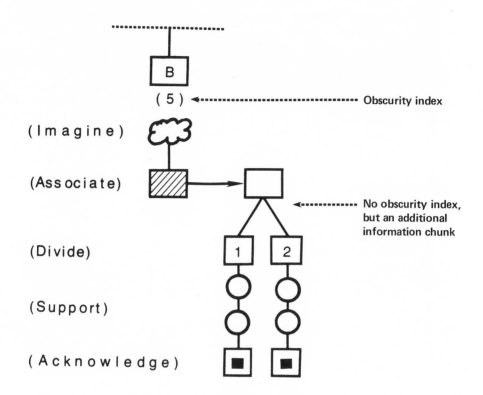

(Imagine)

(Associate)

(Divide)

(Support)

(Acknowledge)

Obscurity index

No obscurity index, but an additional information chunk

Chapter 3 Exercise

Exercise 1. Providing and Identifying Supports

Importance and Purpose of the Exercise

Many novice message designers confuse points and supports. This confusion results in erroneous estimates of the number of information chunks which in turn results in inaccurate estimates of the message's information load. The purpose of this exercise is to clarify the function of supports at the application level that such confusion will forever be laid to rest.

A. Providing Supports

Instructions

Select a single statement regarding a topic with which you are very familiar. That statement will be your *single point* to be supported. DO NOT SUB–DIVIDE THAT POINT! Now provide a support for that point from each of the following categories. You may create or borrow the supports, but be sure they fit the category: Repetition, paraphrase, description, narration, list of brief examples, explanation, numerical data, quotation, authoritative opinion (testimony), document, example, comparison, contrast, definition, visual support.

Evaluation of Your Efforts

Have your instructor or study partner check your supports for compliance with the definitions of these supports in Chapter 3.

B. Identifying Supports

Instructions

Search newspapers, news magazines, and textbooks for an example of each of the supports listed above. Write in a complete sentence the point of being supported in each instance.

Evaluation of Your Efforts

Have your instructor or a study partner review your collected examples noting especially whether they fit the attributed category and whether they support the point you identified.

Chapter 3 Exercise

Exercise 2. Counting Information Chunks

Importance and Purpose of the Exercise

An "information chunk" is a convenient construct which enables us to quantify the useful information in a message. It, along with the obscurity index, enables us to estimate the information load of a message. The ability to identify and count the number of information chunks is therefore central to designing a message that optimizes the balance between information load, message complexity, and message duration. The purpose of this exercise is to enable you to identify and quantify the information chunks in any given message.

Instructions

Select a documentary or instructional audio- or videotape or a film and outline it. It may be useful to audio record the sound-track for easy repetition of sections. Disregard the introductory, framing, and concluding portions. In other words, identify the body and outline it in box-outline format. Be sure to distinguish between points and supports. When you are satisfied with your outline, count the number of information chunks.

Evaluation of Your Efforts

This exercise is best done in a group. After all have counted their information chunks, find out who has the greatest number of chunks and who has the fewest. Have those two people explain their thinking to the rest of the group. Invite group response to their explanations. Given this dialogue, re-assess your own effort.

Chapter 3 Exercise

Exercise 3. Editing Information-Overloaded Messages

Importance and Purpose of the Exercise

"Information overload" means that the message contains more information than can be processed by the receiver. When confronted with information overload, listeners resort to various strategies for coping with it, but many of the strategies are counterproductive, and all of them result in some loss of information. The purpose of this exercise is to experience what is entailed in the basic editing options. The underlying assumption here is that it is better for the message designer to select which information will be sacrificed than for the receiver to do so.

Instructions

Select a central idea that can be subdivided into at least 12 information chunks, some of which are developed on sub- or sub-subpoints. Your task is to reduce the number of information chunks to six in each of two strategies. First, preserve the original scope of the message by eliminating some subdivision and by combining points at a higher level of abstraction. Then, give up scope for detailed development of fewer points. In this latter case, you will have to revise your central idea to accommodate the narrower scope.

Evaluation of Your Efforts

Continue working on this exercise until you have reduced the number of chunks to six in each case. Then assess the cost of your editing decisions in terms of your feelings about having to eliminate material you wanted to include. State explicitly the assumptions underpinning your decisions and evaluate them as parts of your ideal value system.

Chapter 3 Exercise

Exercise 4. Interpreting the Body Structure Matrix

Importance and Purpose of the Exercise

The order of presentation of information in the message body alone can account for different levels of message effectiveness. The appropriate basis for selecting patterns of body structure stems from the interaction of information load and receiver readiness. Given information regarding these two dimensions, the prescription is easily identified, but it requires some practice to interpret the prescription. The purpose of this exercise is to make the Body Structure Matrix (Figure 3.5) a usable tool of design for you.

Instructions

    A. Review the general rules at the bottom of the matrix and the section entitled "Order of Presentation." Then write a paragraph explaining why the cell defined by high readiness and high information load is appropriate.

    B. Write a paragraph explaining how to fill the prescription contained in the medium readiness/medium information load cell.

    C. Outline the body of a message on a topic of your choice according to the prescription for the low readiness/low information load cell.

    D. Analyze a message of your choosing and assign it to the cell of nearest fit. Then using the matrix, judge whether it is appropriately adapted to the intended receivers and whether the information load is appropriate.

Evaluation of Your Efforts

Share your efforts with a study partner or in a class discussion and seek the impressions of others regarding your use of the matrix. Subtle refinements of the matrix are possible only through use and discussion of the matrix.

Chapter 3 Exercise

Exercise 5. Identifying Outline Weaknesses

Importance and Purpose of the Exercise
As a practicing message designer, you will frequently be asked
to evaluate the ideas of clients and colleagues as they are expressed
in outline format. If weaknesses can be detected at the outline
stage, a great saving of time and other resources can accrue. The
purpose of this exercise is to provide you with practice in
identifying weaknesses in box-outlines and sentence outlines, and
in detecting incompatibility between the two.

Instructions
Review the Chapter 2/Number 1 exercise. Use a box-outline
created there as the basis for this exercise, but now, develop that
outline with information chunks. You may use any other
fully-developed box-outline you have at your disposal. Next,
translate the box-outline into a complete-sentence outline according to the format in the text. When you and two study partners
have completed both outlines, share yours with the other two and
have them look for any weakness described in Table 3.2 and for
any inconsistency between the box- and sentence-outlines. Then
rotate so that you become a critic for the other two study
partners. Discuss differences of interpretation until the differences
are resolved.

Evaluation of Your Efforts
The evaluation is an inherent part of this exercise. By the time
you have worked through it, you will know the quality of your
work.

Name ....

Section .... Date ....

Chapter 4 Exercise

Exercise 1. Learning the Conceptual Atmosphere Matrix

Importance and Purpose of the Exercise

The contextual atmosphere that flavors the whole message is determined by the balance you establish between diversity and density. To the extent that these factors are selected by design rather than by chance, you have greater control over the impact of your message. Since these considerations must be made for every message you design, it will be economical of your time to commit this matrix to memory. The purpose of this exercise is to assist you in learning this matrix at the free-recall level.

Instructions

Photocopy several copies of the blank matrix on the following page. Then after studying the Conceptual Atmosphere matrix, fill out the matrix without reference to the text: First, write the major cell descriptor in the upper 1/3 of each cell; then write the correlated cognitive pattern in the middle 1/3 of each cell; finally, write the appropriate social context in the remaining 1/3 of each cell.

Example:

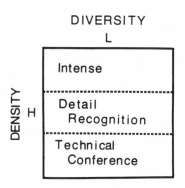

Evaluation of Your Efforts

When you reach the criterion of two consecutive perfect recitations, you may claim mastery.

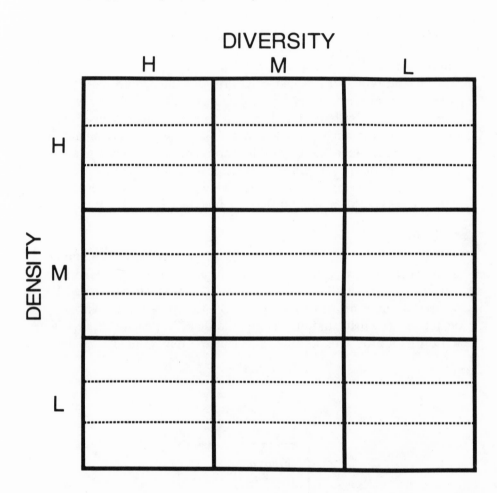

Chapter 4 Exercise

Exercise 2. Interpreting Diversity/Density Profiles

Importance and Purpose of the Exercise

With your developing expertise in designing messages, you are likely to be invited from time to time to criticize a slide show, a videotape, a film, etc. A useful critical method is to profile the complexity of the message and then describe on the basis of your profile interpretation what impact the message is likely to generate. The purpose of this exercise is to develop your skill in interpreting the diversity/density profiles.

Instructions

Select a short film or video recording and play it to a class-sized group. During the viewing, you scale diversity and density. If other reliable raters are present, have them rate also and average your ratings. After the viewing, have the rest of the group complete the response sheet on the following page. Before looking at a summary of their responses, write your predictions (based upon the profile) regarding: (1) the kind of contextual atmosphere it will create, and (2) the kind of cognitive activity the message will require. Finally, compare your predictions with the group's appraisal. If there are differences, what explanations can you offer?

Evaluation of Your Efforts

Ideally, your predictions will match the group's assessment rather closely. *Note*: You may have to interpolate between cells if your profiles do not fit the matrix in whole numbers.

Reaction Questionnaire

I. Circle the number of the item which best describes the kind of "atmosphere" this viewing created.

1. Ecstatic   6. Methodical
2. Challenging   7. Exciting
3. Intense   8. Intriguing
4. Compelling   9. Thorough
5. Routine

II. Circle the number of the item which best describes the kind of cognitive activity required during this viewing. (If more than one seems to have been required, select the one that was dominant.)

1. Detail recognition   6. Analogy recognition
2. Solution recognition   7. Pattern recognition
3. Achievement recognition   8. System recognition
4. Concept recognition   9. Stereotype recognition
5. Position recognition

III. Place an X in the appropriate space for each of these scales:

A. (Affection) How well did you like the message presentation?

Much : 7 : 6 : 5 : 4 : 3 : 2 : 1 : Little

B. (Cognitive Strain) How hard did you have to work to get this message?

Much : 7 : 6 : 5 : 4 : 3 : 2 : 1 : Little

Name ....

Section .... Date ....

Chapter 4 Exercise

Exercise 3. Rating Diversity and Density

Importance and Purpose of the Exercise

The matrix prescriptions are only of conceptual value until you are able to scale the message complexity elements precisely and reliably. Learning to rate these elements refines the concepts in tacit ways that you may not be able to explain, but in ways that will affect the consistency of your ratings. The importance of estimating diversity and density is that given accurate measures of these two elements, you will be able to control the contextual atmosphere generated by these signal characteristics. The purpose of this exercise is to develop your ability to scale diversity and density consistently with your own ratings and with those of others who are trained in the use of the complexity model.

Instructions

Photocopy several copies of the rating scale on the following page. Spend an evening or two rating television commercials on the six dimensions related to diversity and density. As you watch each commercial, make notes of the diversity and density characteristics you notice immediately. Then think back over the message with special attention to each scaled dimension. At this point, commit yourself to a rating by checking on the broken line at the appropriate place. Pay close attention to the polar descriptors (sometimes they are reversed). Do not try to deal with fractions or between-the-interval check marks. Also, do not think about scale numbers at this point; just check on the scale between the polar descriptors for each dimension. When you have checked each scale, translate each check mark into a numerical rating by looking at the number at the top of the column. Then average the three diversity dimensions and record the average diversity score. Do the same with density.

When you feel confident with commercials, move to other types of messages: books, magazines, news shows, movies, etc. Work in a group when possible; class-sized groups are ideal.

Evaluation of Your Efforts

When working alone on television commercials, you can check your reliability of rating by rating the same commercial after the passage of time. If your compared ratings are within one-half of a scale point, your progress is satisfactory. When working in groups, ask the highest rater and the lowest rater to engage in dialogue. Listen carefully to their reasons for rating as they did and re-examine your own ratings. After several practices in the group, calculate the group's average on both elements. Compare your averages with the group's. You should be within one-half a scale point of the group's average.

Scaling Practice

Message .... Date ....

DIVERSITY

Audible Variety	$\overline{X} =$	Low _ _ _ _ _ _ _ High
Visual Variety		Low _ _ _ _ _ _ _ High
Structural Variety		Low _ _ _ _ _ _ _ High

DENSITY

Rate of Change	$\overline{X} =$	Low _ _ _ _ _ _ _ High
Redundancy		High _ _ _ _ _ _ _ Low
Structural Depth		Low _ _ _ _ _ _ _ High

Signal Characteristics

Notes

Chapter 5 Exercise

Exercise 1. Rating Sophistication and Readiness

Importance and Purpose of the Exercise

Two of the most important things you can know about your receivers are their sophistication and readiness levels. Given that information, you can prescribe several features of a message designed for them. But central to acquiring that information is the ability to scale these factors reliably. The purpose of this exercise is to develop your skill in scaling the sophistication and readiness levels reliably for any given audience and to determine which kind of audience would be optimal for receiving any given message.

Instructions

Photocopy several copies of the scale on the following page. Then select ten to 12 magazines intended for various audiences. For each magazine, sample and scan it for about ten minutes. Finally, scale the magazine on the six dimensions and average the sophistication dimensions, and again, average the readiness dimensions.

Next, select television commercials and other programming to scale in the same manner. Finally, view a short film with a group of study partners or in class and discuss and compare your ratings.

Evaluation of Your Efforts

Check your own reliability in scaling by repeating selected ratings after the passage of time. Also, continue this exercise until your ratings are within one-half of a scale point from the group's average.

Scaling Practice

Message .... Date ....

SOPHISTICATION

Abstraction   Low _ _ _ _ _ _ _ _ High
Implicitness $\overline{X} =$ _____   Low _ _ _ _ _ _ _ _ High
Precision   Low _ _ _ _ _ _ _ _ High

READINESS

Framing Provided   High _ _ _ _ _ _ _ _ Low
Relevance Provided $\overline{X} =$ _____ High _ _ _ _ _ _ _ _ Low
Mnemonics Provided   High _ _ _ _ _ _ _ _ Low

Organismic Capabilities

Chapter 5 Exercise

Exercise 2. Interpreting Sophistication/Readiness Profiles

Importance and Purpose of the Exercise

Design decisions based upon the audience's sophistication/readiness characteristics directly involve the overall structure of the message, the selection of graphics, and the choice of language style. These essential message qualities should be readily prescribed (at least in general terms) from any given sophistication/readiness profile. A practicing message designer will be expected to deliver "thumbnail" prescriptions without reference to external sources. The purpose of this exercise is to assist your mastering the general cell traits of the matrix by committing them to your free-recall memory.

Instructions

First review Figures 5.2 and 5.3. If you are unclear on the meanings of any of the cell descriptors, re-read the text relative to those concepts. When you feel ready, complete the exercise on the following page.

Evaluation of Your Efforts

Mastery implies perfection. The criterion for this exercise is therefore a flawless performance. Photocopy some extra copies of the exercise and continue the exercise until you have completed two consecutive perfect performances at least one day apart.

Mastery Drill for the General
Sophistication/Readiness Matrix

Instructions. Below are three lists of cell descriptors—each of which is to be matched with SOP/REA profile information. Write the letter of the appropriate term in the proper column and row.

			List #1	List #2	List #3
SOP		REA			
H	—	H			
H	—	M			
H	—	L			
M	—	H			
M	—	M			
M	—	L			
L	—	H			
L	—	M			
L	—	L			

A Rank and file
B Lay audience
C Displaced expert
D Professional
E Elite
F Mass audience
G Modal
H Under-achiever
I Over-achiever

A Erudite/full
B Elegant/subtle
C Plain/austere
D Plain/subtle
E Elegant/austere
F Erudite/subtle
G Elegant/full
H Plain/full
I Erudite/austere

A Dedicated
B Popular
C Quick starter
D Expert
E Slow starter
F Common denominator
G Adult workforce
H Responsible
I Competent

Chapter 5 Exercise

Exercise 3. Prescribing and Interpreting Dispositional Patterns

Importance and Purpose of the Exercise

Just as the order of presentation is important within the body of a message, the overall arrangement of parts is important also. While the disposition matrix may be consulted as needed during the designing of a message, the specialized language used in the matrix should be recognized without review. The purposes of this exercise are to insure your understanding of the matrix-cell vocabulary and to guide your efforts to recognize their application in any given message.

A. Dispositional Matrix Vocabulary

Instructions
Write a definition for each of the following terms:
1. Exordium
2. Expository background
3. Central idea
4. Division
5. Body
6. Refutation
7. Peroration
8. Transition
9. Digression

Evaluation of Your Efforts

Check your definitions against those in Chapter 5. Note any differences and recite the revised definitions until you can define each one fully without hesitation.

B. Interpreting Dispositional Patterns

Instructions
View a short film or video recording and identify the dispositional elements employed in it. Then match that pattern to the matrix cell that comes closest to it. Finally,

draw inferences about the readiness and sophistication levels of an appropriate audience for this message.

Evaluation of Your Efforts

Either check with your instructor, a study partner, or class members to see how your inferences compare with theirs. Several repetitions of this exercise will refine your skill.

Chapter 5 Exercise

Exercise 4. Matching Graphics and Audiences

Importance and Purpose of the Exercise

Too often graphics are provided for messages on the basis of convenience rather than design. If you have a good cartoonist or a photographer available, it is easy to think in terms of cartoons or color slides. But the non-verbal aspects of graphics appeal to different audiences differently, and selection should not be left to whim or intuition. The purpose of this exercise is to increase your sensitivity to the graphic requirements of different audiences.

A. Prescribing Graphics

Instructions

Select three audiences at random from the following list and describe the appropriate graphic rendering of a common object or situation for each audience. For example: Describe how a typewriter might be portrayed for an elite, a lay, and a rank and file audience. Or, how would you depict a parent and child interaction for each of these audiences?

1. Elite   4. Displaced expert   7. Under-achiever
2. Professional   5. Modal   8. Rank and file
3. Over-achiever   6. Lay audience   9. Mass audience

Evaluation of Your Efforts

Check your prescriptions against Figure 5.4, or ask a study partner for a critique of your prescriptions.

B. Classifying Graphics

Instructions

Collect 30-40 pictures, illustrations, cartoons, etc., from a wide range of magazines: *Newsweek, People, Money, Popular Mechanics,* and *Psychology Today* are good choices. Then lay out a large blank matrix, and assign each picture to a cell. When you are finished, look for the similarities within cells and the differences between cells.

Evaluation of Your Efforts

It is best to do this exercise with others so that you may discuss your differences. If you agree, fine; if you do not, discuss your choices and re-evaluate your position. You may find that interpolation between cells is required.

Chapter 5 Exercise

Exercise 5. Identifying Prose Styles

Importance and Purpose of the Exercise

Both as a critic and a designer, you need to classify prose styles so that you may match them appropriately with various communication strategies. For example: the plain style is generally appropriate for teaching, the middle style for proving, and the grand style for moving the passions. Recognizing these general categories should become second-nature for you. The purpose of this exercise is to enable you to assign any given bit of prose to one of four categories or to recognize the combination of types within a single passage. In general, this exercise increases your sensitivity to the nuances of language.

Instructions

Review Step 14 carefully and while referring to the text, write a concise definition of the plain, forcible, elegant, and grand styles *in the style being defined.* That is, your definition of plain style should be written in the plain style. Then for two or three days, pay close attention to the language you encounter during your daily routine. When you sense that you have a paradigm example, classify it. Recorded examples are sometimes more appropriate for close examination.

Evaluation of Your Efforts

After classifying an example spontaneously, review your definition of that style to determine the closeness of fit. Again, if you can work on this exercise with others, the refining of the concepts will be hastened.

Chapter 5 Exercise

Exercise 6. Matching Language Difficulty and Interest Levels with Audiences

Importance and Purpose of the Exercise

A professional message designer, copywriter, or scriptwriter soon develops a sense of whether the language of a given message fits the intended audience. This is an essential skill for a professional to possess. The purpose of this exercise is to direct your attention precisely and systematically to the analysis of language and to its appropriate application.

Instructions

Photocopy a full page of text from each of three sources. An academic or scientific journal, a digest-type magazine, and a tabloid. For each source, count out a 100-word sample and draw a slash mark at the end of the sample. Then find the nearest period and circle it. Within the 100-word samples, count: (1) the number of "personal words" (defined in Chapter 5) and (2) the number of syllables. Next, locate the circled period and count the number of whole sentences in the sample. Determine how many of those sentences are "personal sentences" (defined in Chapter 5), and count the average number of words per sentence. Finally, consult the matrix (Figure 5.7) and see whether your findings match the respective cells.

Evaluation of Your Efforts

If there is a mismatch between your findings and the matrix prescriptions, re-tabulate your findings. If your count was reliable, attempt an explanation of the inconsistency.

Chapter 6 Exercise

Exercise 1. Learning the Basic Response-Style Matrix

Importance and Purpose of the Exercise

Every message manifests some degree of tension and aloofness through its non-verbal characteristics. The interaction of the message's tension and aloofness levels shapes to a large extent the kinds of responses the receivers will give when receiving the message. To the extent that you can control these elements in your messages, you will increase the probability of achieving the responses desired by the source. The purposes of this exercise are to increase your sensitivity to common personality traits and to associate them with specific matrix cells.

A. Spontaneous Response Styles

Instructions

Watch several television situation-comedy shows where the characters are fairly clearly stereotyped (for example: *Barney Miller, MASH, Love Boat*, or re-runs of the *Mary Tyler Moore Show*). Study the characters one at a time and rate them as high, moderate, or low both in tension and aloofness. Then consult Figure 6.1 and see whether the cell descriptor fits that character.

Evaluation of Your Efforts

This exercise will have been successful when you begin to observe people in your everyday situations and are able to classify their response styles either by descriptors or by matrix variables.

B. Compulsive Response Styles

Instructions

Search your memory for paradigm examples of each cell

descriptor in Figure 6.2. Without referring to the matrix, estimate their tension and aloofness levels. Then compare your estimates with the matrix classifications.

Evaluation of Your Efforts

If your judgments do not match the matrix, re-examine your original classification of the behavior. If you are convinced that your judgment is better than the matrix classification, amend the matrix for your future personal use.

Chapter 6 Exercise

Exercise 2. Rating Aloofness and Tension

Importance and Purpose of the Exercise

Response styles, the third major division of message complexity, must be scaled with the same degree of accuracy and reliability for contextual atmosphere and receiver-imposed constraints. When aloofness and tension can be rated as well as you have learned to rate the other elements, you will be able to rate the total message complexity of any given message. The purpose of this exercise is to reduce the variance in your ratings of tension and aloofness.

Instructions

Photocopy several copies of the rating scale on the following page. Select several instances representing a wide variety of television programs or films and rate each for aloofness and tension. Longer programs might profitably be divided into episodes, scenes, etc., so that each can be rated separately. Sometimes the overall averaging obscures the range manifested in different segments. For an overall rating, that averaging effect is appropriate; but, for purposes of drill, the separate ratings will probably be more beneficial. Be sure to average the three aloofness dimensions to get an overall aloofness score. Do the same with tension.

You may find it helpful to list the specific cues of tension and aloofness during the viewing and commit yourself to ratings following reflection after the viewing. Also, repeated viewings during early practice is often useful. With practice, you will be able to rate each dimension during a single viewing.

Evaluation of Your Efforts

If you are working alone, your best estimate of your rating

reliability is to re-rate a piece after a delay of two or three days. If you are working in a group (which is preferable), your best basis for evaluation is to compare your ratings with the group's average. Always discuss your excessive deviations in order to refine your definitions of tension and aloofness. These concepts become more precise with critical usage. A rule-of-thumb criterion, whether you are working alone or in a group, is that your ratings are satisfactory if they fall within one-half a scale point from your comparison rating.

Scaling Practice

Message .... Date ....

ALOOFNESS
> *Reward* High _ _ _ _ _ _ _ Low
> *Involvement* High _ _ _ _ _ _ _ Low
> *Frustration* High _ _ _ _ _ _ _ Low

TENSION
> *Shock* Low _ _ _ _ _ _ _ High
> *Suspense* Low _ _ _ _ _ _ _ High
> *Conflict* Low _ _ _ _ _ _ _ High

Response Requirements

Notes

Chapter 6 Exercise

Exercise 3. Matching Music and Response Styles

Importance and Purpose of the Exercise

The selection of music to be used in a message is often made on either superficial or preferential bases rather than in a thoughtful attempt to create certain response styles. The difference is that of an amateur selection as opposed to a professional one. Music properly selected is one of the most powerful non-verbal effects available to the designer. The purpose of this exercise is to develop your ability to select musical passages that predispose your receivers to respond according to the source's desires.

Instructions

This exercise is best done as a class project. Have each member of the class draw a cell description from the matrix presented in Figure 6.4. If there are fewer than 18 members in the class, have each member draw enough times to provide at least 18 cells. Each cell should be represented at least twice.

Now have each class member find a recorded sample of music that would fit his or her cell(s). In class, play a 60-90 second sample of each selection without announcing the basis of its selection. Have the rest of the class rate each selection on tension and on aloofness.

Select a committee to rank order the selections on the aloofness levels reported. Then divide the ranked list into three equal parts to establish a high, a middle, and a low category of aloofness selections. Do the same on the tension ratings. Next, assign each selection to a matrix cell according to these two classifications. Now, randomly select one selection from each cell and play it to the class without disclosing to which cell it belongs. Each class member should assign each of the nine selections to the matrix.

Evaluation of Your Efforts

Locate your score with the following chart.

Number of Correct Classifications	*Your Standing as a Music Classifier*
9	Excellent: You are a "pro."
7-8	Good: Try just a little harder.
4-6	Fair: Keep working at it.
2-3	Poor: Are you sure you were able to hear the music?
0-1	Awful: You have a "tin ear"; leave the selection of music to others.

Chapter 6 Exercise

Exercise 4. Matching Colors and Response Styles

Importance and Purpose of the Exercise

Most people when asked can identify rather precisely the colors they like and those they dislike. There is even some convincing evidence to suggest that their color preferences are related to some of their personality characteristics. Indeed, much of the color selection for visual messages is based upon the subjective preferences of the designer or the artist. But selecting colors to elicit selected response styles is a different assignment from selecting colors on the basis of personal preference. A message designer will do well to select colors that predispose his or her receivers to respond in a manner compatible with the source's purpose, irrespective of what either the designer or the receivers' preferences may be. The purpose of this exercise is to demonstrate the compatibility of selected colors with certain behavioral response styles.

Instructions

You will need a tablet of construction paper containing a wide range of colors and a collection of expendable magazines, corporate annual reports, brochures, etc. Collect a large number of pictures of people photographed individually. Cut out the pictures, removing all of the background possible. Then spread these out over a large surface on a page of each paper color. One at a time, place the pictures against each colored background and select the color that "best fits" the picture. Note which pictures fit which colors. Then assign the pictures to cells on either Figure 6.1 or Figure 6.2. Record the aloofness/tension cell description for each picture; then turn to Figure 6.5 (the response-style color matrix) and see whether the selected color matches the prescribed color.

Evaluation of Your Efforts

The best evaluation would be to compare your findings with those of others—preferably several others. It is possible that if your findings deviate too far from the matrix prescriptions, you are judging from your preferences (aesthetically) rather than from your sense of response-style compatibility. If this is the case, repeated practice, with frequent reference to the matrices, may be useful.

Chapter 6 Exercise

Exercise 5. Matching Visual Composition and Response Styles

Importance and Purpose of the Exercise

Many of the commonsense and practical experience "rules-of-thumb" have been synthesized into the response-style matrix for visual composition. Beyond merely identifying possibilities and establishing simple and random qualities of various visual composition alternatives, this matrix clusters choices into patterns that relate to identifiable response styles. The thoughtful use of this matrix can contribute significantly to making a message work to satisfy the source's requirements. The purpose of this exercise is to build your confidence in the validity of this design instrument.

Instructions

This rather elaborate exercise calls for three photographic lights, a camera, and a table-top stage set. The set can be built by cutting away a cardboard carton and lining the three walls with a different piece of cloth depending upon the shot. The stage can be set to create a simple scene involving one or two figurines and appropriate stage "props." You will vary several visual aspects of the stage set (without rearranging the items on the set) to create five distinct scenes: one for the central cell of the matrix and one of each of the corner cells. Once the cell prescription is filled in each instance, photograph the scene. The photographs will be presented to a panel of judges (who are unfamiliar with the response-style matrix) who will be asked to select from a list of nine response-style descriptors the one that best fits each photograph.

Follow these prescriptions for setting the stage for each scene:
A. Using a neutral gray cloth to cover the walls:
    1. Set-up for the moderate aloofness/moderate tension shot:

Set-up an over-the-shoulder shot at eye-level and a medium distance. Light the set to preserve detail in the shadowed areas. Frame the shot for visual balance.

B. Using a black cloth to cover the walls:
2. Set-up for the high aloofness/high tension shot: This will be a long shot from a low angle and with the camera tilted to create imbalance. Light for high contrast and long dark shadows falling on the right side only. Maximize the depth of field.
3. Set-up for the low aloofness/high tension shot: This will be a close-up, low angle shot. It should also be from a subjective viewpoint; that is, the camera should be thought of as the eye of one of the characters. Light for high contrast and deep shadows falling in one direction only. Tilt the camera to create imbalance. Use a shallow depth of field.

C. Using a white cloth to cover the walls:
4. Set-up for the high aloofness/low tension shot: Use a high-angle long-shot with a deep field depth. Frame the picture to maximize the feeling of stability. Flat light in order to minimize shadows.
5. Set-up for the low aloofness/low tension shot: Shoot it close-up from a high angle and a subjective viewpoint. Flat light for minimal shadowing. Frame the shot to maximize stability. Use a shallow depth of field.

Evaluation of Your Efforts

If you have followed the instructions carefully, your panel of judges should be able to match the cell descriptors with the appropriate photographs with little difficulty.

Chapter 7 Exercise

Exercise 1. Mastering Message Profiles

Importance and Purpose of the Exercise

An advantage to being able to think in complexity profiles is that given a profile, you can anticipate rather remarkably what the effect of a message so designed will be. The savings in time and resources can be substantial if you eliminate inherently weak designs before investing in production. The purpose of this exercise is to have you experience both the prognosis and the prescription applications of a complexity profile.

A. The Prognosis Experience

Instructions

Given the following profile, consult the appropriate matrices to determine the probable contextual atmosphere, the receiver-imposed constraints, and the response style for a message designed accordingly. Write your conclusions as if you were reporting the probable outcome of a proposed message to a client. PROFILE: DIV = 5.3, DEN = 5.1, SOP = 4.0, REA = 3.5, ALO = 5.7, TEN = 2.3.

Evaluation of Your Efforts

Compare your prognosis with the prognosis of others who have attempted it. Discuss differences in your findings and re-assess your original effort following the discussion.

B. The Prescription Experience

Instructions

Using the same profile presented above, describe in detail how you might manifest this profile into a message. Write a paragraph for each of the six complexity elements.

Evaluation of Your Efforts

   Discuss with your instructor or a study partner the feasibility
and workability of your prescription.

Chapter 7 Exercise

Exercise 2. Creating a Message Plan

Importance and Purpose of the Exercise

The message plan provides you with the first tangible conceptualization of the integrated message. It coordinates the content and
the message complexity along a time line. With a message plan,
you can determine at any moment what information is being
presented and how that information is being shaped non-verbally
to optimize its effectiveness. Again, the message plan allows for
modifications in the design before the actual production and
evaluation of the message. All of the important considerations can
be adjusted and traded off at this stage, until there is unity,
coherence, and proper emphasis in the design. The purpose of this
exercise is to acquaint you with the process of creating a message
plan—to de-mystify the process—without having to design a
message from the beginning.

Instructions

Using the box-outline from Chapter 3, Exercise 5, and the
message prescription you generated in Chapter 7, Exercise 1,
create a message plan using Figure 7.3 as a model. Photocopy one
or more copies of the message plan form on the following page.
You may glue two or more together if you need more space. First,
assign time units to the vertical divisions, then fit your box-outline
to the time line. Finally, while consulting your prescription, design
the message complexity elements so that they are coordinated
with the information chunks. Use Figure 7.3 as a model.

Evaluation of Your Efforts

Check to see whether the main and subpoints have been
assigned the amount of time that establishes their relative levels of
importance. Also check to see whether the fluctuations in level for

each message complexity element average out to the level
prescribed by the complexity profile.

Chapter 7 Exercise

Exercise 3. Translating the Message Plan into a Storyboard

Importance and Purpose of the Exercise

The storyboard permits us to translate the abstract and conceptual design into a concrete and observable format. The storyboard forces us to make some refining and specific commitments and decisions. It not only allows us to see which decisions have to be made, but it also allows us to communicate our intentions to clients and to those responsible for the production. In other words, the storyboard helps us to refine our own ideas and to communicate them to others. The storyboard can be developed at different aesthetic levels according to the purpose it is serving. The purpose of this exercise is to have you experience: (1) translating a point on the message plan into a visual image; (2) providing instructions to the producer; and (3) rendering the visual image at different levels of definition.

Instructions

Photocopy three copies of the storyboard form on the following page. Cut the pages to form six storyboard pages. Then select two time-points from the message plan from Chapter 7, Exercise 2, for development. At the bottom of each storyboard page, write in the "page time" and the complexity element levels as determined from the message plan. Consult the appropriate matrices according to the complexity profile at the bottom of the page, and write notes in the appropriate box regarding composition, color, diversity, etc. For two of the pages, sketch the visuals to the limit of your artistic ability; for another two, stage the visual and photograph it (perhaps with a Polaroid camera) and affix the photos to the pages. For the remaining two pages, trace on tracing paper the essential features of the photographed images. Then trim and affix the tracings to the storyboard pages. Write special instructions to the producer or artist to assist him or her in creating the image you desire.

Evaluation of Your Efforts

Have someone study your storyboard pages one-by-one and describe in some detail the shot in the final production that stimulates his or her imagination. Then you must determine whether the image received was the one you intended to send. Also, examine the reactions of your study partner to see whether the different visual formats generated different reactions.

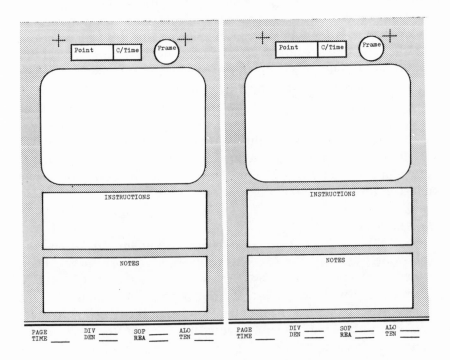

Chapter 7 Exercise

Exercise 4. Visualizing the Message from a Storyboard

Importance and Purpose of the Exercise

Creativity has been defined as the ability to look at one thing and to see another. Visualizing the message from a storyboard is therefore an inherently creative act. Anyone who communicates is creative because all of the messages we receive must be re-created from our own experiences before they are meaningful. The purpose of this exercise is to make that inherently creative process more conscious and to discover ways of using it willfully so that you may edit the message in your mind—before it has been produced for others to see. This ability leads to conserved resources and better directing of the production.

Instructions

Select six events involving yourself that occurred this morning between the time you arose and the time you ate lunch. Reconstruct each one as vividly in your memory as you can and sketch it with simple stick figures in the upper portion of the six "thumbnail" storyboard pages on the following page. Under each sketch, write very briefly what is happening. Now, exchange papers with a study partner.

Study the page frame-by-frame until you can recall each cell quickly at will. Now, take four to five minutes to relax by any standard process. During this period, think only about how your relaxing muscles feel. Then close your eyes and call up each sketch in turn and substitute real people, objects, and settings. Let it be a "freeze-frame." Study the details; change the colors; re-arrange the elements. Next start at the beginning and introduce action, voices, sounds.

When you have control of each frame (shot—scene), select the first three and create a continuity or transition between each so that they flow. Then drop the first frame and add the fourth.

Again, create continuity between the three. Continue until all sets of three have continuity.

Again, return to the beginning, but this time run through the whole sequence. Hear it; see it; smell it; taste it; feel it.

If you want more experience, change the characters and the setting, but preserve the relationships and action. Maybe you would like to try a "flashback" by re-sequencing the frames.

Evaluation of Your Efforts

Only you can tell whether you made it work. If so, practice visualizing often. If it did not happen for you, forget it for today and try again soon.

"Thumbnail"   Storyboard

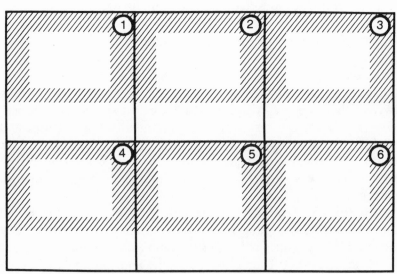

Chapter 7 Exercise

Exercise 5. Writing for the Ear

Importance and Purpose of the Exercise

Most writing is intended to be read rather than heard. We are trained throughout our education to write according to formal writing style. Nearly everything we read has been written in a style that is qualitatively different from the way we speak. (A transcript of a public speech is a notable exception.) But a *script* is typically only a written vehicle for producing an aural message. Thus, when most people start writing scripts, they sound like essays rather than talk. The purpose of this exercise is to sensitize you to the qualitative differences between written and oral style.

Instructions

Gain permission from a friend to tape-record a lengthy conversation. After a few minutes, the tape recorder will be forgotten and the conversation will become more natural. Select a sample of three to five minutes from the latter portion and transcribe it *verbatim*. You are likely to notice soon that we do not always speak in conventional sentences. (You may have to create some new means of punctuation.) Study the phrase or sentence structure, the selection of words, the rhythms generated by the phrases, the contractions, the idioms, etc.

Next, select a few paragraphs from a news magazine (such as *Newsweek*). Read a paragraph aloud two or three times listening as you read. Then paraphrase the thought of the paragraph as you would report its essence to a friend. Tape-record your paraphrases for all of the selected paragraphs. Finally, transcribe your paraphrases *verbatim*. Then compare your version with the original.

Carry this exercise one step further by converting your paraphrase into dialogue. Select two different personality types and make their words fit their personalities.

Evaluation of Your Efforts

Record the original, your paraphrase, and your dialogue, and play it to a group for their reactions. If they prefer your paraphrase or dialogue over the original, you are probably adequately sensitized to the qualitative differences between writing intended for the eye and writing intended for the ear.

Chapter 7 Exercise

Exercise 6. Translating the Storyboard into a Production Script

Importance and Purpose of the Exercise

While the storyboard is an excellent vehicle for communicating with the client and the producer, the director works best from a production script during actual production and post-production. It becomes necessary, therefore, to translate the storyboard faithfully into a script which specifies all of the design features that influence production. The purpose of this exercise is to have you experience translating a storyboard into a production script.

Instructions

Return to Chapter 7, Exercise 3, and write the words that are to be spoken on the back of two pages that represent different time-points on the message plan. Make your words consistent with the complexity profile at the bottom of the pages. That is, write at the appropriate density level, sophistication and readiness levels, and at the appropriate aloofness and tension levels.

Next, write a production script according to the models in Chapter 7. If your time-points are contiguous, write one script incorporating both pages in the format of either model. If they are not contiguous, write an example of each format using only one storyboard page for each.

Evaluation of Your Efforts

Compare your script with those of others, or ask your instructor or a director/producer for suggestions for improvement.

Name ....

Section .... Date ....

Chapter 8 Exercise

Exercise 1. Learning from the Professionals

Importance and Purpose of the Exercise
One of the distinguishing marks of a professional is his or her ability to discriminate quality products from inferior ones. Amateurs, given time, may be able to discriminate also, but for the professional, time equals money. From the consumer's standpoint, the professional can reduce the cost of delivering a quality product by recognizing acceptable efforts instantly. This kind of discrimination can be *learned*; the better you can do it, the more professional you are. The purpose of this exercise is to improve your ability to discriminate professional from non-professional quality in minimal time.

Instructions
Have each member of your class bring a sample of his or her best color slides from his or her private collections. Borrow an equal number from your library's slide collection or from professionally-produced slide shows. The total sample should include between 200-300 slides. Randomly mix the slides and place them in slide trays. Invite a professional photographer to be your consultant. Show a slide; have class members judge it as professional or not by marking (P) or (N) by the number of each; then have the professional state his or her opinion. Students mark the incorrect (i.e., non-compliant) judgments and calculate their percentages at the end.

Repeat the exercise limiting the time each slide is projected to five seconds. Repeat again at two-second intervals.

You may wish on the initial presentation to have the consultant explain why he or she judged so, but it is not essential for developing discrimination.

Similar exercises may be created for discriminating between professional and amateur recordings, graphics, recorded script

307

passages, slide sequences, video shots, acting, etc. Set up one or several exercises according to your needs.

Evaluation of Your Efforts

As a rule-of-thumb, we may assume that a professional should be able to discriminate slides at the rate of one each three seconds with 90 percent accuracy. By the way, you may notice some disagreement between your consultant's appraisals and the actual source of the slides. If your consultant has an established credential, it might be better to favor his or her judgment. It is possible that some of the amateur contributors sometimes achieved professional quality, and it is possible that some items that pass for professional quality are indeed inferior.

Chapter 8 Exercise

Exercise 2. Selecting and Coaching Talent

Importance and Purpose of the Exercise
Some producers/directors like to work closely with the designer in order to render the design faithfully. Some designers also serve as producer/director for their own projects. In either case, it is important for the designer to feel comfortable in audition and coaching/rehearsal situations. The purpose of this exercise is to de-mystify the processes of selecting and coaching talent by providing a direct experience of both processes.

Instructions
Divide your class or study-group into thirds. One-third will serve as talent; one-third will be audition critics; and one-third will be coaches. Using a portion of a suitable script (one of your own creation or a borrowed one), conduct an audition of the talent, each of whom is trying out for the same part. A narrator's role is a good one for this purpose. The critics, in a prior meeting, should study the script and agree upon a suitable interpretation. They should also standardize a critique form so that all will be looking for the same qualities.

After the audition, the critics should confer and make a final selection—justifying their selection among themselves. Videotaping the tryouts, if possible, is a convenience during the selection process.

Regardless of who is selected, talent and coaches should be paired off. The coach and the talent should jointly study the critiques for that particular performer and determine what special areas require coaching. The coach should establish appropriate coaching strategies and rehearse the talent privately.

Evaluation of Your Efforts
Conduct a second audition just as before and compare the more

recent critique sheets with the earlier ones. If the areas emphasized during the coaching are rated higher in the latter evaluation, both the coach and the talent may take a bow.

Chapter 8 Exercise

Exercise 3. Analyzing Photographs and Graphics

Importance and Purpose of the Exercise

Although a message designer *per se* is not expected to be a graphic artist or a photographer, it is important for the designer to understand some of the technical possibilities in both areas so that he or she may design more appropriately and assess the products of the artist and photographer realistically. The purpose of this exercise is to provide an experience for you of analyzing both graphic art and photography at a level beyond the lay person's practice.

Instructions

Select a half dozen of both graphic displays and photographs from a quality magazine. Analyze each according to the suggestions below and attach your written analysis to the original.

For the graphics, look for such things as: special techniques for generating images; letter size, type, and spacing; eye-movement patterns; white-space usage; balance; color. Then infer what the probable impact will be and to which audience it will probably appeal.

For the photographs, try to determine: the type of lens used; the depth of field; the f-stop and exposure speed; the use of special filters; etc. For each photograph, sketch a diagram showing camera and light placement. Is there evidence of photo retouching?

Evaluation of Your Efforts

Exchange your samples with another student and see whether your conclusions are in agreement. If not, try to resolve disagreements through discussion. Failing to reach agreement this way, seek a third opinion.

311

Chapter 8 Exercise

Exercise 4. Evaluating Sound-Tracks

Importance and Purpose of the Exercise

As with graphics and photography, the designer must be able to recognize the implications of the technical aspects upon the aesthetic. By being able to identify common flaws in recording, you may be able to design around the causes and recognize unacceptable treatments. The purpose of this exercise is to sensitize your ear to some of the finer aspects of recording quality.

A. Controlled Variation

Instructions

In this part of the exercise, you will create your own material for analysis and evaluation. First, take a quality portable tape recorder into several locations where the ambient noise varies. Some examples: a freeway, out-of-doors, a classroom, a living room, a hard-surfaced public hallway, etc. Play the samples sequentially listening carefully for the varying qualities. Each segment should have a recorded voice in a portion of it so that you may notice the effects of the environment on the vocal quality.

In another sample, record at the appropriate recording level, then increase the volume so that the distortion from over-modulation can be heard. Do the same for an under-modulated signal by reducing the recording volume below optimal.

Record a spoken segment under optimum conditions, then "dub" the master to produce five generations of recording. First compare the first and the fifth. When the quality differences are clear, listen to the first and the fourth. Continue in this manner until you can discriminate a two-generation gap.

Evaluation of Your Efforts

Your ability to refine your listening ability will be reflected by the frequency with which you can identify the different properties per number of attempts. Listen to the recordings of others who have done this exercise and score yourself.

B. Real-Life Recordings

Instructions

Listen to a video recording or a film without watching the picture and pay close attention to the following items: ambient sound, modulation level, cueing and transitional techniques, and microphone type and use. It would also be useful to compare amateur and professionally prepared sound-tracks in the same manner.

Evaluation of Your Efforts

You are likely to "know" when you are able to discriminate without external confirmation of that fact. But, if objective verification is needed, do the exercises with others and strive for agreement in judgment. Discuss differences until they are resolved or until an impass is reached.

Chapter 8 Exercise

Exercise 5. Testing, Trouble-Shooting, and Revising a Message

Importance and Purpose of the Exercise

Careful design of a message can increase the degree of confidence that it will work to serve the source's requirements, but a factual statement about its workability can be made only *after* it has been tried on receivers. By the time a mediated message can be tested on a sample audience, a great deal of time and resources will have been invested in it. If it does not produce the desired results, something should be done to salvage the investment. This exercise suggests what can be done. The purpose of this exercise is to familiarize you with the recommended processes for testing, trouble-shooting, and revising a message.

Instructions

Create a simple information message in one of two ways: (1) either write a message describing how to assemble a moderately complex structure from various shaped building blocks or "Tinker-Toys"; or (2) write a message describing the assembly or use of some commercial product. (You may elect to use the manufacturer's instructions as your message.)

Tape record the message as appears appropriate for a receiver to follow it while complying with the instructions. Use no visual aids, but do supply the listener with the required materials to complete the task.

Next, select five or six receivers who are unfamiliar with the task and have them perform the task as they listen to the message. Allow no replays or questions. When the message is finished, the task should be completed. See whether the receiver's efforts match the instructions *exactly* to produce the desired product. For each failing attempt, attempt to locate the source of failure by working through the "Algorithm for Trouble-Shooting Messages" in Chapter 8. Finally, review the recorded message according to the algorithm's prescription and repeat it with the original receiver.

Evaluation of Your Efforts

The criterion for your message is perfect performance. Continue reworking the message until your listeners (working individually) meet the task criterion flawlessly.

Suggested Major Design Projects

Project I. Original Design

Given a client, topic, and audience of your own choosing, design, produce, and evaluate a 15-minute slide/sound message in which you follow explicitly each of the 21 steps in the design process.

This project provides an excellent opportunity to integrate the entire process into a documented statement of your message-design ability. It is suitable as a term project in a college course, or (with expansion of scope and production format) it merits credit for a "special problems" course. Several of my students have found such projects invaluable in job interview situations. This project is to the message designer/producer what an artist's portfolio is to the artist.

Project II. Message Analysis and Evaluation

Given a film or video-recording of an instructional, promotional, or motivational message, perform an exhaustive written analysis and evaluation involving each of the 21 steps of the design process.

This project provides the same opportunity as Project I to integrate the entire process and to document your understanding of it. The emphasis is placed upon your ability to understand how a message of someone else's design works. Thus, it avoids considerations of production skill and expense. The written report of such an analysis with accompanying recommendations for revisions is a valuable exhibit for display during a job interview. The scope of this project is also suitable as a major term project for college credit.

Project III. Message Reconstitution

Select a fable, a short story, or a poem of moderate length and reconstitute it into a script and storyboard for either a sound/slide show or a videotape. Reconstitution requires first reducing the original to its essential qualities (for example, reducing a short story to its plot line and character list). Then, retaining those elements, shift to a different situation or environment and build a new message from the old structure. You may either generate your own complexity profile or you may borrow one from a message of someone else's design. Borrowing one from elsewhere is also an exercise in reconstitution.

The practice of reconstitution is well-established. Writers of plays, novels, and short stories are often inspired by someone else's work; for instance, "West Side Story" is a reconstitution of "Romeo and Juliet." Musicians' compositional exercises of creating variations on a theme are a form of reconstitution also. Reconstitution is a basic creativity process, and its products may be manifested in art, dance, music, public speeches, essays, lectures, etc.

This project will be testimony to your ability to "look at one thing and see another." In other words, it will document your ability to be creative on demand. That skill is especially valuable in assignments which require adaptation of one message format to another: a case in point would be the adaptation of a novel to the requirements of a film script.

"Any theory is at best a 'convenient fiction'."

"It is not the function of science to discover 'ultimate truths'. . . . The function of science is simply to enable us to predict, to explain, and to control selected aspects of our environment."

Chapter 10

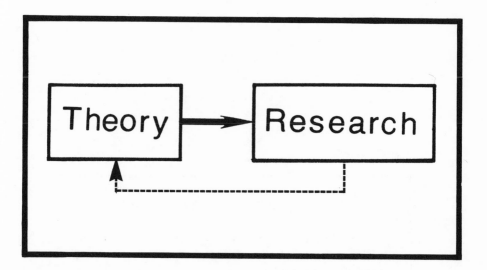

Central Idea

This axiomatic theory identifies and organizes axioms, postulates, propositions, and hypotheses derived from the basic model in such a way as to generate research which will either validate the theory or indicate required modifications in theory. In other words, this theory consists of a coherent set of statements that can guide future research. They spring directly from the model upon which this book is based. The main advantage of this approach is that even though some of the hypotheses drawn from these axioms may be borne out when tested, even *that* knowledge will be used to revise and strengthen the theory.

Chapter Contents

1. Theory-then-research approach.
2. Requirements of an axiomatic theory.
3. An axiomatic theory of message design.

Chapter 10

Applications in Research:
A Formal Theoretical Statement

Any theory is at best a "convenient fiction." It is inherently fictitious because its function is to simplify (and thus distort) reality in order to render it manageable by our limited cognitive processes. Just as any act of perception screens out detailed data about the thing observed, any theory, in seeking the essential characteristics of a thing, distorts by abstraction. Yet, in so far as our theories allow us to function better in our environment, these fictions are convenient and useful.

It is not the function of science to discover "ultimate truths" or "first principles," although many labor under this misconception. The function of science is simply to enable us to predict, to explain, and to control selected aspects of our environment. To the extent that our theories serve these functions, they are justified, even though they *are* merely convenient fictions. In the words of Jacob Bronowski:

> Science is a very human form of knowledge. We are always at the brink of the known, we always feel forward for what is to be hoped. Every judgment in science stands on the edge of error, and is personal. Science is a tribute to what we can know although we are fallible. (Bronowski, 1973)

An axiomatic theory seems appropriate for formalizing a set of constructs about designing messages. The more popular practice, and in my view an inappropriate one, is to state theoretical constructs as "covering laws." Covering laws attempt to postulate universal, invariant relationships; they tend to provide linear explanations. Communication phenomena, including messages, are more appropriately understood within the context of systems because of their inherently complex interrelationships. But our understanding of communication is not yet sufficient to construct practical general-systems theories. The best compromise, given the present "state of the art," is an axiomatic theory. It provides a manageable stepping-stone from where we are to where we ultimately would like to be.

Central Idea

This axiomatic theory identifies and organizes axioms, postulates, propositions, and hypotheses derived from the basic model in such a way as to generate research which will either validate the theory or indicate required modifications in theory. In other words, this theory consists of a coherent set of statements that can guide future research. They spring directly from the model upon which this book is based. The main advantage of this approach is that even though some of the hypotheses drawn from these axioms may not be borne out when tested, even *that* knowledge can be used to revise and strengthen the theory.

Theory-Then-Research Approach

Until World War II, practically all research on messages was critical (as opposed to empirical), and it was based largely on the precepts of Aristotle and his disciples. But research for military purposes, or propaganda, rumor, etc., introduced the methods of social science to the rhetorical scholars. Within a short time after the war, scholarly journals began reporting findings from simple experiments related to isolated inquiries about communication. After a few years, hundreds of research reports were accumulating in the journals, and critics began attempts to synthesize the findings into integrated theoretical statements. It did not work. The studies had been conducted at different levels of abstraction, without standardized definitions or instruments, and under varied levels of control. Efforts to discover principles under these conditions were rendered useless by virtue of overgeneralization or imprecision and resulted in frustration and failure.

Only in the last decade have we realized the importance of developing an internally consistent theory first and then generating hypotheses for research from the theory. The most obvious advantage of this "theory-then-research" approach is that all of the hypotheses generated are of a known level of abstraction. They can be operationalized with standardized definitions and instruments, and they can be compared and integrated when confirmed. Even the unconfirmed hypotheses point directly at theoretical weaknesses so that they can be modified.

It is for these reasons that this theory is advanced at this time. It is granted that several of the positions hypothesized here are speculative and that some are not likely to be supported by empirical data. But, they are *testable*, and once tested, they will strengthen the theory, either by confirming it or by identifying its misconceptions. In this light, this theory is a prototype.

Requirements of an Axiomatic Theory

To be regarded as valid, an axiomatic theory must meet both logical and empirical requirements. This theory has been developed with these requirements as guidelines.

Logical Requirements

The logical, or deductive, structure of an axiomatic theory must begin with a set of axioms which do not contradict each other. Axioms are the "givens" or "self-evident truths" on which the theory is founded. They are not to be tested directly, but rather assumed. Axioms may be revised or abandoned as a result of their indirect testing through hypotheses, but such adjustment substantially modifies the theory.

No axiom may be derived from another axiom. Postulates may be derived from axioms, and postulates may have corollaries, but axioms represent cardinal positions. Postulates may be divided and developed at a lower level of abstraction (i.e., more concretely) in the form of propositions. A proposition may be regarded as a research hypothesis, but in my usage, a hypothesis will be an operationalized tentative conclusion.* Incidentally, this theoreti-

---

*The convention of preceding "hypothesis" with the indefinite article "an" is derived from British practice, where the "h" is silent and requires an elision. In American practice, we say "an hour" ("h" is silent) and "a house" ("h" is pronounced). Accordingly, American writers will more properly write and say "a hypothesis," since they pronounce the "h."

cal statement is developed only through the proposition level of abstraction, although examples of hypotheses will be provided.

The set of axioms must be necessary and sufficient for the deduction of all theorems. A theorem is a logical extrapolation from axioms, thus each premise in the extrapolation must be rooted in an axiom. Further, no statement is qualified as an axiom if it does not allow such extrapolation to be made with it.

Axioms should assert some form of implication, but that relationship need not be causal. That is, the relationship could be correlative without accounting for cause.

Empirical Requirements

The empirical (or inductive) characteristics of an axiomatic theory are rooted in "facts" as opposed to "self-evident truths." Since statements of fact are only possible *after* an observation has been made, the level of confidence we can place in such statements is relative to the quality of the observation on which they are based. Consequently, the variables used in the deduced theorems must be operationalized and measured. Further, the validity and reliability of all measures must be established by conventional standards.

If causal relationships are posited, conventional experimental designs must be incorporated in the research. Essentially, causality can only be inferred when all variables are controlled between comparison groups or conditions, except those deliberately manipulated by known amounts by the investigator.

An Axiomatic Theory of Message Design
AXIOM 1.0 The tactics associated with each strategy are functions of two dimensions.

POSTULATE 1.1   The tactics associated with the strategy "to inform" are: (1) the receiver's knowledge level, and (2) the receiver's awareness of knowledge level.

POSTULATE 1.2   The tactics associated with the strategy "to stimulate" are: (1) the receiver's knowledge level, and (2) the receiver's awareness of knowledge level.

POSTULATE 1.3   The tactics associated with the strategy "to interpret" are: (1) the receiver's knowledge level, and (2) the receiver's awareness of knowledge level.

POSTULATE 1.4   The tactics associated with the strategy "to instruct" are: (1) the receiver's knowledge level, and (2) the receiver's awareness of knowledge level.

POSTULATE 1.5   The tactics associated with the strategy "to persuade" ("to promote") are functions of the degree of: (1) acceptance of issues by the receiver, and (2) acceptance of issues by the source.

POSTULATE 1.6   The tactics associated with the strategy "to entertain" are functions of: (1) the receiver's seriousness level, and (2) the source's seriousness level.

POSTULATE 1.7   The tactics associated with the strategy "to solve" are functions of: (1) the level of goal definition by the source, and (2) the level of goal attainment.

POSTULATE 1.8   The tactics associated with the strategy "to argue" are functions of: (1) the elements of the source's argument, and (2) the receiver's willingness to grant those elements.

POSTULATE 1.9   The tactics associated with the strategy "to transform" are functions of the receiver's reliance on: (1) left-brain functions, and (2) right-brain functions.

AXIOM 2.0 The tactics associated with each strategy are ordered into unique sequences according to the entry level and destination on the matrix.

POSTULATE 2.1   The strategy "to inform" is associated with the sequence of tactics progressing from "to imagine" to "to associate" to "to divide" to "to amplify" to "to acknowledge."

POSTULATE 2.2   The strategy "to stimulate" is associated with the sequence of tactics progressing from "to imagine" to "to extrapolate" to "to acknowledge."

POSTULATE 2.3   The strategy "to interpret" is associated with two sequences depending upon the cell of entry.

POSTULATE 2.31   When the cell of entry is defined by the receiver's moderate knowledge level and low awareness of knowledge level, the sequence is from "to shadow" to "to extrapolate" to "to paraphrase" to "to acknowledge."

POSTULATE 2.32   When the cell of entry is defined by the receiver's high knowledge level and low awareness of knowledge level, the sequence is from "to reframe" to "to paraphrase" to "to acknowledge."

POSTULATE 2.41   The strategy "to instruct" (general) is associated with a sequence of tactics assigned to each matrix cell.

POSTULATE 2.411   The tactical sequence for the cell labeled "ingenuous" is: (1) to build confidence in the process, and (2) to present the "full treatment."

POSTULATE 2.412   The tactical sequence for the cell labeled "naive" is: (1) to take a quick assessment, (2) to confirm receiver's suspicions of inadequate knowledge, and (3) to present the "full treatment."

POSTULATE 2.413   The tactical sequence for the cell labeled "sophomoric" is: (1) to begin at the terminal level of the sequence, (2) to confront the receiver with his or her ignorance, and (3) to present the "full treatment."

POSTULATE 2.414   The tactical sequence for the cell labeled "cognizant" is: (1) to acknowledge known areas, (2) to isolate weak areas, and (3) to present the "accelerated treatment."

POSTULATE 2.415   The tactical sequence for the cell labeled "dilettantish" is: (1) to make a quick assessment, (2) to confirm the receiver's suspicions of inadequate knowledge, (3) to isolate the weak areas, and (4) to present the "accelerated treatment."

POSTULATE 2.416   The tactical sequence for the cell labeled "superficial" is: (1) to begin at the terminal level of the sequence, (2) to confront weaknesses, and (3) to present the accelerated treatment.

POSTULATE 2.417   The tactical sequence for the cell labeled "profound" is: (1) to acknowledge the receiver's knowledge level, and (2) to proceed to the next item.

POSTULATE 2.418   The tactical sequence for the cell labeled "knowledgeable" is: (1) to probe suspicions of inadequate knowledge, (2) to quiz at the terminal level of the "full treatment," and (3) to reassure of knowledge adequacy.

POSTULATE 2.419   The tactical sequence for the cell labeled "dormant" is: (1) to quiz at the terminal level of the accelerated treatment, (2) to deny ignorance, and (3) to reassure of knowledge adequacy.

POSTULATE 2.42   The strategy "to instruct" (concepts) involves both a "full treatment" and an "accelerated treatment" tactical sequence.

POSTULATE 2.421   The tactical sequence for the "full treatment" (concepts) is: (1) to present definition, (2) to present initial matched set of examples/non-examples, (3) to identify critical attributes, (4) to present a practice matched set, and (5) to present a terminal matched set.

POSTULATE 2.422   The tactical sequence for the "accelerated treatment" (concepts) is: (1) to present a hand and convergent matched set of examples/non-examples, (2) to isolate the critical attributes, and (3) to present the detailed concept definition.

POSTULATE 2.43   The strategy "to instruct" (details) involves both a "full treatment" and an "accelerated treatment" tactical sequence.

POSTULATE 2.431   The tactical sequence for the "full treatment" (details) is: (1) to preview the whole, (2) to conduct recitation, (3) to isolate problem areas, (4) to suggest mnemonic devices for problem areas, (5) to drill with problem-set using reinforcement, and (6) to conduct recitation to the criterion level.

POSTULATE 2.432   The tactical sequence for the "accelerated treatment" (details) is: (1) to drill with reinforcement, (2) to provide the correct response for each error immediately, and (3) to conduct recitation to the criterion level.

POSTULATE 2.44   The strategy "to instruct" (relationships) involves both a "full treatment" and an "accelerated treatment" tactical sequence.

POSTULATE 2.441   The tactical sequence for the "full treatment" (relationships) is: (1) to identify the terminal task, (2) to present an overview of the complete network or process, (3) to identify the governing rule or underlying principle, (4) to present the simplest usable case, (5) to isolate the elements of that case, (6) to present increasingly complex cases, and (7) to present an elaborated rule or underlying principle.

POSTULATE 2.442   The tactical sequence for the "accelerated treatment" (relationships) is: (1) to present a complex case of the network or process, (2) to isolate the elements of that case, (3) to identify the relationships of the elements, and (4) to present the elaborated rule or underlying principle.

POSTULATE 2.5   The strategy "to persuade" is associated with tactical sequences according to the intended outcome of the persuasive effort.

POSTULATE 2.51   The tactical sequence employed for "gaining acceptance" of a position is: (1) to move the receivers with pathetic appeals, (2) to prove a case with enthymemes and examples, and (3) to acknowledge the identity of the source's and the receiver's positions.

POSTULATE 2.52   The tactical sequences employed for "moderating a position" are related to the receiver's initial position.

POSTULATE 2.521   When the receiver's initial position is more favorable than the source supports, the tactical sequence is: (1) to minimize the receiver's warrant's backing, (2) to list exceptions to the receiver's warrant, and (3) to qualify the claim.

POSTULATE 2.522   When the receiver's initial position is

less favorable than the source supports, the tactical sequence is: (1) to provide rhetorical backing for the source's warrant, (2) to provide inartistic verification for the source's data, and (3) to state a qualified claim.

POSTULATE 2.53   The tactical sequence employed for "dissuading" a receiver from acceptance of a position is: (1) to create doubt by cross-examination, (2) to discredit rejected argument by refutation, and (3) to inoculate by ethos-supported assertions.

POSTULATE 2.6   The strategy "to entertain" has not been developed at the tactical level.

POSTULATE 2.7   The strategy "to argue" is associated with tactical sequences related to the elements of the source's argument.

POSTULATE 2.71   The tactical sequence related to establishing the validity of the source's data is: (1) to state the data, (2) to verify or document the data, and (3) to test the data's verification.

POSTULATE 2.72   The tactical sequence related to establishing the validity of the source's warrant is: (1) to state the warrant, (2) to offer direct backing and exceptions for the warrant, and (3) to trace the backing to its factual roots.

POSTULATE 2.73   The tactical sequence related to establishing the validity of the source's claim (granting the source's data and warrant) is: (1) to state the claim, (2) to qualify the claim, and (3) to relate the qualifications to the warrant's exceptions.

POSTULATE 2.74   The tactical sequence related to establishing the validity of the source's claim when the receiver grants neither the warrant nor the data is: (1) to state the verified and tested data, (2) to state the backed and excepted warrant, and (3) to state the qualified claim.

POSTULATE 2.75   The tactical sequence related to establishing the validity of the source's claim when the receiver grants only the data or the warrant is: (1) to state the granted element, (2) to prove fully the ungranted element, and (3) to state the claim in which qualifications are related to the exceptions to the warrant.

POSTULATE 2.8   The strategy "to solve" is executed either by employing the "full reflective thinking sequence" or by modifying it according to the relative differences between goal definition and goal achievement levels.

POSTULATE 2.81   The tactical sequence related to the "full sequence" is: (1) to define and delimit the problem, (2) to analyze symptoms for causes, (3) to establish goal-related criteria for evaluating solutions, (4) to list possible solutions, (5) to select the best solution, and (6) to implement the solution.

POSTULATE 2.82   The tactical sequence related to the "modified sequence" is: (1) to modify the full reflective-thinking sequence according to cell prescriptions, and (2) to employ the modified sequence.

POSTULATE 2.821   The sequence modification prescribed for the cell labeled "reinforce" is to abandon efforts to solve the problem further.

POSTULATE 2.822   The sequence modification prescribed

for the cell labeled "refine goals" is to specify objectives.

POSTULATE 2.823   The sequence modification prescribed for the cell labeled "formalize goals" is to induce goals from successful cases.

POSTULATE 2.824   The sequence modification prescribed for the cell labeled "narrow goal" is to delimit the problem by establishing priorities.

POSTULATE 2.825   The sequence modification prescribed for the cell labeled "employ truncated process" is to eliminate the step related to analysis of the symptoms for causes.

POSTULATE 2.826   The sequence modification prescribed for the cell labeled "brain storm" is to list possible solutions without prior analysis and to withhold evaluation until the list is completed.

POSTULATE 2.827   The sequence modification prescribed for the cell labeled "risk radical departure" is to attempt a "second-order change," Watzlawick *et al.* (1974), by stepping out of the present frame, i.e., by reframing the apparent problem.

POSTULATE 2.828   The sequence modification prescribed for the cell labeled "refine solutions" is to retain the present solutions but to isolate and correct their inefficiencies.

POSTULATE 2.9   The strategy "to transform" is associated with a tactical sequence which progresses from: (1) "candidate status" to (2) "apprentice status," to (3) "warrior status," to (4) "luminous-being status."

POSTULATE 2.91   The "candidate status" is associated with the tactical sequence of: (1) to create a "safe space," (2) to "grab the

	will," and (3) to forewarn the receiver of an irreversible change.
POSTULATE 2.92	The "apprentice status" is associated with four tactical sequences according to the cell of entry.
POSTULATE 2.921	The tactical sequence prescribed for the "apprentice a-1" cell is: (1) to require receiver to "clean-up personal space," (2) to explain the necessity of "agreement," (3) to explain the cost of pride, and (4) to promote apprentice to a-2 status.
POSTULATE 2.922	The tactical sequence prescribed for the "apprentice a-2" cell is: (1) to encourage the expansion of "safe public space," (2) to introduce activities requiring the development of strength and temperance, and (3) to promote the apprentice to "warrior-1" status.
POSTULATE 2.923	The tactical sequence prescribed for the "apprentice b-1" cell is: (1) to create the conditions necessary for the apprentice to experience "transportation" from present space, (2) to introduce appropriate "power objects," and (3) to promote the apprentice to b-2 status.
POSTULATE 2.924	The tactical sequence prescribed for the "apprentice b-2" cell is: (1) to assist in the creation of the apprentice's "personal space," (2) to create the conditions necessary to "stopping the internal dialogue," and to promote the apprentice to "warrior-1" status.
POSTULATE 2.93	The "warrior status" is associated with three tactical sequences according to the cell of entry.

POSTULATE 2.931   The tactical sequence prescribed for the "warrior-1" cell is: (1) to test the receiver's commitment by staying an encounter with a "worthy opponent," (2) to continue the encounter until the criterion is met, and (3) to promote the receiver to the "warrior-2" status, which represents the area of greater deficiency.

POSTULATE 2.932   The tactical sequence prescribed for the "warrior a-2" cell is: (1) to disassemble the receiver's "personal space" into categories, (2) to reassemble the categories to create new relationships, and (3) to promote the receiver to the "luminous-being" cell.

POSTULATE 2.933   The tactical sequence prescribed for the "warrior b-2," cell is: (1) to argue for the necessity of developing "impeccability" (integrity, quality, ownership), (2) to stage a test case requiring demonstrated impeccability in the performance of a task, (3) to transfer task-related impeccability to interpersonal relationships, (4) to stage a test case at the relationship level, and (5) to promote the receiver to the status of luminous being.

POSTULATE 2.94   The tactical sequence prescribed for the "luminous-being" cell is: (1) to enlist the aid of a "benefactor" who administers the remainder of the sequence, (2) to demonstrate limited instances of creative interpretation, (3) to guide the receiver through a variety of creative tasks, (4) to establish confidence within limits of ability to create interpretations, and (5) to promote self-initiated expansion of the limits of creativity.

AXIOM 3.0 The calculation of a message's information load is a function of: (1) the number of "information chunks," and (2) the average "obscurity index" of the message.

POSTULATE 3.1   Under conditions of stable obscurity index, information load increases as the number of information chunks increases.

POSTULATE 3.2   Under conditions of a constant number of information chunks, the information load increases as the obscurity index decreases.

POSTULATE 3.3   The same information load may be created through different assignments of number of information chunks and obscurity indexes.

PROPOSITION 3.31   An information load comprised of a "low number of chunks" and a "low obscurity index" is equivalent to one comprised of a "moderate number of chunks" and a "high obscurity index."

PROPOSITION 3.32   An information load comprised of a "moderate number of chunks" and a "low obscurity index" is equivalent to one comprised of a "high number of chunks" and a "high obscurity index."

AXIOM 4.0 The prescriptions for structuring the message's body are functions of "information load" and "receiver readiness."

POSTULATE 4.1   The degree of "imbeddedness" employed in the body structure is a function of the information load.

PROPOSITION 4.11   Highly "imbedded" body structures are more effectively applied to messages of "high information load" than to those of "low information load," whereas primal structures are better suited to messages of "low information load."

POSTULATE 4.2   The arrangement of information chunks in the body of a message is a function of a receiver's readiness.

PROPOSITION 4.21   Receivers of high readiness are better served by message bodies which are developed with climactic arrangement.

PROPOSITION 4.22   Receivers of moderate readiness are better served with body structures which relegate weaker information chunks to the middle of the message, thus presenting stronger ones at the beginning and the end.

PROPOSITION 4.23   Receivers of low readiness are better served by body structures which are developed in an anticlimactic arrangement.

POSTULATE 4.3   The manner of supporting a point is a function of the receiver's readiness.

PROPOSITION 4.31   Receivers of high readiness are better served by points supported directly (i.e., the supports follow the statement of the point).

PROPOSITION 4.32   Receivers of moderate readiness are better served by a combination of direct and indirect supports.

PROPOSITION 4.33   Receivers of low readiness are better served by indirect (implicative) support of points (i.e., the presentation of supports precedes the statement of the point).

POSTULATE 4.4   The degree of support in an information chunk is a function of the message's information load.

PROPOSITION 4.41   Messages of high information load are more effective when the number and/or size of supports is minimized.

PROPOSITION 4.411   Messages of high information load where supporting material is minimized are more effective when supports are specific and/or literal.

PROPOSITION 4.412   Messages of moderate information load are more effective when support types are mixed.

PROPOSITION 4.413   Messages of low information load are more effective when supports are arranged from general to specific and/or from figurative to literal.

POSTULATE 4.5   The use of transitions in a message body is a function of receiver readiness.

PROPOSITION 4.51   Receivers of low readiness are better served by message bodies developed with elaborate transitions.

PROPOSITION 4.52   Receivers of moderate readiness are better served by message bodies developed with moderate transitions.

PROPOSITION 4.53   Receivers of high readiness are better served by message bodies developed with minimal or no transitions.

AXIOM 5.0 The "complexity level" of a message is a function of: (1) the signal's characteristics, (2) the constraints imposed by the receivers, and (3) the response style desired by the source.

AXIOM 5.1 The signal characteristics of the message determine the "contextual atmosphere" created by the message.

POSTULATE 5.1   The signal characteristics of "diversity" and "density" interact to determine the contextual atmosphere of the message.

POSTULATE 5.11   "Diversity" is the sum of: (1) visual variety, (2) audible variety, and (3) structural variety where each dimension is weighted equally.

POSTULATE 5.11   The degree of affection for a message is positively related to the degree of diversity in the message.

POSTULATE 5.12   "Density" is the sum of: (1) the rate of change, (2) the degree of non-redundancy, and (3) the structural depth of the message where each dimension is weighted equally.

POSTULATE 5.121   The degree of cognitive strain associated with a message is positively related to the degree of message density.

POSTULATE 5.13   The matrix cells created by the interface of diversity and density discriminate both emotional and cognitive states.

PROPOSITION 5.131   High diversity and high density generate an "ecstatic" atmosphere which is conducive to pattern recognition.

PROPOSITION 5.132   Moderate diversity and high density generate a "challenging" atmosphere which is conducive to concept recognition.

PROPOSITION 5.133   Low diversity and high density generate an "intense" atmosphere which is conducive to detail recognition.

PROPOSITION 5.134   High diversity and moderate density generate a "compelling" atmosphere which is conducive to system recognition.

PROPOSITION 5.135 Moderate diversity and moderate density generate a "routine" atmosphere which is conducive to position recognition.

PROPOSITION 5.136 Low diversity and moderate density generate a "methodical" atmosphere which is conducive to process/problem recognition.

PROPOSITION 5.137 High diversity and low density generate an "exciting" atmosphere which is conducive to stereotype recognition.

PROPOSITION 5.138 Moderate diversity and low density generate an "intriguing" atmosphere which is conducive to achievement recognition.

AXIOM 5.2 The receiver-imposed constraints determine: (1) the message dispositional pattern, (2) the type of graphics, and (3) the language style which maximizes effectiveness.

AXIOM 5.21 Receiver-imposed constraints are a function of: (1) the receiver's sophistication level, and (2) the receiver's readiness level.

POSTULATE 5.211 "Sophistication" is the sum of: (1) the receiver's ability to handle abstraction, (2) the receiver's ability to interpret implicitness, and (3) the receiver's ability to tolerate precision where each dimension is equally weighted.

POSTULATE 5.212 "Readiness" is the sum of: (1) the degree of framing required by the receiver, (2) the degree to which the receiver needs the relevance stressed, and (3) the degree to which the receiver requires mnemonic aid where each dimension is equally weighted.

AXIOM 5.22 The dispositional pattern of a message is a function of: (1) the receiver's degree of sophistication, and (2) the receiver's degree of readiness.

POSTULATE 5.221   For an "elite" (expert) audience (High SOP/High REA), the most effective dispositional pattern is: (1) to state the central idea, and (2) to develop the body fully.

POSTULATE 5.222   For a "professional" (responsible) audience (Moderate SOP/High REA), the most effective dispositional pattern is: (1) to present a brief expository background, (2) to state the central idea, and (3) to develop the body fully.

POSTULATE 5.223   For an "over-achiever" (dedicated) audience (Low SOP/High REA), the most effective dispositional pattern is: (1) to develop a full expository background, (2) to state the central idea, and (3) to develop the full body.

POSTULATE 5.224   For a "displaced expert" (quick starter) audience (High SOP/Moderate REA), the most effective dispositional pattern is: (1) to state a brief exordium, (2) to present the central idea, (3) to develop the full body, and (4) to supply a brief peroration.

POSTULATE 5.225   For a "modal" (competent) audience (Moderate SOP/Moderate REA), the most effective dispositional pattern is: (1) to present a brief exordium, (2) to present a brief expository background, (3) to present the central idea, (4) to develop a moderate body, (5) to employ either a division step or transitions, and (6) to present a brief peroration.

POSTULATE 5.226   For a "lay" (popular) audience (Low SOP/Moderate REA), the most effective dispositional pattern is: (1) to present a brief exordium, (2) to present a full expository background, (3) to present the central idea, (4) to develop a division step, (5) to develop a moderate body, (6) to employ transitions, and (7) to present a brief peroration.

POSTULATE 5.227   For an "under-achiever" (slow starter) audience, the most effective dispositional pattern is: (1) to present a full exordium, (2) to present a brief exposition, (3) to state the central idea, (4) to develop a moderate body, (5) to present a brief peroration, and (6) to use optional digressions.

POSTULATE 5.228   For a "rank and file" (adult workforce) audience (Moderate SOP/Low REA), the most effective dispositional pattern is: (1) to present a full exordium, (2) to present a brief expository background, (3) to present the central idea, (4) to employ either a division step or transitions, (5) to present a full peroration, and (6) to employ optional digressions.

POSTULATE 5.229   For a "mass" (common denominator) audience, the most effective dispositional pattern is: (1) to present a full exordium, (2) to present a full expository background, (3) to state the central idea, (4) to develop a brief body, (5) to present a full peroration, and (6) to employ optional digressions.

AXIOM 5.23 The type of graphics employed in a message is a

function of: (1) the receiver's degree of sophistication, and (2) the receiver's degree of readiness.

POSTULATE 5.231   The degree to which reality can be
represented effectively is a function of
the receiver's level of sophistication.

PROPOSITION 5.2311   Receivers of low sophistication are
best served by graphics, which
represent objective reality.

DEFINITION 5.2311   "Representational or objective reality"
is defined as graphics which are real-
istic, objective, concrete, and employ
minimal verbalization.

PROPOSITION 5.2312   Receivers of moderate sophistication are best served by graphics
which distort or interpret objective reality.

DEFINITION 5.2312   "Interpreted or distorted reality" is
defined as graphics which interpret
reality subjectively, translate it into
symbols or analogs, and typically employ visual verbalization.

PROPOSITION 5.2313   Receivers of high sophistication
are best served by graphics, which
abstract objective reality.

DEFINITION 5.2313   "Abstracted reality" is defined as
graphics which are generalized, sugges-
tive, schematic, digital, transformed,
conceptual, and typically employ a
high degree of visual verbalization.

POSTULATE 5.232   The degree of graphic definition required to maximize effectiveness is a
function of the receiver's level of readiness.

PROPOSITION 5.2321   Receivers of low readiness are best
served by graphics of high defini-
tion.

DEFINITION 5.2321   "High definition" is defined as a graphic which is framed broadly, retains the context, presents sharp detail, and employs full representational color.

PROPOSITION 5.2322   Receivers of moderate readiness are best served by graphics of moderate definition.

DEFINITION 5.2322   "Moderate definition" is defined as a graphic which moderately frames the subject, de-emphasizes the context, uses color for mood, makes simple associations (montage, or clustering), and employs screened images (half-tone).

PROPOSITION 5.2323   Receivers of high readiness are best served by graphics of low definition.

DEFINITION 5.2323   "Low definition" is defined as a graphic which is framed narrowly, suppresses the context, employs color for emphasis (if any), suggests isolation, and typically has a neutral background with line drawing.

AXIOM 5.24 The language style in a message is a function of: (1) the receiver's degree of sophistication, and (2) the receiver's degree of readiness.

POSTULATE 5.241   The appropriate length of words and sentences is a function of the receiver's sophistication level.

DEFINITION 5.241   "Normal word and sentence lengths" are defined by the research of Rudolf Flesch.

PROPOSITION 5.2411   Receivers of low sophistication are best served by language style which employs short words and short sentences.

PROPOSITION 5.2412   Receivers of moderate sophistication are best served by language

style which employs average
length words and sentences, or
which employs a range of word
and sentence lengths which average to the norms.

PROPOSITION 5.2413   Receivers of high sophistication
are best served by language style
which employs a higher than normal proportion of polysyllabic
words in lengthy sentences.

PROPOSITION 5.2414   The appropriate usage of "personal" words and sentences is a func-
tion of the receiver's level of
readiness.

DEFINITION 5.242   "Personal words and personal sentences" are defined operationally by
Rudolf Flesch.

PROPOSITION 5.2421   Receivers of low readiness are best
served by language style which
employs a greater than normal
number of "personal words" and
"personal sentences."

PROPOSITION 5.2422   Receivers of moderate readiness
are best served by language style
which employs the normal degree
of "personal words" and "personal sentences."

PROPOSITION 5.2423   Receivers of high readiness are
best served by language style
which employs a minimal degree
of "personal words" and "personal sentences."

AXIOM 5.3   The response style desired by the source determines:
(1) the musical effects, (2) the color selection, and
(3) the elements of visual composition which maximize effectiveness.

AXIOM 5.31   Response styles are a function of: (1) the message's
aloofness level, and (2) the message's tension level.

POSTULATE 5.311   "Aloofness" is the sum of the polar opposites of: (1) reward, (2) involvement, and (3) frustration.

POSTULATE 5.312   "Tension" is the sum of the polar opposites of: (1) shock, (2) suspense, and (3) conflict.

AXIOM 5.32 Basic behavioral responses generated by aloofness and tension levels are influenced by a "spontaneous-compulsive" dimension.

POSTULATE 5.321   The basic responses generated on the "spontaneous" matrix are: regimented, heuristic, emotional, provocative, calculating, contemplative, lethargic, productive, and creative.

PROPOSITION 5.3211   "Regimented" responses are generated by high aloofness and high tension.

PROPOSITION 5.3212   "Heuristic" responses are generated by moderate aloofness and high tension.

PROPOSITION 5.3213   "Emotional" responses are generated by low aloofness and high tension.

PROPOSITION 5.3214   "Provocative" responses are generated by high aloofness and moderate tension.

PROPOSITION 5.3215   "Calculating" responses are generated by moderate aloofness and moderate tension.

PROPOSITION 5.3216   "Contemplative" responses are generated by low aloofness and moderate tension.

PROPOSITION 5.3217   "Lethargic" responses are generated by high aloofness and low tension.

PROPOSITION 5.3218   "Productive" responses are generated by moderate aloofness and low tension.

PROPOSITION 5.3219   "Creative" responses are generated by low aloofness and low tension.

POSTULATE 5.322   The basic responses generated by the "compulsive" matrix are: aggressive/submissive, hostile, manic, withdrawn, defensive, vigilant, depressed, ingratiating, and solipsistic.

PROPOSITION 5.3221   "Agressive/submissive" responses are generated by high aloofness and high tension.

PROPOSITION 5.3222   "Hostile" responses are generated by moderate aloofness and high tension.

PROPOSITION 5.3223   "Manic" responses are generated by low aloofness and high tension.

PROPOSITION 5.3224   "Withdrawn" responses are generated by high aloofness and moderate tension.

PROPOSITION 5.3225   "Defensive" responses are generated by moderate aloofness and moderate tension.

PROPOSITION 5.3226   "Vigilant" responses are generated by low aloofness and moderate tension.

PROPOSITION 5.3227   "Depressed" responses are generated by high aloofness and low tension.

PROPOSITION 5.3228   "Ingratiating" responses are generated by moderate aloofness and low tension.

PROPOSITION 5.3229   "Solipsistic" responses are generated by low aloofness and low tension.

AXIOM 5.33 Music, selected according to its aloofness and tension properties, generates predictable response styles.

POSTULATE 5.331   The basic moods generated by the

musical matrix are: unsettling, exciting, passionate, provocative, evocative, invigorating, lethargic, nostalgic, and innovative.

POSTULATE 5.332   The basic musical moods are associated with basic behavioral responses.

PROPOSITION 5.3321   "Unsettling" music (High ALO/High TEN) generates regimented, aggressive/submissive responses.

PROPOSITION 5.3322   "Exciting" music (Moderate ALO/High TEN) generates heuristic, hostile responses.

PROPOSITION 5.3323   "Passionate" music (Low ALO/High TEN) generates emotional, manic responses.

PROPOSITION 5.3324   "Provocative" music (High ALO/Moderate TEN) generates provocative, withdrawn responses.

PROPOSITION 5.3325   "Evocative" music (Moderate ALO/Moderate TEN) generates calculating, defensive responses.

PROPOSITION 5.3326   "Invigorating" music (Low ALO/High TEN) generates contemplative, vigilant responses.

PROPOSITION 5.3327   "Lethargic" (primal) music (High ALO/Low TEN) generates lethargic, depressed responses.

PROPOSITION 5.3328   "Nostalgic" (mood) music (Moderate ALO/Low TEN) generates productive, ingratiating responses.

PROPOSITION 5.3329   "Innovative" (novel) music (Low ALO/Low TEN) generates creative, solipsistic responses.

AXIOM 5.34 Selected colors generate predictable response styles.

POSTULATE 5.341   Certain colors are related to specific cells of the aloofness/tension matrix.

PROPOSITION 5.3411   High ALO and High TEN colors include white and lime-green.

PROPOSITION 5.3412   Moderate ALO and high TEN colors include orange.

COROLLARY 5.3412   The combination of primary red and primary yellow produces secondary orange, which increases the aloofness properties and retains the high tension properties.

PROPOSITION 5.3413   Low ALO and high TEN colors include the primary colors: red, yellow, and green.

PROPOSITION 5.3414   High ALO and moderate TEN colors include: black and pink.

PROPOSITION 5.3415   Moderate ALO and moderate TEN colors include: light-green, Kelly-green, and violet.

PROPOSITION 5.3416   Low ALO and moderate TEN colors include: purple.

COROLLARY 5.3416   The combination of primary red and primary blue produces secondary purple which decreases tension without increasing aloofness.

PROPOSITION 5.3417   High ALO and low TEN colors include: light blue and brown.

PROPOSITION 5.3418   Moderate ALO and low TEN colors include: forest-green and gray.

PROPOSITION 5.3419   Low ALO and low TEN colors include: heather-green and tan.

COROLLARY 5.3419   Neutral colors tend to be low-tension colors.

POSTULATE 5.342   Colors prescribed by the ALO/TEN matrix cells generate related behavioral and mood responses.

PROPOSITION 5.3421   White and lime-green generate regimented, aggressive/submissive response styles.

PROPOSITION 5.3422   Orange generates heuristic, hostile response styles.

PROPOSITION 5.3423   The primary colors (red, yellow, and blue) generate emotional, manic response styles.

PROPOSITION 5.3424   Black and pink generate provocative, withdrawn response styles.

PROPOSITION 5.3425   Light-green, Kelly-green, and violet generate calculating, defensive response styles.

PROPOSITION 5.3426   Purple generates contemplative, vigilant response styles.

PROPOSITION 5.3427   Light blue and brown generate lethargic, depressed response styles.

PROPOSITION 5.3428   Forest-green and gray generate productive, ingratiating response styles.

PROPOSITION 5.3429   Heather-green and tan generate creative, solipsistic response styles.

AXIOM 5.35 Visual composition, created according to its aloofness and tension properties, generates predictable response styles.

POSTULATE 5.351   Certain compositional elements are related to specific cells of the aloofness/tension matrix.

PROPOSITION 5.3511   Visual compositional elements related to the high ALO/high TEN cell are: long shot, low angle, off-balance, objective viewpoint, zoom or dolly-out, high contrast, dark background, and deep field.

PROPOSITION 5.3512   Visual compositional elements related to the medium ALO/high TEN cell are: Medium shot, low angle, off-balance, mixed viewpoint, jump-cut in and out, high contrast, dark background, and moderate field.

PROPOSITION 5.3513   Visual composition elements re-

	lated to the low ALO/high TEN cell are: close-up, low angle, off-balance, subjective viewpoint, zoom or dolly-in, high contrast, dark background, and shallow field.
PROPOSITION 5.3514	Visual compositional elements related to the high ALO/moderate TEN cell are: long shot, eye level, unfixed balance (i.e., neutral stability), objective viewpoint, zoom or dolly-out, details in shadows, deep field.
PROPOSITION 5.3515	Visual compositional elements related to the moderate ALO/moderate TEN cell are: medium shot, eye-level, neutral stability, mixed viewpoint, jump-cut in and out, detail in shadows, and moderate field.
PROPOSITION 5.3516	Visual compositional elements related to the low ALO/moderate TEN cell are: close-up, eye-level, neutral stability, subjective viewpoint, zoom or dolly-in, detail in shadows, and shallow field.
PROPOSITION 5.3517	Visual compositional elements related to the high ALO/low TEN cell are: long shot, high angle, stable (secure), zoom or dolly-out, no shadows, light background, deep field.
PROPOSITION 5.3518	Visual compositional elements related to the moderate ALO/low TEN cell are: medium shot, high angle, stable, mixed viewpoint, jump-cut in and out, no shadows,

light background, and moderate field.

PROPOSITION 5.3519   Visual compositional elements related to the low ALO/low TEN cell are: close-up, high angle, stable, subjective viewpoint, zoom or dolly-in, no shadows, light background, and shallow field.

POSTULATE 5.352   Visual composition created by matrix cell prescriptions generates related behavioral and mood responses.

PROPOSITION 5.3521   Visual composition created according to the high ALO/high TEN cell prescription generates regimented, aggressive/submissive response styles.

PROPOSITION 5.3522   Visual composition created according to the moderate ALO/high TEN cell prescription generates heuristic/hostile response styles.

PROPOSITION 5.3523   Visual composition created according to the low ALO/high TEN cell prescription generates emotional/manic response styles.

PROPOSITION 5.3524   Visual composition created according to the high ALO/moderate TEN cell prescription generates provocative/withdrawn response styles.

PROPOSITION 5.3525   Visual composition created according to the moderate ALO/moderate TEN cell prescription generates calculating, defensive response styles.

PROPOSITION 5.3526   Visual composition created according to the low ALO/moderate

	TEN cell prescription generates contemplative, vigilant response styles.
PROPOSITION 5.3527	Visual composition created according to the high ALO/low TEN cell prescription generates lethargic, depressed response styles.
PROPOSITION 5.3528	Visual composition created according to the moderate ALO/low TEN cell prescription generates productive, ingratiating response styles.
PROPOSITION 5.3529	Visual composition created according to the low ALO/low TEN cell prescription generates creative, solipsistic response styles.

Example of Hypothesis Generation

AXIOM 5.1   The signal characteristics of the message determine the "contextual atmosphere" created by the message.

POSTULATE 5.1	The signal characteristics of "diversity" and "density" interact to determine the contextual atmosphere of the message.
POSTULATE 5.11	"Diversity" is the sum of: (1) visual variety, (2) audible variety, and (3) structural variety where each dimension is weighted equally.
POSTULATE 5.111	The degree of affection for a message is positively related to the degree of diversity in the message.
HYPOTHESIS 5.111	Given a sample of short messages designed from complexity profiles that differ only in diversity values, subjects will assign higher affection values on a standardized semantic differential scale to those messages having higher diversity values.

POSTULATE 5.12   "Density" is the sum of: (1) the rate of change, (2) the degree of non-redundancy, and (3) the structural depth of the message where each dimension is weighted equally.

POSTULATE 5.121   The degree of cognitive strain associated with a message is positively related to the degree of message density.

HYPOTHESIS 5.121   Given messages on the same topic and with the same complexity profile except for varying density values, subjects receiving the higher density messages will: (a) report higher cognitive strain on an appropriate semantic differential scale; (b) be judged by trained stress analysts to be experiencing higher stress, and (c) will require more repetitions of the message to achieve a criterion of perfection on an appropriate achievement test.

POSTULATE 5.13   The matrix cells created by the interface of diversity and density discriminate both emotional and cognitive states.

PROPOSITION 5.131   High diversity and high density generate an "ecstatic" atmosphere which is conducive to pattern recognition.

HYPOTHESIS 5.131a   Given a message of high diversity and high density, subjects will select "ecstatic" as the descriptor from a list of nine cell descriptors which best describes the atmosphere generated by the message.

HYPOTHESIS 5.131b   A content analysis of reaction papers written by subjects immediately after receiving a message of high diversity and high density will reveal a predominant level of pattern-recognition.

Appendix A: Theoretical Refinement

Appendix A-1

The Instructional Message:
A Theoretical Perspective

Patrick O. Marsh is professor of communication studies at California State University, Sacramento, CA 95819.

This article presents a theoretical model for message design proved capable of improving the quality of instruction while increasing cost effectiveness. Integrating classical rhetoric, information theory, contemporary media criticism, social psychology, and the psychology of human information processing, the model directs the designer to design a block of time that optimizes the information load and message complexity within the constraints of the receiver's abilities and experience, the requirements of the source, and the capabilities and limitations of the medium.

ECTJ, VOL. 27, NO. 4, PAGES 303–318
ISSN 0148–5806

In light of current taxpayer revolts, one message is unmistakable: We must increase the quality of instruction with seriously reduced resources. Some recent successes in college instruction by radio (Koegel & Marsh, 1978) prompt me to share the model by which these high-quality/low-cost materials were designed. This model, although still prototypic, has been evolving over the past decade. I believe the time is right for sharing, not only from the standpoints of the political/economic currents and the model's initial successes, but also from the direction the state of our art seems to be moving.

The model enables the design of a given block of time to optimize the probability of achieving the source's purpose by systematically adapting the content to both the receiver's cognitive requirements and the capabilities of the medium. Both a practical and a theoretical tool, the model not only enables the designer to prepare a detailed prescription to guide the message's production; but also provides a theoretical perspective from which an integrated theory may direct, and be tested by, empirical research.

My purpose is to present the model briefly, but in sufficient detail to make it usable to both designer and researcher. My position regarding the nature of instructional messages and their design represents a significant but necessary departure from tradition. Torkelson's (1977) commendable critique of the first quarter century's contribution to the "educational communication field" provides direction and context for my perspective.

Given the philosophical, methodological, and substantive trends Torkelson has identified, I believe the model is timely not only because it focuses on the instructional message (regardless of the medium), but also because this theoretical perspective can be developed into an integrated axiomatic theory that adequately treats the message complexities that have thwarted earlier attempts to control message variables in experimental situations. This integrated theory permits the generation of researchable hypotheses at known levels of abstraction so that independently conducted studies may be compared meaningfully, thus supporting or challenging the theory's basic assumptions.

Torkelson's survey identified a number of issues that have influenced the field's evolution. Rather than taking a position on each issue separately, I shall state the credo that underpins my theoretical perspective:

An instructional message can best be prescribed by a communication model that takes into account the complex, systemic, and uniquely human processes of cognition by adapting information relevant to the learner's needs to the learner's capacities; this should be done in ways that provide the appropriate degree of external guidance to contribute (in verifiable ways) to the systematized programs that provide continuing progress toward the learner's independence.

ROOTS OF THE THEORETICAL MODEL

Although I strongly prefer generating research from a "theory, then research" approach rather than attempting to synthesize isolated empirical studies into theory, I do not believe that the process of synthesis at the theoretical level shares the shortcomings of synthesis at the empirical level. On the contrary, I believe that the joining of perspectives from various disciplines, and schools within disciplines, provides a more mature, more integrated, and generally more realistic point of departure.

ture. I have selected elements from some theories and reconceptualized their relationships according to thrusts derived from other theories that on the surface appear incompatible.

Mathematical Models

To illustrate, Shannon and Weaver's (1949) mathematical model of communication provides an adequate point of departure because of its broad scope and generality. When it is adjusted to accommodate the criticisms of McLuhan (1964) and Schwartz (1974) it serves as the overall context for my model. McLuhan criticized the linear quality of communication models fashioned after Shannon and Weaver, and Schwartz challenged the "transportation" metaphor implicit in such models. When the elements of the Shannon and Weaver model are conceived of as being systematically related, both internally and externally, the linear characteristic disappears. Similarly, this conception accounts for meanings being *elicited* rather than *delivered*.

Shannon's mathematical model, which resulted in "information theory," influenced my thinking in another way. Mathematical information theory, while directly limited to nonhuman physical communication channels, postulates some signal properties and some relationships among time, information load, and signal complexity that will serve this model. According to Valentine (1963):

The actual formula for information most widely used is: amount of information $= \log\left(\dfrac{S+N}{N}\right)$ 2TW or 2TW $\log\left(\dfrac{S+N}{N}\right)$. Translated into conventional verbal symbols the formula means: "The amount of information in a speech wave is proportional to the duration of the speech, to the range of frequency components involved, and to the logarithm of the number of discriminable steps in amplitude" (Miller, 1951, p. 45). Thus, in order for a speaker to increase the amount of information he is attempting to present, he must do one or more of the following: (1) talk longer; (2) talk with a wider range of frequencies (greater variety) in the speech spectrum; or (3) talk so that there are finer distinctions in the intensity of his utterances. (p. 169)

Translating this quotation into a slightly higher level of abstraction, we discover that the amount of information contained in a message is proportional to the duration of the message and the signal complexity. Signal complexity is a function of signal diversity (channel width) and signal density. For more convenient application to this emerging model, an algebraic arrangement leads to this relationship: The optimal duration of a message is a function of the ratio between amount of information and signal complexity. This relationship, when adjusted to include the organismic and response variables inherent in the human cognition models (to be identified shortly), is central to my theoretical perspective.

Proceeding along similar lines of thought, Hsia (1971) has stated succinctly both the mission of message designing and a method of achieving that mission. Both observations have contributed to my concept. Defining the mission, he says:

Evidently, input information can be manipulated and adjusted at the initial stage to maximize efficiency in order to control and reduce possible subsequent equivocation and error. (p. 57)

Continuing, he says:

Implicitly, equivocation is proportionate to the excess information. An obvious way to reduce equivocation is to reduce information loading; but a more efficient way seems to optimize the ratio of information and redundancy which presumably helps establish memory trace (Barlow, 1959) and facilitates the passage of information across synapses, presumably utilizing both facilitation and disinhibition neural pathways. (pp. 57–58)

Cognitive Models

Another major root supporting my theoretical perspective comes from the psychology of perception, cognition, and human information processing. I prefer cognitive theories that account for stimulus, organismic, and response variables operating systematically. Neisser (1976) provides one of the most acceptable perspectives of cognition from my point of view. He defines his central concept — the perceptual cycle — this way:

In my view, the cognitive structures crucial for vision are the anticipatory schemata that prepare the perceiver to accept certain kinds of information rather than others and thus control the activity of looking. Because we can see only what we know how to look for, it is these schemata (together with the information actually available) that determine what will be perceived. Perception is indeed a constructive process, but what is constructed is not a mental image appearing in consciousness where it is admired by an inner man. At each moment the perceiver is constructing anticipation of certain kinds of information that enable him to accept it as it becomes available. Often he must actively explore the optic array to make it available, by moving his eyes or his head or his body. These explorations are directed by the anticipatory schemata, which are plans for perceptual action as well as readinesses for particular kinds of optical structure. The outcome of the explorations — the information picked up — modifies the original schema. Thus modified, it directs further exploration and becomes ready for more information. (pp. 20–21)

Machamer elaborates Neisser's concept in an informal working model shown in Figure 1.[1] Although Machamer criticizes his own model for inadequately depicting the complex systemic nature of the perceptual processes and for making the process appear more linear than it actually is, it is useful in explaining my model. Thus, a momentary elaboration of Machamer's model seems justified.

A human motivated by a complex of needs, desires, and purposes — the source of which might be evolutional, cultural, or personal — explores the environment for information relevant to those purposes. The search results in sampling events or objects in the environment which become relevent stimuli that display their information arrays upon the receptors, thus activating short-term storage. The short-term storage facilitates later recognition by allowing comparison with stored schemata and also furthers the selection of attributes to direct further exploration. Use of schemata in this way also modifies them, thus keeping them current with the or-

[1] This model was generated on the blackboard during an NSF short course for college teachers at Stanford University, November 21–22, 1977.

FIGURE 1
Machamer's Model of Cognition

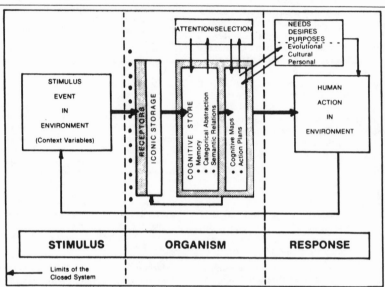

ganism's experience. Once a stimulus array has been selected and matched against appropriate schemata, has been assimilated at the appropriate categorical abstraction level, and has been associated with appropriate semantic processes, it may be used to construct cognitive maps and action plans consistent with the organism's needs, desires, and purposes. Again, a human action is taken within the environment, and the process continues its systemic, interacting cycle.

This model of cognition is central to my theoretical perspective of an instructional message because it incorporates humans—dynamic, growing, changing humans who interact continuously with their environment and their experience—into the source and receiver roles of the overall communication model derived from Shannon.

I am also indebted to the team of psychologists who related selected "set" factors to the concept of "environmental complexity" and ultimately defined the relationship between the ability to "integrate" information and environmental complexity to be that of an inverted U-curve. Schroder, Driver, and Streufert (1967) have contributed directly to my concept of message complexity (which plays a critical role in my model) as well as to my empirical generation of "U-curves" for college students (Marsh, 1973; Marsh & Kowitz, 1975). The significance of U-curves in designing instructional messages is that they objectify the trade-off between economy and achievement. Their function will become clearer as I describe my model.

Classical Rhetoric Models

The third major root of this theoretical perspective is found in the "classical concept of rhetoric." It is difficult to pinpoint the contributions of any one person since the concepts useful to any model are found at differing levels of refinement among various authors. The principal sources that have contributed to the classical concept—a well-understood concept among rhetoricians, but a difficult one to compress to a few words—include Aristo-

FIGURE 2
Stage 1—Source-Receiver Interaction

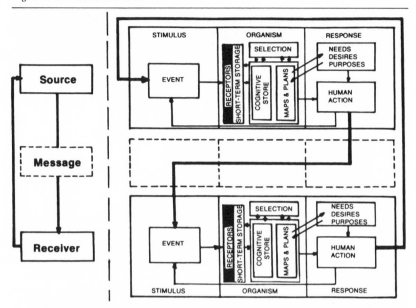

tle, Cicero, Quintilian, and the anonymous author of *Rhetorica ad Herennium.*

The principal shortcoming of classical rhetoric for our purposes is that its sole function is to serve persuasive strategies. Since instruction and persuasion are, in my opinion, very different processes, rhetorical concepts must be extended beyond their original contexts to be useful in producing instructional messages. Yet the expository counterparts of persuasive devices serve my model well, particularly in the realm of information management. At least one contemporary psychologist shares with me this recognition of the practical application of classical rhetoric. Norman (1976) asserts that modern science, with all its power, has added little to our knowledge about the practical art of remembering things. I would add to Norman's assertion that modern science has added little to our knowledge about the practical arts of (a) analyzing a proposition (or central idea) into its issues (or essential elements of information), (b) determining the *stasis* of a controversy (or defining the information

gap between the source and receiver), (c) discriminating between points and supports, (d) disposing (or arranging) the content into organism-required structures and sequences, and (e) prescribing language styles appropriate to strategic requirements. These are the areas of classical rhetoric on which I have relied particularly.

From these roots of mathematical communication theory, cognitive psychology, and classical rhetoric, the following model has evolved.

THE THEORETICAL MODEL

This model is presented in four developmental stages. Stages 1 and 2 are at similar levels of abstraction and are integrated into the complete model at Stage 3. Stage 4 focuses on the "message" component of the model in order to amplify its elements to a practical level of abstraction.

Stage 1

Figure 2 elaborates a simplified version of

the Shannon model by incorporating Machamer's cognitive model within the human elements of Shannon's schematic. The message element is undeveloped and is represented by broken lines to permit focusing on the cognitive processes of the source and receiver and their interaction. Shannon's elements of transmitter, channel, and noise need not be considered at this point; we will treat them as if they were characteristics of the message in transit and deal with that complex later.

Actually, the source's cognitive processes may be tapped at any point in the model, given its systemic nature, but for simplicity we begin at the stimulus input stage. Typically, the source explores the environment (as previously explained), matches short-term memory against unique schemata, selects relevant perceptions as data for determining an action plan consistent with needs, and then determines a purpose of a message to be communicated to the receiver. The purpose is held in cognitive store while other data are sought from the environment or recalled from memory so that the message may be adapted to the situation (including the receiver). Another cycle through the process prepares the planned message for transmission.

Now, let us assume that the message has been conceived by the source and its transmission is in progress. The receiver receives the message in competition with any number of other stimuli in the environment and through a quick cognitive cycle selects the message as the dominant stimulus in the environment. In subsequent cycles the receiver matches the short-term signal storage with the schemata held in long-term storage; selects aspects of the signal for further processing; develops cognitive maps or action plans according to his or her needs, desires, purposes, etc., and ultimately takes some sort of action. The source perceives that action, perhaps evaluates it according to his or her own purposes or expectations, and decides either to continue or to terminate the process. Thus we find feedback loops operating both within and between the humans in the model.

Stage 2

Given the interaction between the source and the receiver explained by a cognitive model that incorporates stimulus-, organismic-, and response-oriented theories into a systemic equality, now we can focus on the nature of the message. I choose to regard the message as being compatible with the cognitive processes of the source and the receiver. Accordingly, I conceive of both the informational component and the complexity component of the message as requiring adaptation to the stimulus, organismic, and response aspects of cognition. Before the design of either the information or the complexity aspects is complete, consideration must be given to the stimulus, organismic, and response properties of the message. Their particular influences are discussed at Stage 3.

The relationship discussed earlier—that the effective time of a message (i.e., duration) is a function of the ratio of information load over message complexity—is incorporated as the overall organizing principles of this portion of the model; thus in Figure 3 information load is depicted as the numerator and message complexity as the denominator (i.e., $T = I/C$). The significance of this feature is that it reminds us that message time can be reduced by either reducing the amount of information or by increasing the complexity of the message. The option is, of course, a design choice influenced by the several requirements of the communication situation.

To be usable either to a researcher or to a message designer, both information load and message complexity must be quantifiable. Without dwelling on the details of quantifying them at this stage, let me merely indicate the necessary considerations. To quantify information load, we must know not only how many units of information the message contains but also how salient that information is. Some information can be recalled from memory banks or associated with other familiar information, while other information must be introduced from a position of "no previous background or knowledge." I call this

FIGURE 3
Stage II—Overview of Message Component

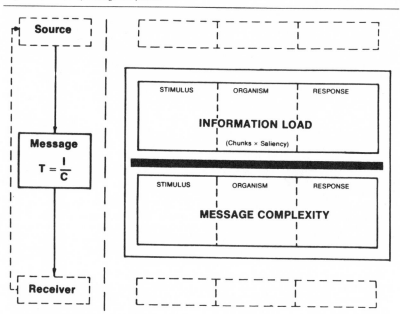

variable a "saliency" factor. Perhaps a more obvious requirement is a count of information units contained in a message; such counting is problematic. The "bit" measure from mathematical information theory has not proved very useful for quantifying gross messages of an instructional nature. I have come to use the "information chunk," defined as a terminal division point in an outline at which supporting materials are added. This notion, while compatible with Miller's concept (1969), is a larger unit than he had in mind. Mellon (1974) has speculated on the matter of chunk magnitude, but more technically than I find useful.

Message complexity is perhaps the most original part of this model. My definition of it was inspired by mathematical information theory as it deals with channel width and signal density. While that concept is appropriate for analyzing signals within a physical communication channel (such as a telephone wire), it neglects the variables of human factors which limit human information-processing channels. Schroder et al. (1967) led me to introduce what they call "set" factors. Several years of theorizing and some multivariate as well as applied research have produced a definition of message complexity with which I am sufficiently comfortable to include in this theoretical perspective. Its nature will become clearer as the model is developed. Bradac, Desmond, and Murdock (1977) have used variables of "diversity" and "density," but their effort was directed to defining "linguistic complexity" rather than the overall complexity of a message.

Stage 3

Stages 1 and 2 have been necessary to place the integrated model of Stage 3 into perspective. Figure 4 represents the complete model at a rather high level of abstraction. A sequential explanation will establish the

FIGURE 4
Stage III – The Integrated Model
(Abbreviations are defined in the text.)

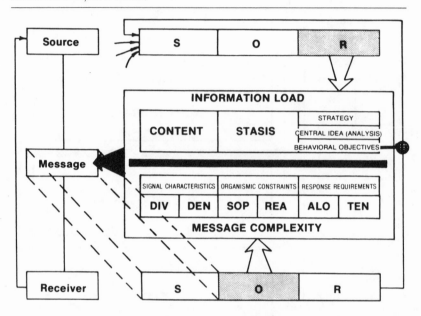

general rationale for the approach I have taken.

Having decided, through several cognitive operations, to prepare (i.e., design) a message, the source *responds* by making several commitments to this decision—and may manifest this commitment behaviorally by writing a *purpose statement*. This statement specifies a desired *strategy* (e.g., to instruct), identifies the intended *receiver*(s) with sufficient specificity to facilitate adaptation of the message to its needs, specifies a *central idea* which inherently distinguishes necessary from irrelevant information to be contained in the message, and, finally, lists the *behavioral objectives* that provide a basis for the measurement of the message's effectiveness. Thus, the source's response at the moment of commitment in the cognitive process establishes the basic requirements that must be met in designing a message.

Similarly, the receiver, as identified in the purpose statement, imposes certain constraints on the designer by virtue of his or her organismic state. These *organismic constraints* affect the manner in which the information will be developed by virtue of what needed information is known or unknown by the receiver; they also shape that component of message complexity that is governed by the receiver's levels of general sophistication (SOP) and readiness (REA) to learn.

The reconciliation of the source's requirements with the receiver's organismic constraints narrows the designer's range of freedom. This limitation on the "degrees of freedom" is a blessing rather than a curse, for up to this point there have been innumerable options for developing the message; but ultimately all of the alternatives must be rejected so that only one finalized message is delivered. Message designing is concerned with making that final choice (or sequence of choices) from among all of the possibilities, with choosing the one that will serve both the source's requirements

FIGURE 5
A Scale of Message Complexity

			1	2	3	4	5	6	7	
Signal Characteristics	**DIVERSITY**									
	Audio Variety	Lo	—	—	—	—	—	—	—	Hi
	Visual Variety	Lo	—	—	—	—	—	—	—	Hi
	Structural Variety	Lo	—	—	—	—	—	—	—	Hi
	DENSITY									
	Rate of Change	Lo	—	—	—	—	—	—	—	Hi
	Redundancy	Hi	—	—	—	—	—	—	—	Lo
	Structural Depth	Lo	—	—	—	—	—	—	—	Hi
Organismic Capabilities	**SOPHISTICATION**									
	Abstraction	Lo	—	—	—	—	—	—	—	Hi
	Implicitness	Lo	—	—	—	—	—	—	—	Hi
	Precision	Lo	—	—	—	—	—	—	—	Hi
	READINESS									
	Framing Provided	Hi	—	—	—	—	—	—	—	Lo
	Association Provided	Hi	—	—	—	—	—	—	—	Lo
	Continuity Provided	Hi	—	—	—	—	—	—	—	Lo
Response Requirements	**ALOOFNESS**									
	Reward	Hi	—	—	—	—	—	—	—	Lo
	Involvement	Hi	—	—	—	—	—	—	—	Lo
	Frustration	Lo	—	—	—	—	—	—	—	Hi
	TENSION									
	Shock	Lo	—	—	—	—	—	—	—	Hi
	Suspense	Lo	—	—	—	—	—	—	—	Hi
	Conflict	Lo	—	—	—	—	—	—	—	Hi

Note: All scale items are framed to represent message qualities, not receiver requirements.

and the receiver's limitations most effectively.

The process of reconciliation of source with receiver states was called *stasis* by classical rhetoricians; its impact is that it determines both the content of the message and tactics of its development. With *content* and *tactics* identified, the essential information-control functions of message design are completed.

However, two components of message complexity remain to be determined. One of these components is related to the stimulus portion of the cognitive model. Specifically, it is at this point that consideration must be given to the signal characteristics of the message once it is to become encoded and transmitted. Of concern is the diversity (DIV) of the stimulus that impinges upon the receiver as well as the density (DEN) of the information encoded in that signal. These message-complexity elements are directly analogous to the channel-width and signal-density components of information theory. I have defined

them operationally through factor-analytic studies. In practical terms, these complexity elements guide design decisions regarding the degree of audible, visual, and structural variety and the amount of redundancy, the depth of structure, and the rate of change that is appropriate.

The remaining complexity component is associated with the response aspect of the cognitive process. The behavioral objectives, specified by the source, direct the design of the message so that desired or appropriate levels of aloofness (ALO) and tension (TEN) may be elicited in the receiver. Aloofness is similar to Wiener and Mehrabian's (1968) concept of "non-immediacy." Its less awkward polar opposite is "engagement," but engagement decreases rather than increases message complexity when added to the other elements. Tension refers to muscular responses (both smooth and striped) that result from the organism's being stimulated. The overall *response style* can be (so it is hypothesized) significantly determined by the degree to which the receiver is invited to participate (or is exluded from participating) in the presentation of the message and by the degree of tension experienced in the process.

The general function of message complexity is to optimize a compromise between the boredom that results from too low a complexity level and the overload that results from too high a level. Theoretically, it matters little how the compromise is achieved so long as the overall complexity level is optimal. The optimum must be established empirically; this has been done with one population (Marsh, 1973; Marsh & Kowitz, 1975), as noted earlier in the discussion of U-curves. Thus, trade-offs can be made among the complexity components in order to achieve nuances compatible with the source's purpose so long as total complexity is at the appropriate level. Figure 5 displays a scale of message complexity which represents my effort to operationalize the concept.

When information load and message complexity have been appropriately balanced in accordance with the durational limits of the message, the design prescription can be completed. Once that prescription is filled by appropriate message production and the message is transmitted, it should become the dominant stimulus in the receiver's environment. That message stimulus having been designed according to the receiver's organismic needs, the receiver should be able to process it with minimal distortion, and the desired response(s) should be forthcoming. The responses are compared with the behavioral objectives specified in the purpose statement, and the results are fed back to the source, who decides whether to modify or terminate the communication.

Stage 4

A close-up view of the model's message component provides a clearer understand-

FIGURE 6
Stage IV—Closeup of Message Component

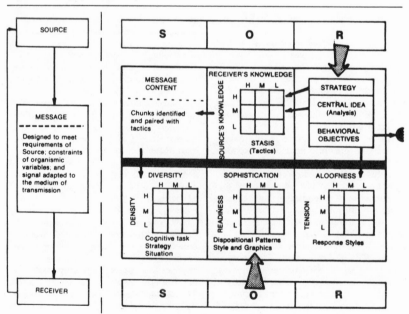

ing of its utility in both research and message design. Figure 6 magnifies that portion of the model and suggests a sequence for making design decisions.

Returning to the purpose statement, the designer focuses on the strategy, the central idea, and the behavioral objectives. Since the concern is exclusively with the strategy "to instruct" (or "to inform"), the other optional strategies of this model (to persuade, argue, promote, move, and transform) will not be considered. Given the strategy "to instruct," the next task is to analyze the central idea into its component elements. This process is analogous to analyzing an argumentative proposition into its issues. The behavioral objectives are reviewed and stored for particular use later.

Each element of the central idea is now located on the "tactics matrix." This matrix compares the receiver's knowledge with the source's knowledge on that information element and prescribes appropriate tactics for developing a given element within the matrix cells. The tactics I have generated by a priori analysis are shown in Figure 7.

As each element is paired with its appropriate tactic, and its corresponding saliency value is discovered, the required message content becomes clearer. Some of the information elements may require subdivision; when that is accomplished the information chunks can be identified. Then the information load — the number of chunks × the average saliency value — can be calculated. This process leads to the discovery of "what to say" and "how to say it."

The designer now turns toward management of message complexity. The order of development is either arbitrary or based on the relative strength of assessments and commitments. For the sake of continuity, I will arbitrarily select the "signal characteristics" component as a starting point. The cells of the diversity-density matrix (see

FIGURE 7
Tactics Matrix (for strategy to inform/instruct)

| | Receiver's Knowledge of Given Information Element | | |
	High	Medium	Low
High (Source's)	Acknowledgment Recall, Symbolize, Recognize, Reinforce (1)	Clarification Amplify divisions, Support (2)	Analysis Divide, Reduce, Dissect, Abstract (3)
Medium	Reframing Shift focus, Change context (2)	Sharing Integrate, Adapt, Combine, Conceptualize (3)	Initiation Associate, Simulate (4)
Low	Inquiry Probe, Interview, Reflect, Research (3)	Paraphrasing Translate, State in other words (4)	Imagination Transform, Create, Hypothesize, Guess, (5) Vicarious experience

(left axis: Source's Knowledge of Given Information Element)

Sequence 1: Imagination, initiation, analysis, clarification, acknowledgment.
Sequence 2: Imagination, sharing, acknowledgment.
Sequence 3: Imagination, paraphrasing, inquiry, reframing, acknowledgment.

Note. Numbers in parentheses represent saliency index values. The sequences represent tactical chains for developing a content item from the cell of entry to acknowledgment of completion or adequate development.

FIGURE 8
Signal Characteristics Matrix

		Diversity High	Diversity Medium	Diversity Low	
Density	High	To inspire (to move, over-whelm, transport) Pattern recognition (psychedelic or hypnotic overload) Multi-media barrage	To abstract (to brief, conceptualize) Concept recognition Briefing	To document (to argue, convince) Detail recognition Technical conference	High ↑
Density	Medium	To integrate (to organize, systematize) System recognition Caucus	To persuade (to direct, promote) Position recognition Assembly	To solve (to exhaust, analyze, synthesize, evaluate) Problem/Solution recognition Task-team	Cognitive Strain
Density	Low	To entertain (to experi-ence, identify with) Stereotype recognition Cocktail party	To stimulate (to activate, retrieve) Analogy recognition Church service	To inform (to retain, expose, store) Achievement recognition Classroom	↓ Low

High ◄————————— Affection —————————► Low

Note. Contained in each cell are the strategy and appropriate cognitive task and a typical communication situation.

Figure 8) relate to the basic strategies discussed previously and some additionally refined strategies. The strategy of best fit is located in its cell, and the row and column then identify the appropriate levels of diversity and density. Of course, if either density or diversity is determined by situational factors, the strategic choice may require amendment. My a priori assignment of strategies provides the cell contents. I speculate that the degree of affection a receiver has for the message increases in proportion to its diversity, and that the degree of cognitive strain increases with message density. This working matrix includes, within the cells, not only strategies, but also appropriate cognitive tasks and typical communication situations.

Now we address the "response requirement" component of message complexity. The matrix in this component is used in conjunction with the behavioral objectives

we can retrieve from the initial step in this sequence. The complexity elements that define this matrix are *aloofness* and *tension*. These axes define "response style" cells. My a priori response styles are listed below, with tension coded first and aloofness second:

H × H   Automated (Compulsive)
H × M   Heuristic (Interpretive)
H × L   Emotional (Expressive)
M × H   Inquiring (Probing)
M × M   Calculating (Methodical)
M × L   Contemplative (Evaluative)
L × H   Bored (Apathetic)
L × M   Productive (Supportive)
L × L   Creative (Introspective)

Finally, we determine the organismic-constraint component of message complexity. Estimates of the receiver's *sophistication* and *readiness* define the matrix (see Figures 9 and 10), and the cells display appropriate language styles, dispositional patterns,

FIGURE 9
Organismic Constraint Matrix

	Sophistication		
	High	**Medium**	**Low**
Readiness — High	EXPERT (Elite) No expository background Central idea Several points Develop with montage ——— Abstracted graphics Black & white line drawings	PROFESSIONAL Brief expository background Central idea Several points Develop with montage and supports ——— Distorted graphics in black & white (caricatures)	OVERACHIEVER Elaborate expository background Central idea Several points Develop with supports ——— Representational graphics low definition Black & white
Readiness — Medium	DISPLACED EXPERT No exordium Brief expository bkgd. Central idea Several points Develop with montage Brief conclusion ——— Abstracted graphics with color for emphasis	MODAL Brief exordium Brief expository bkgd. Central idea; Either division or transitions Few points; Develop with montage and supports Brief conclusion ——— Distorted graphics with color for emphasis	LAY AUDIENCE Brief exordium Elaborate expository bkgd. Central idea; Division Few points Develop with several supports; Transitions Brief conclusion ——— Representational graphics with color for emphasis
Readiness — Low	UNDERACHIEVER Elaborate exordium Brief expository bkgd. Central idea Division Few points Develop with montage Full conclusion ——— Abstracted graphics in real color	RANK AND FILE Elaborate exordium Brief expository bkgd. Central ideas Either division or transitions; Few points Develop with supports Full conclusion ——— Distorted graphics in real color	MASS AUDIENCE Elaborate exordium Elaborate expository background Single or few points Develop with montage and supports Brief conclusion ——— Representational graphics in real color

Note. Described in each cell are dispositional pattern and appropriate verbal presentation and physical (rather than conceptual) graphics.

and graphic modalities. Exhaustive descriptions of these dimensions are not justified here, but a single example may clarify this aspect of message complexity. Assume an audience of low sophistication and moderate readiness (a lay audience) (refer to Figures 9 and 10). The cell prescription for this dispositional pattern requires a brief exordium, a well developed expository background, an explicit statement of the central idea followed by a division of the information elements in the form of a preview, the presentation of a few simple information chunks joined by explicit transitions, and finally a restatement of the central idea. The language should be at the level of a "how to do it" magazine (i.e., digest style) with sentences averaging 8–14 words and each group of 100 words containing 120–140 syllables. The graphics should be over-simplified photographic representations using color for arousal and emphasis.

If the tentative complexity profile generated from the matrices deviates from expectations established either by U-curve optimums or from profiles of successful models, trade-offs must be made according

FIGURE 10
Organismic-Constraint Matrix — Interest and Difficulty Levels

		Sophistication		
		High	Medium	Low
Readiness	**High**	EXPERT (Elite) < 4% pers words < 5% pers sent > 25 wds/sent < 167 syl/100 wds (Academic, scientific)	PROFESSIONAL < 4% pers words < 5% pers sent 15–24 wds/sent 141–166 syl/100 words	OVERACHIEVER < 4% pers words < 5% pers sent < 9–14 wds/sent < 120–140 syl/100 words
	Medium	DISPLACED EXPERT 5–9% pers words 6–42% pers sent > 25 wds/sent > 167 syl/100 words	MODAL 5–9% pers words 6–42% pers sent 15–24 wds/sent 141–166 syl/100 words (Digests, quality magazines)	LAY AUDIENCE 5–9% pers words 6–42% pers sent < 8–14 wds/sent < 120–140 syl/100 words
	Low	UNDERACHIEVER > 10% pers words > 43% pers sent > 25 wds/sent > 167 syl/100 words	RANK & FILE > 10% pers words > 43% pers sent 15–24 wds/sent 141–166 syl/100 words	MASS AUDIENCE > 10% pers words > 43% pers sent < 8–14 wds/sent < 120–140 syl/100 wds (Comics, pulp fiction)

Note. Adapted from Rudolf Flesch (1946).

to the source's priorities. This exposition completes the model from which this theoretical perspective has been derived.

UTILITY OF THE MODEL

Given the model in its present prototypic state, its matrices can generate over 300,000 potential messages with single-element central ideas. The possibilities literally become innumerable as the messages become more typical in scope. Looking at this phenomenon in the opposite direction, we can see that the millions of possible ways an instructional message could be created can be reduced systematically to a handful of desirable designs. When the a priori elements of this model have been either validated or replaced by empirical research, the model can be computerized. Computerization is an easy step away when elements and sequences are defined in operational terms. With an adequate computerized operation, message designers of the near future will be able to

generate instructional message prescriptions with such ease that highly individualized instructional messages will be commonplace. Indeed, such high-quality, low-cost message designing may hasten the arrival of widespread learner-directed instruction. The learner can become his or her own message designer.

Lest we get carried away, let us focus on the more immediate possibilities such a model offers. Raymond Koegel and I (Koegel & Marsh, 1978) have demonstrated that this model is both efficient and effective in designing college-level instruction by radio. We compressed an upper division, concept-oriented course into twenty 30-minute radio programs. Subject-matter topics were assigned randomly to a set of seven replicated complexity profiles, which in turn were assigned randomly to nine program formats. Each program was designed and produced strictly in accordance with the prescriptions entailed in the profile assignment.

The regularly enrolled students were assigned to receive instruction either by the traditional classroom lecture format (n = 96) or by the radio format (n = 72). A professional third-party evaluation agency collected all data and conducted the statistical analysis and evaluations. Table 1 summarizes the achievement test results.

Even though the radio group, for whom messages had been designed according to this model, demonstrated significantly superior achievement, even more impressive results may be expected in future studies. In this study topics were randomly assigned to profiles and formats. Yet some combinations were superior to others. If future courses incorporate only the most effective combinations (e.g., high diversity, high density, high aloofness, and low tension in either a demonstrative or classificating lecture) achievement might be even higher.

Just as impressive as the superior achievement resulting from this design process is its efficiency. With its 20 half-hour programs, the radio group achieved more in 10 hours than the classroom lecture group did in 40 hours. And it must be noted that the classroom lecturers were our most seasoned and popular instructors for that course.

With this theoretical perspective established, the next task is to establish a formal axiomatic theory that posits a limited number of axioms from this theoretical perspective. This will make research efficient, especially in light of the condition that empirical support for any one hypothesis tends to support the entire theory. Additionally, the specific operationalized hypothesis can be cast at

TABLE 1
Achievement Test Means

Test	Instruction Format		
	Radio	Classroom	Probability
1	29.86	27.47	.003
2	26.94	24.44	.007
3	31.08	26.54	.001
Mean of Means	29.29	26.15	

similar and known levels of abstraction so that findings from independent studies may be pooled meaningfully. To illustrate, I have taken a single axiom, derived three propositions from it, and translated those propositions into operationalized hypotheses. Bear in mind that these are illustrative and that countless hypotheses can be generated similarly to occupy a program of research indefinitely.

AXIOM: The "contextual atmosphere" of a message is a function of its diversity/density profile.

Proposition 1. Affection for messages, as reported by receivers, increases as message diversity increases.

Hypothesis 1. Given a sample of short messages designed from complexity profiles that differ only in diversity values, subjects will assign higher affection values on a standardized semantic differential scale to those messages having higher diversity values.

Proposition 2. The cognitive strain experienced by receivers increases as message density increases.

Hypothesis 2. Given instructional messages on the same topic and with the same complexity profile except for varying density values, subjects receiving the higher density messages will: (a) report higher cognitive strain on an appropriate semantic differential scale; (b) be judged by trained stress analysts to be experiencing higher stress, and (c) will require more repetitions of the message to achieve a criterion of perfection on an appropriate achievement test.

Proposition 3. The interaction of affection and cognitive strain generates a variety of contexts discriminately compatible with given cognitive tasks.

Hypothesis 3a. Given a blank diversity/density matrix and the nine randomized cognitive task descriptors derived from the model's matrix, subjects will assign the descriptors to cells beyond chance probability as prescribed by the model.

Hypothesis 3b. Subjects who are presented with an argumentative message designed with low diversity and high density will demonstrate higher detail-recognition achievement than will subjects who receive an argumentative message designed with high diversity and low density.

It is clear, then, that meaningful and needed research can be conducted from this perspective. This is possible largely because this model has isolated the significant and relatively invarient aspects of messages without becoming bogged down by their unique qualities which render them noncomparable for experimental purposes.

One further practial application of the model is its use as a tool of analysis and criticism. Messages of known degrees of success may be profiled (especially in terms of their message complexity). These profiles permit recognition of the differences between successful and unsuccessful messages and thus provide models to be followed by designers.

Finally, I believe the theory that will grow from this perspective will promote the credo from which it sprang. I submit that item by item it complies with that statement, which I repeat here as a way of emphasizing my commitment to it and this perspective's compliance with it:

An instructional message can best be prescribed by a communication model that takes into account the complex, systemic, and uniquely human processes of cognition by adapting information relevant to the learner's needs to the learner's capacities; this should be done in ways that provide the appropriate degree of external guidance to contribute (in verifiable ways) to the systematized programs that provide continuing progress toward the learner's independence.

REFERENCES

Anonymous. *Rhetorica ad herennium*.

Aristotle. *Rhetoric*.

Bradac, J. J., Desmond, R. J., & Murdock, J. I. Diversity and density: Lexically determined evaluative and informational consequences of linguistic complexity. *Communication Monographs*, 1977, *44*, 273–283.

Cicero. *De oratore*.

Flesch, R. *How to write, speak, and think more effectively*. New York: New American Library (Signet), 1946.

Hsia, H. J. The information processing capacity of modality and channel performance. *AV Communication Review*, 1971, *1*, 51-75.

Koegel, R., & Marsh, P. *Demand access instructional radio: A report on an innovative project for the CSUC system*. January 15, 1979. (Available from: California State University and Colleges, Office of the Chancellor, Fund for Innovative Instruction, 400 Golden Shore, Long Beach, CA 90802.)

Marsh, P. O. *Final report of the U-curve plotting project*. 1973. (Available from: California State University and Colleges, Office of the Chancellor, Fund for Innovative Instruction, 400 Golden Shore, Long Beach, CA 90802.)

Marsh, P. O., & Kowitz, A. C. *Toward a model of message complexity*. Paper presented at the annual convention of the Western Speech-Communication Association, Seattle, November 1975. (Copies available on request from: Patrick O. Marsh, Department of Communication Studies, California State University, Sacramento, CA 95819.)

McLuhan, M. *Understanding media: The extensions of man*. New York: McGraw-Hill, 1964.

Mellon, R. K. How big is a chunk? *Science*, 1974, *138*, 482–487.

Miller, G. A. *Language and communication*. New York: McGraw-Hill, 1951.

Miller, G. A. The magical number seven plus or minus two: Some limits on our capacity for processing information. In G. A. Miller (Ed.), *The psychology of communication: Seven essays*. Baltimore: Penguin Books, 1969.

Neisser, U. *Cognition and reality: Principles and implications of cognitive psychology*. San Francisco: W. H. Freeman, 1976.

Norman, D. A. *Memory and attention: An introduction to human information processing*. New York: Wiley, 1976.

Schroder, H. M., Driver, M. J., & Streufert, S. *Human information processing*. New York: Holt, Rinehart and Winston, 1967.

Schwartz, T. *The responsive chord*. Garden City, N.Y.: Anchor Press/Doubleday, 1974.

Shannon, C., & Weaver, W. *The mathematical theory of communication*. Urbana: University of Illinois Press, 1949.

Torkelson, G. M. AVCR—One quarter century: Evolution of theory and research. *AV Communication Review*, 1977, *25*, 317–358.

Quintilian. *Institutio oratoria*.

Valentine, M. Information theory and the psychology of speech. In J. Eisenson, J. J. Auer, & J. V. Irwin (Eds.), *The psychology of communication*. New York: Appleton-Century-Crofts, 1963.

Wiener, M., & Mehrabian, A. *Language within language: Immediacy, a channel in verbal communication*. New York: Appleton-Century-Crofts, 1968.

Appendix A-2

Explanation and Justification for
Using a Seven-Point Scale

The seven-point scale is the most common psychometric instrument used in the behavioral sciences. Three- and five-point scales often fail to provide a satisfactory degree of discrimination. Nine, 11, and 13-point scales seldom provide significantly more useful estimates than seven-point scales, yet they are more time-consuming and tedious to use. Also, seven items are easily managed within the memory and judgment channel capacities of the human information processing system.

It is important to have a scale with an odd number of intervals so that a middle category can be identified. On a seven-point scale, that middle value is "4," and it is typically where the scaling effort should begin. There is some ambiguity associated with the rating "4," however, for it may be selected either because one judges the thing rated as "average," or it may simply be the least inaccurate response if the dimension is perceived as irrelevant to the object.

Although the seven intervals are defined as equal, we should not conclude that one-seventh of the cases judged should be aligned with any given interval. There is a tendency for things to cluster around the average and to be less frequently represented by higher or lower ratings. For instance, approximately one-third of the objects judged will be considered "average" (scale value "4") when a large sample of random cases is scaled. One of the remaining one-thirds will be *unevenly* distributed among ratings 5, 6, and 7. The other one-third will be similarly distributed between ratings 3, 2, and 1. Ratings 1 and 7 should therefore be reserved for clearly *extreme* cases. You should also expect to rate more often at the 3 and 5 intervals than at the 2 and 6 intervals.

The 3 x 3 matrices used in this book assume "high" values to be scaled "6," "middle" values to be scaled "4," and "low" values to be scaled "2." Of course, interpolation on the matrices is possible and has been suggested.

Perhaps the best approach to using a seven-point scale is to work through this sequence mentally:

1. "Does this object being rated match my internalized notion of the average or typical case?" (If "yes," rate it "4.")

2. If you answered "no" to question No. 1, ask this question: "Does it fall above or below the average?"

3. If you perceive it as below (above) average, ask yourself to what degree: "Slightly below (above)?" "Definitely below (above)?" Extremely below (above)?" Translate your answers into numerical ratings accordingly: 3(5), 2(6), or 1(7), respectively.

The best we can expect by this method of scaling is reliability (or consistency) of judgments. If you rate the same items the same ways over extended time intervals, your rating behavior is reliable. Further, if you and other raters rate an item the same, you have established interrater reliability (consistent agreement). Usually, you can increase your reliability by discussing with other raters why they rated an item differently. Such discussions tend to refine the concepts. Since there is seldom an objective standard against which to test the validity of your judgment (as there would be if you were judging physical weights), we have to define values ultimately according to agreement among raters.

Appendix A-3

A Scale of Cognitive Styles

Based on research reported by Ausburn and Ausburn (1978)

1 2 3 4 5 6 7

1. Active   _ _ _ _ _ _ _   Passive

2. Analytic   _ _ _ _ _ _ _   Global

3. Narrow focus   _ _ _ _ _ _ _   Broad focus

4. Risks exclusion   _ _ _ _ _ _ _   Risks inclusion error
error

5. Many conceptu-   _ _ _ _ _ _ _   Few conceptual
al groupings   groupings

6. Responds reflec-   _ _ _ _ _ _ _   Responds impulsive-
tively   ly

7. Concreteness   _ _ _ _ _ _ _   Abstractness

8. Many dimen-   _ _ _ _ _ _ _   Few dimensions
sions

9. Structural depth   _ _ _ _ _ _ _   Structural shallow-
ness

10. Retains discrete   _ _ _ _ _ _ _   Merges new impres-
    and differential   sions with older
    images   ones

11. Concentrates on   _ _ _ _ _ _ _   Susceptible to dis-
    central task   traction

12. Intolerant of un-   _ _ _ _ _ _ _   Tolerant of unreal-
    realistic experi-   istic experiences
    ences

13. Prefers   low   _ _ _ _ _ _ _   Prefers high risk/
    risk/low payoff   high payoff

14. Low reliance on   _ _ _ _ _ _ _   High reliance on vis-
    visual images   ual images

Note: The higher the total score, the greater is the alignment with the
characteristics in the right column. Quantification may be desirable for
studying norms and deviations. Without quantification, comparisons
between individuals can be made graphically by plotting the two sets of
responses in different colors and connecting similarly colored points
with lines. The similarities and contrasts are thus readily apparent.

Appendix A-4

Evolution of Quintilian's Classical Structure

Aristotle stated that the *essential* components of a message are: (1) to state your case, and (2) to prove it. We can interpret this to mean to state your central idea and to support it. But Aristotle's teacher, Plato, argued that: "Every discourse is a living creature having its own head and body and feet—having its own beginning, middle, and end." Thus, Plato insisted that a message should have an introduction, a body, and a conclusion. Aristotle responded that while all that is essential is the body (consisting of the central idea and its support), he would grant that often it is convenient (not necessary) to have an introduction (proem) and a conclusion (epilogue).

Quintilian, who was more concerned with the receivers' thought processes than with essence or convenience, elaborated Aristotle's four parts according to specific and discrete functions. He believed it important to single out from the proem the exordium and the narration. The exordium prepares the listeners to hear the message, and the narration provides information needed in order to see the speaker's case (or message) in its proper context. Quintilian then analyzed the central idea into the proposition and the division (an analysis of the proposition into its issues). Then the confirmation was assigned the function of supporting each of the issues with appropriate proofs and appeals. The mirror image of the confirmation, whose function is to build one's constructive case, is the refutation. The refutation's function is to destroy the credibility of opposing positions. Aristotle's "body" was thus divided into four discrete functions. Finally, Quintilian retained the conclusion or epilogue and called it the peroration.

We should note that while the focus of classical rhetoric was on persuasion, several of Quintilian's elements may be adapted to other forms of discourse. Using terms that do not connote persuasion, we can describe a general disposition model as consisting of: (1) an exordium, (2) an expository background, (3) a central idea, (4) a preview, (5) the body, and (6) the peroration or conclusion.

CLASSICAL STRUCTURE

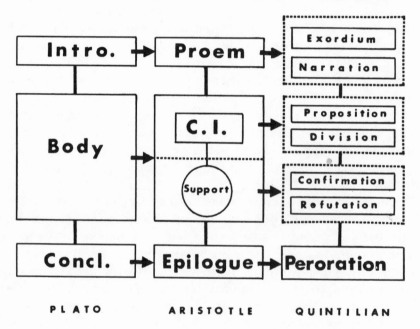

PLATO   ARISTOTLE   QUINTILIAN

Appendix A-5

Research Support for Table 5.2:
"Rules-of-Thumb for Selecting Visual Supports"

Francis M. Dwyer's extensive research into effective use of visual supporting material reports some findings that are contrary to popular expectations. I have abstracted what appear to me to be his most useful findings from his book, *A Guide for Improving Visualized Instruction*, State College, Penn.: Learning Services, 1972. I have retained his words in reporting the findings to prevent misinterpretation. Following that abstract, I have summarized the items employed in Table 5.2 in my own words.

Dwyer's Findings
1. "Generally, the more realistic illustrations were found to be the least effective in complementing oral instruction. In fact, they were no more effective than the oral instruction alone." (p. 22)
2. "The realistic photograph was least effective in complementing oral instruction." (p. 23)
3. "The simple line drawing presentation was found to be the single most effective in complementing oral instruction." (p. 23)
4. "For the teaching of specific types of educational objectives (terminology and comprehension tests), oral instruction without visualization is as effective as visualized instruction." (p. 23)
5. "For specific objectives and for students in certain grade levels (advanced grades, terminology test), color appears to be an important instructional variable for improving student achievement." (p. 27)

379

6. "In general, the differential effects attributed to the different visualized treatments on the immediate retention tests disappeared on the delayed retention tests." (p. 27)
7. "The results of these studies substantiate the hypothesis that reality may be edited for instructional purposes." (p. 27)
8. ". . . the effectiveness of discrimination learning promoted by the addition of relevant stimuli may be limited by the information processing capacity of the organism, with learning reaching an early peak and then diminishing with the addition of relevant, but superfluous, cues." (p. 30)
9. "More realistic presentations are at a disadvantage when the time is limited." (p. 30)
10. ". . . merely increasing the size of instructional illustrations by projecting them on larger viewing areas does not automatically improve their effectiveness. In fact, for certain learning objectives, the use of the larger images inhibited student achievement." (p. 39)
11. "The success of the line drawings complemented by motion . . . (may be a function of time). The line drawings presented succinctly the relevant information, and the use of motion focused the students' attention on the important aspects of instruction." (p. 41)
12. "The use of questions to focus students' attention on relevant visual learning cues in the more realistic visual displays is not an effective instructional technique for increasing students' achievement." (p. 43)
13. "The use of questions to complement simple line illustrations is an effective instructional technique for increasing student achievement on criterial measures to the ones used in this study." (p. 43)
14. "The effectiveness of the photographic presentation (in self-paced instruction) may be explained by the fact that the photographs contained more realistic detail than the other types of visual illustrations and thereby possessed more inherent information which could be transmitted to the students who were interacting with them." (p. 55)
15. "Students receiving the textbook—like treatments alone (in

self-paced instruction)—achieve as well as those receiving the programmed treatments on the immediate and delayed tests." (p. 54)

16. ". . . the photographic presentation was more effective than the programmed presentation without visuals in facilitating achievement on the identification and drawing tests . . . " (p. 54)

17. ". . . students who received the programmed instruction complemented by the line drawings required significantly more time to complete their instruction than did students who received the programmed instruction alone and those who viewed the detailed drawing presentation (color)." (p. 56)

18. " . . . the simple line presentation was found to be the most effective presentation in facilitating student achievement (for slide presentations): however, in the programmed instruction study, the realistic photograph presentation was found to be most effective." (p. 86)

Summary of General Conclusions

1. Determine whether visual supports are justified. (For learning terminology or for general comprehension, they tend to contribute little.)
2. Edit reality as much as the situation will allow when viewing time is controlled or limited.
3. Add color to edited visual to heighten attention.
4. Do not expect increased delayed retention effects from visual supports.
5. Larger images do not necessarily add to instructional effectiveness.
6. Motion tends to focus attention to desired parts of a visual.
7. Questions do not make very effective attention focusers in realistic visuals.
8. Questions help to focus attention on simpler illustrations.
9. Realism for self-paced instruction; simplicity for oral supplement.

Appendix A-6

An Empirically-Derived "U-Curve"
for Students at California State University, Sacramento

(Marsh, 1973)

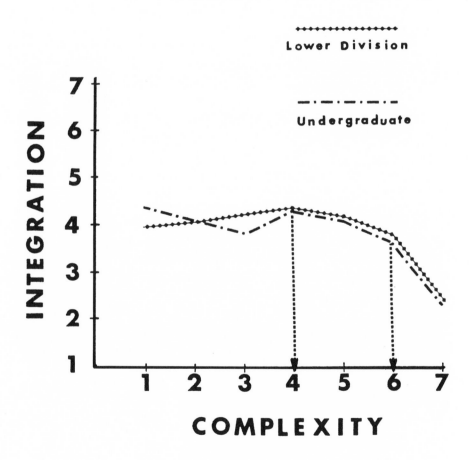

Appendix B: Less Common Usages

Appendix B-1

"Awareness of Knowledge Level" Calculations

Confidence Level

$$AKL^* = \underline{\hspace{5cm}} = \ldots\ldots\ldots\ldots$$

Demonstrated Knowledge Level

(Note: Convert both confidence and demonstrated knowledge levels to a seven-point scale.)

	Extremely	Definitely	Slightly	
Over-Confident	5.31 - 7.00	2.71 - 5.30	1.10 - 2.70	1.00
Under-Confident	.140 - .383	.383 - .749	.750 - .990	
	L	M	H	

*Awareness of Knowledge Level

Demonstrated Knowledge Level Conversion Scale

% SCORE		SCALE VALUE
0.00 - 14.3%	1	
14.4 - 28.7%	2	
28.8 - 43.1%	3	
43.2 - 57.3%	4	
57.4 - 71.7%	5	
71.8 - 86.1%	6	
86.2 - 100%	7	

Appendix B-2

Matrix for Strategy: To Solve

Desired State: Level of Goal Definition

	H	M	L
H	**REINFORCE** Strive for more of the same (1)	**REFINE GOALS** Specify objectives (2)	**FORMALIZE GOALS** Induce goals from successful cases. Must be doing something right, what is it? (3)
M	**REFINE SOLUTIONS** Retain present solution, but isolate inefficiencies (2)	**EMPLOY REFLECTIVE THINKING PROCESS** Use full Dewey sequence (5)	**NARROW GOALS** Delimit problem; establish priorities (4)
L	**RISK RADICAL DEPARTURE** "Second-order change," step out of frame (3)	**BRAINSTORM** List possible solutions while withholding judgment for the moment (4)	**EMPLOY TRUNCATED PROCESS** Use "no cause" sequence (3)

Actual State: Level of Goal Attainment

The appropriate tactics for messages related to solving problems are identified according to the level of goal definition (desired state) and the level of goal attainment (actual state). The cells contain brief prescriptions. The central cell of the matrix provides the best starting place for explanation and elaboration of these prescriptions, since it involves the entire reflective thinking sequence.

Employ reflective thinking process. Dewey's (1933) well-known problem-solving sequence is more complete than many others because it insists upon identifying causes for the problem's symptoms. Although paraphrased, its essentials are:

1. Define and delimit the problem.
2. Analyze the problem in search of causes for the identified symptoms.
3. Establish a set of criteria by which possible solutions may be evaluated.
4. List the possible solutions.
5. Select and implement the best solution.

Refine goals. When goal attainment is high and goal definition is only moderate, there is a need to refine the goals—to specify objectives. The implementation facilities are very functional and need more specific goals in order to maximize their effectiveness. Since problems are initially defined in terms of the gap between "what is" and "what ought to be," the more refined the goal, the more precise the problem definition will be. One might argue: "If our achievement is high regardless of vague goals, what is the problem?" The problem in this instance is that the system is not achieving its potential—there is room for improvement.

Formalize goals. Although it seems paradoxical, some instances can be identified where attainment is high, yet no one can cite the goals. For instance, President Eisenhower once appointed a commission to identify "Goals for Americans." Also, universities and similar institutions form task groups and commission to formalize goals even when the systems are functioning at a high level. They must be doing something right, but what is it?

This is not to say they are without goals; the goals simply are not formalized. By analyzing different aspects of the system, particular objectives can be identified and those can be induced into broader goal statements. It is a commonplace saying that the real goals of a system are related to those activities that get rewarded. Sometimes the *de facto* goals are completely at odds with the goals *de jure*. The importance of formalizing goals is not limited to knowing and communicating "where you are going," but bears directly on the ability to identify criteria (derived from goals) by which possible solutions may be evaluated.

Narrow goals. If goals are ill-defined and achievement is only moderately satisfactory, the appropriate tactic is to narrow the goals—delimit them. A common fault in problem solving is an effort to accomplish too much. Unlimited goals tend to become superficial and ineffective. To narrow goals, one should analyze the global goals and establish priorities. Limits on resources must determine how far down the priority list one can go.

Employ truncated process. When both goal attainment and goal definition are low, the problem should be approached as a whole rather than in terms of concentrating on goals or solutions. This process should be more global than the reflective thinking process. These two processes differ not only in precision, but also fundamentally: the truncated process, adapted from Harris and Schwahn (1961), seeks a solution without attempting to identify causes for the problem. The truncated process asks these basic questions:

1. What is the single question, the answer to which is all the group needs to know to accomplish its purpose?
2. What sub-questions must be answered before we can answer the single question we have formulated?
3. Do we have sufficient information to answer confidently the sub-questions?
4. What are the most reasonable answers to the sub-questions?
5. Assuming that our answers to the sub-questions are correct, what is the best solution to the problem?

Brainstorm. Coon (1957) defined brainstorming as ". . . a technique for stimulating the generation of ideas and facilitating their expression . . . . It usually involves cooperative thinking by groups and is usually directed to the solution of specific problems." He also identifies four basic brainstorming rules:

1. Adverse criticism is taboo.
2. "Free-wheeling" is welcome.
3. Quantity of ideas is desired.
4. Combination and improvement of ideas are sought.

Brainstorming is appropriate when there is a moderately defined goal, but goal attainment is low. The emphasis is upon identifying solutions without following a structured sequence or process. Judgments are withheld until the brainstorming function is completed. At that time, the solutions may be evaluated on a comparative, advantageous basis.

Risk radical departure. Watzlawick, Weakland, and Fisch (1974) define a radical departure from the reflective-thinking sequence (which in their language produces "first-order change").* For knotty problems, as opposed to mere difficulties, they propose the use of "second-order change." A situation of high-goal definition and low-goal attainment appears an appropriate target for this tactic. They summarize the essence of second-order change as follows:

a. Second-order change is applied to what in the first-order change perspective appears to be a solution, because in the second-order change perspective this *"solution" reveals itself as the keystone of the problem* whose solution is attempted.

b. While first-order change always appears to be based on common sense (for instance, the "more of the same" recipe), second-order change usually *appears weird,* unexpected, and uncommon-sensical; there is a puzzling, paradoxical element in the process of change.

c. Applying second-order change techniques to the "solution" means that the situation is dealt with in the *here and now.* These techniques deal with effects and not with their presumed causes; the crucial question is "what?" and not "why?"

d. The use of second-order change techniques *lifts the situation out* of the paradox-engendering trap created by

*From the book, *Change: Principles of Problem Formation and Problem Resolution*, by Paul Watzlawick, John Weakland, and Richard Fisch, Copyright © 1974, W.W. Norton and Company, Inc., New York.

the self-reflexiveness of the attempted solution and *places it in a different frame* (as is literally done in the solution of the nine-dot problem).

Refine solutions. When goals are highly defined and goal attainment is only moderate, the suggested tactic is to retain the present solutions, but isolate and correct causes of inefficiency. Barnes (1944), a pioneer in time and motion study, specifies four basic tactics for developing a better method; he says to:

a. Eliminate all unnecessary work.
b. Combine operations or elements.
c. Change the sequence of operations.
d. Simplify the necessary operations.

Numerous management techniques such as PERT and "fault-tree analysis" are available for this purpose, but in essence, Barnes' list identifies the appropriate tactics.

Reinforce. When goals are well-defined and goal attainment is high, the appropriate tactic is to reinforce the present efforts with recognition, payment, or privilege in order to maintain this satisfactory level of performance.

Appendix B-3

Matrix for Strategy: To Argue
(i.e., to test the validity of a claim)

RECEIVER'S WILLINGNESS TO GRANT:

	H	M	L

CLAIM H row:
- STATE CLAIM — C (1)
- QUALIFY CLAIM — C / Q (3)
- RELATE CLAIM QUALIFICATIONS TO EXCEPTIONS — C / Q / EX (5)

WARRANT M row:
- STATE WARRANT — W (1)
- OFFER DIRECT BACKING AND EXCEPTIONS FOR WARRANT — W → Ex / B (3)
- TRACE BACKING FOR WARRANT TO FACTUAL ROOTS — W / Fact ← B (5)

DATA L row:
- STATE DATA — D (1)
- VERIFY DATA (Document) — D / V (3)
- TEST DATA — D / Test ← V (5)

SOURCE'S ARGUMENT

The "obscurity index" is the average of the indexes for data, warrant, and claim.

395

The "obscurity index" is the average of the indexes for data, warrant, and claim.

It is important to remember the distinction between the strategies "to argue" and "to persuade" that were drawn in Chapter 1. Most critical is that argument serves the function of testing the validity of a claim; its function is not to gain commitment to that claim. When this is the source's purpose, the Toulmin model (discussed as a persuasive tactic in the matrix: to persuade) serves the argumentative tactics very nicely. The matrix for the strategy "to argue" is defined in terms of Toulmin's elements: data, warrant, backing, exceptions, qualifications, and claim. If these are not familiar concepts, you may wish to refer to Toulmin, Rieke, and Janik (1979) or to Toulmin (1958).

This matrix identifies the principal elements of the Toulmin model (data, warrant, and claim) in the rows; the columns identify the receiver's willingness to grant those elements. The willingness to grant may vary with these elements, but I will explain the matrix only in terms of high, moderate, and low willingness to grant the whole argument comprised of all three elements. The other possible combinations should be obvious following these explanations.

High willingness to grant. Once a receiver has granted a position, it is unnecessary and generally undesirable to submit proof of that position. Thus, the appropriate tactic for the "high" column is simply to state clearly the data, the warrant, and the claim.

Moderate willingness to grant. When the willingness to grant is moderate, the entire basic Toulmin model, with one addition, provides the best tactic. The addition is to specify the "verification" (or documentation) for the data. The other elements are included just as Toulmin has specified: the source offers direct backing and exceptions for the warrant—all stated explicitly, and the claim is qualified to account for the exceptions.

Low willingness to grant. When a receiver is unwilling to grant anything, the source's argument must not only be complete, but it must push each element back to the limits of objectivity. More specifically: (1) The data must not only be verified, but they must also be shown to meet the relevant tests of evidence. (2) The warrant, qualified by exceptions, must be backed and that backing must be supported by corroborating arguments whose data are grounded *in fact.* (3) The claim, of course, must be qualified, and the qualification should be linked explicitly with the exceptions to the warrant.

Appendix B-4

Appendix for Strategy: To Transform

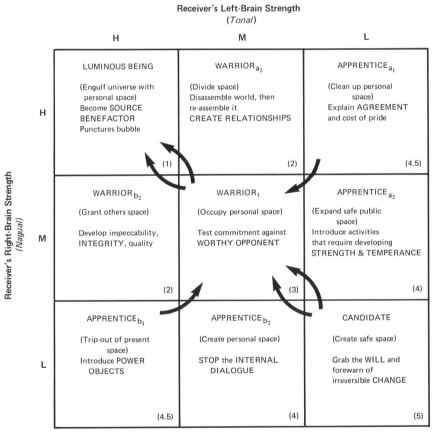

Receiver's Left-Brain Strength
(*Tonal*)

TACTICAL MATRIX

Transformation is a reorientation or reframing of one's way of perceiving one's self and/or world. It is often accompanied by noticeable changes in behavior resulting from changed fundamental beliefs. Transformation changes the context rather than the content of one's life so that the same kind of events are seen and responded to differently after transformation. Religious *conversion* may be the most familiar example. Castaneda (1974) illustrates a pathway leading from "candidate" status to one of the "luminous being"—a course in which transformation takes place. The main events along this course (liberally interpreted) provide the basis for the matrix in Figure 1. Since most of these terms are metaphoric, some definition and explanation are indicated.

The candidate. When the source identifies a candidate, his or her first tactic is to "grab the will," that is, to compel one to decide whether he or she is ready to make a commitment which will lead to irreversible change in the way one sees himself or herself and the world. This choice is made within the context of a "safe space" where no onus is attached to either decision on an issue.

The apprentice. Apprentices are of two types and two degrees. The type-a apprentice is one who is unbalanced as a result of a *tonal* (left-brain) deficiency. If the deficiency is severe, the apprentice-a_1 tactics apply. They serve to help the apprentice "clean up his or her personal space"—i.e., habits of reasoning and personality. The source explains the importance of agreement-keeping and the cost of pride. The a_1 apprentice progresses to the a_2 status, or candidates with less severe deficiencies begin at that level. They are helped *to expand* the security of their "personal space" to include elements of their *public lives* through tactics which require the development of *strength* and *temperance.*

If, however, a candidate is assessed to be severely *nagual* (right-brain) deficient, the apprenticeship begins at the b_1 level. Here "power objects" (any substance or technique that produces a psychodelic state) may be employed to help the apprentice "trip-out" of his or her linear, symbol-dominated world of experience. Less severely deficient and graduated apprentices experience *creating* their own *personal space* at the b_2 level. The tactic for achieving this is one of "stopping the internal dialogue"—experiencing one's environment directly without first translating the perception into language.

The warrior. Upon completing one's apprenticeship, sufficient *tonal-nagual* balance is achieved to allow one to begin acquiring selected talents and character traits shared by disciplined "warriors." At the first level, a warrior must learn to occupy his or her personal space. That is, the warrior must trust and "come from" within oneself. A test of commitment to one's perceptions, beliefs, and principles may be used as a tactic by arranging for a confrontation with a "worthy opponent."

Depending on the performances at the first warrior level, one will advance to the a_2 or b_2 level. The a_2 level strives to refine left-brain functions: notably analytic functions. The warrior learns to divide (compartmentalize) his or her personal space—to disassemble and then to reassemble one's perceptual world. Tactical emphasis is on creating relationships among elements. At the b_2 level, where right-brain capabilities are refined, the emphasis is upon granting others their personal safe space. The tactics focus upon the development of what has variously been described as "quality," "integrity," or "impeccability" by Pirsig (1974), Bartley (1978), and Castenada (1974), respectively.

Luminous being. The transformed person comes to regard himself or herself as "enlightened," "saved," "a man (woman) of knowledge," etc. From such a position, he or she often takes the responsibility for being the "source" of his or her universe, since the personal space of his or her own creation has been expanded to engulf the whole universe. Such an expression as: "the spirit of God is within me" is symptomatic of this transformed state. The chief tactic used to complete the transformation is to enlist a "benefactor" (someone other than the message source who has experienced similar transformation) who "punctures the bubble" that separates one's private space from the universe.

Although the course described here represents a grand strategy in scope, the same tactics can be employed on less ambitious transformation undertakings. They may be compressed into a single message, or (perhaps more typically) they may prescribe a course comprised of separate messages. The process is somewhat analogous to therapy and as such is inherently more time-consuming than other strategic processes.

Appendix B-5

Annotated Examples of Messages Varying in Degree of Erudition (Sophistication) and Austerity (Readiness)

Example 1. High Erudition

It should be recognized that relationships and definitions of relational trajectories are not simply a matter of one partner's expectations; the extent to which the other partner satisfies those expectations, and shares them, is also involved. There may be disagreement over what kind of relationship is being pursued. One partner may define the dating activity as a casual relation; the other may define it as a serious involvement. Much of the dissatisfaction in a relationship often centers around differences in its definition. Thus, in analyzing satisfaction with relationships, the dimensions of judgment that are relevant to each person's definition of the relationship need to be considered.

Analysis and research need to be made of factors that cause a relation to change to a different trajectory. The foregoing supposes that judgments of the other person and behavior toward that person are channeled and organized with reference to a particular relational trajectory. The factors that determine whether a relationship remains on one trajectory or shifts to a different trajectory also need to be explored. Why does the relation to one officemate move from "co-worker" to "potential friend," with the implications for change in social activities and in dimensions of judgment which that movement implies? I suspect there is usually no overt decision to change the direction of the relationship. Instead, altered patterns of activities—such as being thrown into several hours of extra work with a particular person—often promote a change in the relational trajectory. This suggests that a major concern for research ought to be how variations in patterns of social activity affect and are affected by the course of relational growth. (Jesse G. Delia, "Some Tentative Thoughts Concerning the Study of Interpersonal Relationships and Their Development," *The Western Journal of Speech Communication*, 44, Spring, 1980, 101.)

This piece of academic writing reflects the erudite style expected in a scholarly journal. Notice first the abstract nature of the subject matter. Also notice the precision with which words are selected to represent fine discriminations in thought. Finally, observe the rather lengthy and complex sentences and the frequent use of multi-syllable words of Latin and Greek derivation.

Example 2. Low Erudition

If you wear arch supports and are interested in switching to customized shoes, here is some information you might be interested in.

If you lead an active lifestyle (and who doesn't these days?), you can forget about having to change arch supports every time you change shoes, or having them squeak as you walk. There is no problem with their slipping under your feet or rubbing blisters, and customized shoes feel natural—like going barefooted!

Just about every arch support wearer can be fitted for customized shoes these days—but your foot doctor will let you know for sure. There are two kinds, flexible and rigid, and both have easy and uncomplicated systems of cleaning and de-odorizing daily. Rigid soles are cleaned simply by airing them for six hours at room temperature, while flexible soles come with soft pads which are placed in the shoes overnight. Just slip the pads in before going to bed at night!

Customized shoes generally cost from less than $100 to $200 or more—but again, your foot doctor can tell you more. Never put the flexible shoe cleansing pads in when the shoes are wet, and if you know you will be walking through puddles, waterproof them before going out. (This piece was written in the style of a popular teenagers' magazine.)

To contrast the writing in this sample with the "high erudition" selection, first note the differences in word length and sentence length. Also compare the differing levels of abstraction/concreteness. The use of dichotomous categories and broad generalizations that approach universal statements signals much lower precision than its counterpart example.

Example 3. High Austerity

The amendment to #61.48(a)(2) makes clear that the prohibition of that provision applies to entries in logbooks or other records required to show compliance with any requirement for not only the issuance, but also the exercise of the privileges, of a certificate or rating under Part 61. It has been asserted that the rule as presently written is susceptible of the interpretation that it does not prohibit falsification of entries, such as required recent experience, needed for the continuing exercise of the privileges of a certificate or rating. The amendment states the scope of the rule more clearly than the previous language.

Since the former amendment contains an alternative method of compliance that is less burdensome than that which became effective on November 22, 1969, and the latter amendment merely clarifies an existing rule, I find that notice and public procedure thereon is unnecessary, and that these amendments may be made effective on less than 30 days' notice.

In consideration of the foregoing, Part 61 of the Federal Aviation Regulations is amended, effective January 21, 1970.

These amendments are made under the authority of sections 313(a), 601, and 602 of the Federal Aviation Act of 1958 (49 U.S.C. 1354(a), 1421, 1422); and section 6(c) of the Department of Transportation Act (49 U.S.C. 1655(c)). (*Federal Air Regulations*, Volume IX, July, 1970, Part 61, p. 74.)

These regulations assume high readiness on the part of the reader. No one reads them for recreation. The readers consult them with specific objectives in mind, and they wish to find what they are looking for as quickly as possible. Consequently, there is no concern with motivation and only minimal concern with framing. (What framing there is takes the forms of highly codified references and formal outline format.) No aid to memory is offered the reader. The reader must rely upon re-reading the section if long-range retention is required.

Example 4. Low Austerity

After rushing home from the store with your new computer, you may feel as happy and awed as a child discovering his or her first electric train under the Christmas tree. In a short time, however, you may find you are more like the train than the child—you go around in circles trying to figure out what, exactly, this great new gadget can do.

Home computers can become an obsession or a bore. During

the past six years, as the home computer revolution gathered steam, tens of thousands of people have gone "byte bonkers," addicted to their machines, plumbing inner mysteries of operating systems and machine languages, and pontificating in computer code jargon.

On the other hand, tens of thousands of others, who bought computers in breathless, though short-lived, excitement, let their expensive machines gather dust in dark corners. In fact, market surveys show that up to *90 percent* of all home computers are rarely used six months after purchase.

Why? The answer is simple: After they tired of playing games, after the computer was no longer a fad, these once-proud owners found they did not know to what useful purpose to put their marvelous machinery. (Robert L. Perry, "Putting Your New Computer to Work," *Mechanix Illustrated*, August, 1981, 47.)*

The author of this passage appears to have assumed low readiness in his potential readers. Since readers of popular magazines often browse—looking at pictures and captions and sampling lead paragraphs—this author baited his hook with a personalized description with which most general readers could identify. The style is homey and conversational, yet it is fresh and compelling. It invites involvement, suggests active participation and identification, and it provides some framing information. Notice how he puts "you" into the picture he helps you create.

Appendix B-6

Musical Scaling Instruments:
Tension and Aloofness

To facilitate more precise scaling of musical tension and aloofness, two semantic-differential-type scales are included below. The higher the total scores, the higher will be the estimated levels of tension and aloofness, respectively.

Scale of Musical Tension

1 2 3 4 5 6 7

Harmony	_ _ _ _ _ _ _	Dissonance
Resolution	_ _ _ _ _ _ _	Suspension
Softness	_ _ _ _ _ _ _	Loudness
Non-reiteration	_ _ _ _ _ _ _	Repetition of note or theme
Continuity	_ _ _ _ _ _ _	Interruption
Level	_ _ _ _ _ _ _	Climax/retreat

Scale of Musical Aloofness*

1 2 3 4 5 6 7

FORM
De-emphasized	_ _ _ _ _ _ _	Obvious at a glance

MOOD
Depressive/ euphoric	_ _ _ _ _ _ _	Subtle, mildly pleasant

*Adapted from lecture notes from a course taught by Dr. Ward Fenley at California State University, Sacramento, 1973.

DYNAMICS
  Graduated   — — — — — — — — Blocked
RHYTHM$_1$
  Expressive vari- — — — — — — — — Methodical   variation
    ation
RHYTHM$_2$
  Very fast/very   — — — — — — — — Moderate tempo
    slow
TEXTURE
  Rich, "thick"   — — — — — — — — Thin sound
RANGE$_1$
  Highs and lows — — — — — — — — Whole spectrum cov-
    separated   ered at once
RANGE$_2$
  Higher/lower   — — — — — — — — Limited range
USE
  Unusual instru-
    ments; un-   — — — — — — — — Usual instruments used
    usual usages   usually
VIRTUOSITY
  Exploitation of
    technique to
    enhance art- — — — — — — — — Technique balanced by
    ist's skill   musical purpose

Appendix C: Extended Examples

409

Appendix C-1

Example of a Receiver-Profile Questionnaire

An Example: A Truncated Questionnaire

This example is drawn from an actual questionnaire for profiling students in an upper-division college class in preparation for designing a 30-minute tape-recorded lecture on the influence of mass media on society. The knowledge-level portion has been shortened to only two questions for illustrative purposes. The attitude scale has likewise been shortened. Even though the strategy for this message was to inform rather than to persuade, attitudes were estimated to determine effective approaches for raising the "readiness" level if deemed necessary.

QUESTIONNAIRE

You can assist us in preparing a new module for Communication Studies 100A to be entitled: "Mass Media: Our Tools that Shape Us." Each item is important; please respond to all items.

General Demographic Information

1. Age category: (check one)
   .... under 18, ... 18-22, ... 23-30, ... 31-40, ... over 40.
2. Sex: .... Male, ... Female.
3. Citizenship: .... USA, ... other (specify) ....
4. Academic year: .... Fr., ... Soph., ... Jr., ... Sr., Grad.
5. Cumulative Grade Point Average (GPA) ....
6. Check the items which you use regularly.
   .... Black and white TV
   .... Color TV
   .... AM radio
   .... FM radio
   .... Daily newspaper
   .... National or international newspaper
   .... Weekly news magazines
   .... Monthly or quarterly magazines
   .... Electronic computer
   .... Postal information subscription service
7. Are you a Communication Studies Major? .... Minor? ....
8. List other Communication Studies courses you have completed.

Knowledge of Mass Media

Answer each item by circling the correct answer *and* then scale your degree of confidence in the correctness of your answer by blacking in the appropriate scale value on the right.

1. Which person takes the position that mass media are central in the development of civilization, and modern electronic media bring individuals and institutions closer together?

	confidence level
a. Harold Lasswell	1................
b. Marshall McLuhan	2................
c. Wesley C. Clark	3................
d. Walter Lippman	4................
	5................
	6................
	7................

2. As communication technology, industrialization, and literacy continue to grow—

confidence
level

a. Mass media will probably decline.   1....................
b. Specialized media will probably ascend. 2....................
c. Both "a" and "b."   3....................
d. Neither "a" nor "b."   4....................
                                            5....................
                                            6....................
                                            7....................

3. Etc.

* * * * * * * * * *

Attitudes About Mass Media

Indicate your attitude by circling the symbol which best describes your position on each of the following statements:

SA = Strongly Agree
 A = Agree
MA = Mildly Agree
 N = Neutral
MD = Mildly Disagree
 D = Disagree
SD = Strongly Disagree

SA A MA N MD D SD   1. Television is responsible for our declining literacy.

SA A MA N MD D SD   2. We never could have achieved our high standard of living without the mass media.

SA A MA N MD D SD   3. In a capitalistic economy, the "content" of mass media (*i.e.*, programs, news, features, etc.) exists only to provide an audience for the ads and commercials.

4. Etc.

* * * * * * * * * *

SOP/REA Rating Scale

Low 1 2 3 4 5 6 7 High   1. Indicate the level of *abstraction* at which you function best.

Low 1 2 3 4 5 6 7 High   2. What level of implicitness serves your purposes best?

Low 1 2 3 4 5 6 7 High   3. Indicate the level of *precision* you normally employ or prefer.

Low 1 2 3 4 5 6 7 High   4. At what level would you like to have information about mass media *framed* in context?

High 1 2 3 4 5 6 7 Low   5. How *relevant* do you perceive information on mass media to be to your interests?

High 1 2 3 4 5 6 7 Low   6. To what extent do you need assistance in *remembering* mass media related concepts?

Reinforcement Preferences

Rank order your preferences regarding the kinds of rewards you may receive for a job well done.

RANK

....   Recognition
....   Payment
....   Tension reduction
....   Participation
....   Other (specify) ....

Appendix C-2

Example of a Complete Purpose Statement

Strategy: To inform Communication Studies 100A students of the major issues, impacts, performances, and innovations attributable to mass media.

Receivers. The students enrolled in Communication Studies 100A (Survey of Communication Studies) majors account for 30 percent of this population; Social Studies or Humanities majors constitute ten percent, and Business or Public Administration majors five percent of the population. Many have not declared majors. Juniors and seniors comprise 71 percent of the students enrolled. Seventy-four percent are between ages 18-30; 16 percent are between 31-40; the ages of the remainder are unknown. The female/male ratio is 2:1. Fifty-seven percent report GPA's above 3.00. Seventy-one percent are Caucasian with Black, Asian-American, and Mexican-American comprising most of the remainder. Over half of the students carry 15 or more units/semester, and 59 percent work while attending the university.

The students sampled were unable to associate major critics with their position and only slightly more able to recognize the major issues of mass media. They were moderately confident that they could do both. They were knowledgeable about mass media performance and confident of that knowledge. Although their confidence was low regarding their knowledge of social innovations attributable to mass media, they scored moderately high on questions testing that area.

According to self-ratings, the sample audience was moderately high in sophistication and slightly lower in readiness. These ratings were made at the beginning of the semester, and it is likely that readiness will be moderately high by the time this message is presented, since the previous eight messages will probably render the receivers more ready than they were for earlier messages. There appears to be a slight aversion to precision, and there is an indication of some need for framing.

A secondary audience will be students in Communication Studies 140 (Critical Analysis of Social Issues), but since the profiles for the two audiences are assumed to be similar and since it will be used there as introductory material, special efforts to accommodate the secondary audience will not be made.

Central idea. Although some issues related to the impact of our mass media remain unresolved, certain patterns of performance are identifiable in the media which result from and contribute to social and technical innovation.

Performance objectives. After hearing this tape-recorded message and having an opportunity to hear it a second time for review purposes, the receivers should be able to meet these objectives:

1. Given a list of media critics and a list of beliefs about the impact and performance of mass media, match the critics with their positions with 70 percent accuracy or better.
2. Given several examples and non-examples of major unresolved issues among media critics, identify (by circling) the legitimate issues with 70 percent accuracy or better.
3. Given several examples of media usage for information diffusion, needs gratification, and innovation diffusion, classify (by labeling) each example with no errors.

Appendix C-3

Example of the Evolution of
a Sentence Outline from a Purpose Statement

Purpose Statement

Strategy. To inform this audience about the nature and foundation of the martial art of *aikido.*

Receivers. (Description is truncated for this example.) The 20- to 30-year-old mixed sex audience recognizes *aikido* as a martial art and has a vague concept of martial arts in general. They are more familiar with *jujitsu, judo,* and *karate,* but only a few have had any direct experience or training in any martial art. The audience is slightly above average in sophistication and high in readiness.

Central idea. The martial art of *aikido,* the name of which defines its essence, is built upon four fundamental principles.

Performance objectives. After receiving this message, 90 percent of our audience should be able to score 90 percent on a ten-question test derived from the following objectives.

1. Given any syllable in the name *aikido,* select the correct meaning from a list.
2. Given definitions of five martial arts, select the one that best fits *aikido.*
3. Given any of the fundamental principles upon which *aikido* is founded, select a definition from a list which matches it.
4. Given an example of any of the fundamental principles, identify the appropriate principle from a list.

Original Box-Outline

Figure C-3.1 displays the initial analysis of the central idea.

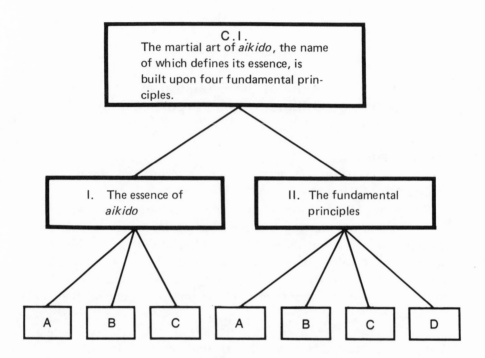

Figure C-3.1. Original Box-Outline.

Notice that it is a simple visual analysis of the central idea.

Box-Outline Adapted for Tactics

Figure C-3.2 shows how each point will be adapted tactically based upon prescriptions from the tactical matrix (Figure 2.5). Points IA and IC call for acknowledgment tactics; that is, once the point is stated, it will be sufficiently clear to the audience that support will not be required. These points, having no supports, are not counted as chunks. Point IB was assigned an obscurity index

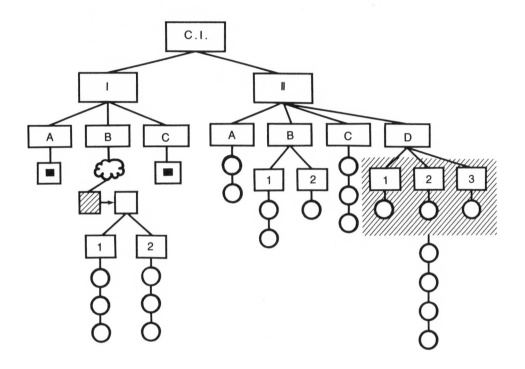

Figure C-3.2. Outline Adapted for Tactics.

of 5 and therefore requires the full tactical sequence: It begins with an imagined situation which then is associated with the point to be made; that point is divided and the subpoints receive the support. Note that the steps preceding the division are preparatory, but are not supports.

Points IIA and IIC were assigned obscurity indexes of 2 so they are developed directly with supports. Point IIB, with an obscurity index of 3, requires a division of that point and then support of the subpoints. Point IID was originally rated 3 on obscurity which calls for division then support, but that division created more chunks than were desired. A design choice required weighing the advantages of employing the prescribed tactic against the disadvantages of information overloading. The decision to edit by reducing structural depth allows us to replace three chunks with one, thus putting the total at seven.

Box-Outline Adapted for Order of Presentation

Reference to the "Body Structure Matrix" (Figure 3.5) permits this final adaptation. Our information load rating is 5; that means the center column is the appropriate one. Incidentally, since 5 is at the high end of the middle range, any extrapolation or bias where options are involved should be toward the "high" column. The appropriate structural pattern for this message is "nested categories" which, according to Table 3.1, is at the medium level (1). Thus, by entering the matrix through the middle row, we can identify the intersected cell. That cell prescribes the following:

2. Use mixed arrangement of points.
3. Use optional point/support order.
4. Use a few supports on terminal points mixing brief and elaborate supports.
4a. Develop with both figurative and literal supports in either order.
4b. Develop with both general and specific supports in either order.
5. Use phrase-type transitions.

These prescriptions have been incorporated into the box-outline in Figure C-3.3. Point I is to be presented primarily in an anti-climactic sequence. The most unfamiliar concept is presented first, and the more familiar ones follow. However, the subpoints are developed before they are integrated into the main point, thus creating a counteracting climactic arrangement. Point II is reversed: the main point is stated first then developed (an anti-climactic quality), yet the subpoints build cumulatively to an integrated development of that point (a climactic quality). A design decision had to be made in point II on the basis of the designer's comparative judgments. Point IIB is the most obscure

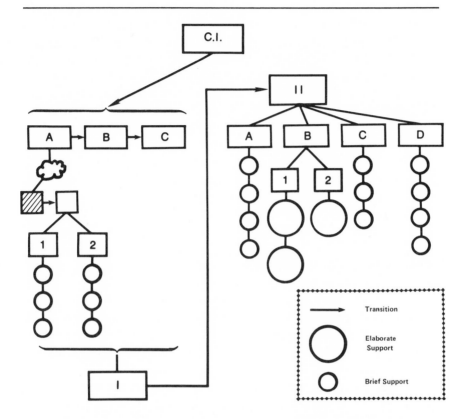

Figure C-3.3. Box-Outline Adapted for Order of Presentation.

one and would therefore typically be placed last in a climactic ordering, but the cumulative building of the order chosen also contributes to the climactic impact. The choice favored the cumulative structure. The subpoints in both points IA and IIB were arranged from less relevant to more relevant which added a climactic tendency. Even though competing ordinal forces were used to moderate an extreme impact, the overall effect is that of a "mixed" structure: the message begins and ends with the strongest elements while weaker ones are relegated to the middle.

Sentence Outline

The sentence outline translates the final version of the box-outline into complete sentences. This process serves not only to insure that the thinking is complete (a sentence expresses a complete thought), but it also facilitates the accurate communication of the designer's message to others involved in its production. Additionally, even the designer's memory may be jogged by the precision of a sentence outline where more cryptic outlines may lose their richness with the passage of time.

Some liberties have been taken with the traditional outline format in the example that follows because of the desire to represent the order-to-presentation features.

Central idea. The martial art of *aikido,* the name of which defines its essence, is built upon four fundamental principles.

A. The syllable "ki" in *aikido,* which means the energy of life itself, is central not only to the word, but to the concept as well.

- *Imagine* a bright, yellow fluid flowing from your body's center out and beyond your fingertips with considerable force.
- *Associate* that image with the concept of *ki*, which is the centralized, coordinated energy used in *aikido*.

1. "Hard" *ki* is the more familiar type of power or energy.

   Visual Support. A board's being broken with hard *ki.*

   Quotation. "Hard *ki* appears sharp and concentrated to a dangerous point of fusion resembling the edge or point of a Japanese blade." (Westbrook and Ratti, 1970, p. 84)

   Example. Bricks broken with the hand.

2. "Soft" *ki* is the kind preferred in *aikido.*

   Visual Support. A board's being displaced, not broken, by tangential, soft *ki.*

   Quotation. "Soft *ki,* by contrast, appears to be evenly diffused, irradiating, and expanding like a huge glove to envelop the target completely or spin tangentially against it." (p. 85)

Description. Of an *aikido* master's appearing to be dancing rather than fighting.

B. The *ai* in *aikido* means harmony or integration in the sense of these words with which you are familiar. (No support needed.)

C. The *do* in *aikido* means path, way, method, or process with no special connotations beyond your meanings. (No support needed.)

I. In essence, therefore, aikido literally means a pathway or method leading to the skill of employing life's centralized, coordinated energy in a harmonious and integrated manner.

(Transition)

II. This defensive art, which applies both to actual attackers and to life's obstacles, is built upon four fundamental principles.

A. The principle of *centralization* identifies the *hara,* center of gravity, around which one orients oneself in order to achieve greater unification and coordination of one's powers.

Visual support. Circle encompassing body with center at *hara.*

Quotation. "Be stably centralized, inwardly and outwardly, in the lower abdomen." (p. 69)

Visual support. Vectors flowing into center of body and then outward.

Narrative. Aikido master remaining centralized during simultaneous attack and after immobilizing attackers, kneels to contemplate his center.

B. The principle of *extension* directs the centralized *ki* through the extremities thereby releasing an almost irresistible and untiring strength.

1. "Static" extension is easier to comprehend than "dynamic."

Example. Demonstration of the "Unbendable arm."

Explanation. The concentration of consciousness and energy from the center to the arm renders it unbendable.

2. "Dynamic" extension is more difficult to comprehend, but is more essential to *aikido*.
Description. The relaxed, flowing, dance-like strength of an *aikido* master.

C. The principle of *leading control* allows one to redirect a powerful, unified attack from its target and to use the force behind the attack to immobilize the attacker.
Comparison. Draw an analogy from a cowboy's heading-off a charging steer until its energy is expended.
Quotation. "This leading motion . . . your attacker's dynamic momentum." (p. 92)
Visual support. Sequence of drawings with vectors suggesting motion.

D. The principle of *sphericity* requires formal definition.
Definition. Sphericity refers to the circular motions which have the *hara* as their center and which characterize all *aikido* strategies.
Explanation. The circular motion around the *aikido* master's center of gravity keeps him collected, centered, and in control of almost anything that enters this sphere of energy.
Visual support. Ying-and-yang symbol and a ripened dandelion blossom.
Example. Ancient Japanese swordsmen who, with their curved swords and circular motion, created an impenetrable sphere of defense about themselves.

Appendix C-4

Hierarchy for Body-Structure Patterns

A. Low-Level Body-Structure Patterns

TYPE	SCHEMA	EXAMPLE
1. Amplification		any "information chunk" that comprises an entire message
2. Topical Clustered		a random grocery list restructured into basic non-related categories: meats, canned-goods, etc.
3. Simple narrative Simple spatial Sequence Simple problem/ solution Simple cause/ effect		one's life story; a report of a trip or tour; a description of an assembly line
4. Syllogistic		I. all men are mortal. II. Socrates is a man. III. Socrates is mortal.
5. Comparison/contrast		any effort to isolate the common ground between two different events, persons, things, etc.: the examination of two court decisions

B. Medium-Level Body-Structure Patterns

TYPE	*SCHEMA*	*EXAMPLE*
1. Nested categories		an organizational chart for business or government
2. Flow chart		general systems schemata
3. Spatial layout (Matrix)		any of the matrices used in this text
4. Problem-solving sequence		Dewey's reflective-thinking sequence; the so-called scientific method
5. Toulmin layout		any application of Stephen Toulmin's six-part model
6. Reframed		any metaphor. A musical reconstituted from a classical play: *West Side Story*

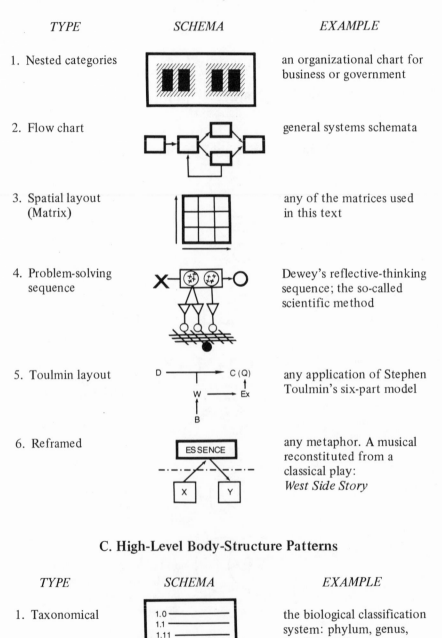

C. High-Level Body-Structure Patterns

TYPE	*SCHEMA*	*EXAMPLE*
1. Taxonomical		the biological classification system: phylum, genus, family, species

2. Circuit

an electronic circuit; a Boolian logic layout

3. Exploded

an auto-parts catalog diagram

4. Algorithmic

any of the "choice points" incorporated in this text

5. Embedded Toulmin layout

a lawyer's brief; a complex, reasoned proposal

6. Pattern/isolate

looking at a cell through three powers of a microscope

7. Compounded

any combination of structural patterns

Appendix C-5

Model Message with Dispositional Elements Identified

The Knapp-White Murder Case*
Daniel Webster

[Exordium]

I am little accustomed, Gentlemen, to the part which I am now attempting to perform. Hardly more than once or twice has it happened to me to be concerned on the side of the government in any criminal prosecution whatever; and never, until the present occasion, in any case affecting life.

But I very much regret that it should have been thought necessary to suggest to you that I am brought here to "hurry you against the law and beyond the evidence." I hope I have too much regard for justice, and too much respect for my own character, to attempt either, and were I to make such attempt, I am sure that in this court nothing can be carried against the law, and that gentlemen, intelligent and just as you are, are not, by any power, to be hurried beyond the evidence. Though I could well have wished to shun this occasion, I have not felt at liberty to withhold my professional assistance, when it is supposed that I may be in some degree useful in investigating and discovering the truth respecting this most extraordinary murder. It has seemed to be a duty incumbent on me, as on every other citizen, to do my best and my utmost to bring to light the perpetrators of this crime. Against the prisoner at the bar, as an individual, I cannot have the slightest prejudice. I would not do him the smallest injury or injustice.

Statement of Position

But I do not affect to be indifferent to the discovery and the punishment of this deep guilt. I cheerfully share in the opprobrium, how great soever it may be, which is cast on those who feel and manifest an anxious concern that all who had a part in planning, or a hand in executing this deed of midnight assassination, may be brought to answer for their enormous crime at the bar of public justice.

*The text of this speech is taken from *Webster's Great Speeches*, edited by Little, Brown and Company, Boston, 1879, pp. 189-226.

[Narration]

Gentlemen, it is a most extraordinary case. In some respects, it has hardly a precedent; anywhere; certainly none in our New England history. This bloody drama exhibited no suddenly excited, ungovernable rage. The actors in it were not surprised by any lion-like temptation springing upon their virtue, and overcoming it, before resistance could begin. Nor did they do the deed to glut savage vengeance, or satiate long-settled and deadly hate. It was a cool, calculating, money-making murder. It was all "hire and salary, not revenge." It was the weighing of money against life; the counting out of so many pieces of silver against so many ounces of blood.

An aged man, without an enemy in the world, in his own house, and in his own bed, is made the victim of a butcherly murder, for mere pay. Truly, here is a new lesson for painters and poets. Whoever shall hereafter draw the portrait of murder, if he will show it as it has been exhibited, where such example was last to have been looked for, in the very bosom of our New England society, let him not give it the grim visage of Moloch, the brow knitted by revenge, the face black with settled hate, and the blood-shot eye emitting livid fires of malice. Let him draw, rather, a decorous, smooth-faced bloodless demon; a picture in repose, rather than in action; not so much an example of human nature in its depravity, and in its paroxysms of crime, as an infernal being, a fiend, in the ordinary display and development of his character.

The deed was executed with a degree of self-possession and steadiness equal to the wickedness with which it was planned. The circumstances now clearly in evidence spread out the whole scene before us. Deep sleep had fallen on the destined victim, and on all beneath his roof. A healthful old man, to whom sleep was sweet, the first sound slumbers of the night held him in their soft but strong embrace. The assassin enters, through the window already prepared, into an unoccupied apartment. With noiseless foot he paces the lonely hall, half-lighted by the moon; he winds up the ascent of the stairs, and reaches the door of the chamber. Of this, he moves the lock, by soft and continued pressure, till it turns on its hinges without noise; and he enters, and beholds his victim before him. The room is uncommonly open to the admission of light. The face of the innocent sleeper is turned from the murderer, and the beams of the moon, resting on the gray locks of his aged temple, show him where to strike. The fatal blow is given! and the victim passes, without a struggle or a motion, from the repose of sleep to the repose of death! It is the assassin's purpose to make sure work; and he plies the dagger, though it is obvious that life has been destroyed by the blow of the bludgeon. He even raises the aged arm, that he may not fail in his aim at the heart, and replaces it again over the wounds of the poniard! To finish the picture, he explores the wrist for the pulse! He feels for it, and ascertains that it beats no longer! It is accomplished. The deed is done. He retreats, retraces his steps to the window, passes out through it as he came in, and escapes. He has done the murder. No eye has seen him, no ear has heard him. The secret is his own, and it is safe!

Ah, Gentlemen, that was a dreadful mistake. Such a secret can be safe nowhere. The whole creation of God has neither nook nor corner where the guilty can bestow it and say it is safe. Not to speak of that eye which pierces through the disguises, and beholds everything as in the splendor of noon, such secrets of guilt are never safe from detection, even by men. True it is, generally speaking, that "murder will out." True it is, that Providence has so ordained, and doth so govern things, that those who break the great law of Heaven by shedding man's blood seldom succeed in avoiding discovery. Especially, in a case exciting so much attention as this, discovery must come, and will come, sooner or later. A thousand eyes turn at once to explore every man, every thing, every circumstance, connected with the time and place; a thousand ears catch every whisper; a thousand excited minds intensely dwell on the scene, shedding all their light, and ready to kindle the slightest circumstance into a blaze of discovery. Meantime the guilty soul cannot keep its own secret. It is false to itself; or rather it feels an irresistible impulse of conscience to be true to itself. It labors under its guilty possession, and knows not what to do with it. The human heart was not made for the residence of such an inhabitant. It finds itself preyed on by a torment, which it dares not acknowledge to God or man. A vulture is devouring it, and it can ask no sympathy or assistance, either from heaven or earth. The secret which the murder possesses soon comes to possess him; and, like the evil spirits of which we read, it overcomes him, and leads him withersover it will. He feels it beating at his heart, rising to his throat, and demanding disclosure. He thinks the whole world sees it in his face, reads it in his eyes, and almost hears its workings in the very silence of his thoughts. It has become his master. It betrays his discretion, it breaks down his courage, it conquers his prudence. When suspicion from without begins to embarrass him, and the net of circumstance to entangle him, the fatal secret struggles with still greater violence to burst forth. It must be confessed, it will be confessed; there is no refuge from confession but suicide, and suicide is confession . . . .

[Division]

Gentlemen, let us now come to the case. Your first inquiry, on the evidence, will be, Was Captain White murdered in pursuance of a conspiracy, and was the defendant one of this conspiracy? If so, the second inquiry is, Was he so connected with the murder itself as that he is liable to be convicted as a *principal*? The defendant is indicted as a *principal*. If not guilty *as such* you cannot convict him. The indictment contains three distinct classes of counts. In the first, he is charged as having done the deed with his own hands; in the second, as an aider and abettor to Richard Crowninshield, Jr., who did the deed; in the third, as an aider and abettor to some person unknown. If you believe him guilty on either of these counts, or in either of these ways, you must convict him.

[Confirmation]

What are the probabilities as to the time of the murder? Mr. White was an aged man; he usually retired to bed at about half past nine. He slept soundest in the early part of the night; usually awoke in the middle and latter part; and his habits were perfectly well known. When would persons, with a knowledge of these facts, be most likely to approach him? Most certainly, in the first hour of his sleep. This would be the safest time. If seen then going to or from the house, the appearance would be least suspicious. The earlier hour would then have been most probably selected.

Gentlemen, I shall dwell no longer on the evidence which tends to prove that there was a conspiracy, and that the prisoner was a conspirator. All the circumstances concur to make out this point. Not only Palmer swears to it, in effect, and Leighton, but Allen mainly supports Palmer, and Osborn's books lend confirmation, so far as possible, from such a source. Palmer is contradicted in nothing, either by any other witness, or any proved circumstance or occurrence. Whatever could be expected to support him does not support him. All the evidence clearly manifests, I think, that there was a conspiracy; that it originated with Joseph Knapp; that the defendant became a party to it, and was one of its conductors, from the first to last. One of the most powerful circumstances is Palmer's letter from Belfast. The amount of this is a direct charge on the Knapps of the authorship of this murder. How did they treat this charge; like honest men, or like guilty men? We have seen how it was treated. Joseph Knapp fabricated letters, charging another person, and caused them to be put into the post office.

I shall now proceed on the supposition, that it is proved that there was a conspiracy to murder Mr. White, and that the prisoner was party to it.

The second and the material inquiry is, Was the prisoner present at the murder, aiding and abetting therein?

This leads to the legal question in the case. What does the law mean, when it says, that, in order to charge him as a principal, "he must be present aiding and abetting in the murder"?

In the language of the late Chief Justice, "It is not required that the abettor shall be actually upon the spot when the murder is committed, or even in sight of the more immediate perpetrator of the victim, to make him a principal. If he be at a distance, cooperating in the act, by watching to prevent relief, or to give an alarm, or to assist his confederate in escape, having knowledge of the purpose and object of the assassin, this in the eye of the law is being present, aiding and abetting, so as to make him a principal in the murder."

"If he be at a distance cooperating." This is not a distance to be measured by feet or rods; if the intent to lend aid combines with a knowledge that the murder is to be committed, and the person so intending be so situate that he can by any possibility lend this aid in any manner, then he is present in legal contemplation. He need not lend any actual aid; to be ready to assist is assisting.

There are two sorts of murder; the distinction between them it is of essential importance to bear in mind: 1. Murder in an affray, or upon sudden and unexpected provocation. 2. Murder secretly, with a deliberate, predetermined intention to commit the crime. Under the first class, the question usually is, whether the offense be murder or man-slaughter, in the person who commits the deed. Under the second class, it is often a question whether others than he who actually did the deed were present, aiding and assisting therein. Offenses of this kind ordinarily happen when there is nobody present except those who go on the same design. If a riot should happen in the court-house, and one should kill another, this may be murder, or it may not, according to the intention with which it was done; which is always matter of fact, to be collected from the circumstances at the time. But in secret murders, premeditated and determined on, there can be no doubt of the murderous intention; there can be no doubt if a person be present, knowing a murder is to be done, of his concurring in the act. His being there is a proof of his intent to aid and abet; else why is he there? . . .

By the counsel for the prisoner, much stress has been laid upon the question, whether Brown Street was a place in which aid could be given, a place in which actual assistance could be rendered in this transaction. This must be mainly decided by their own opinion who selected the place; by what they thought at the time, according to their plan of operation.

If it was agreed that the prisoner should be there to assist, it is enough. If they thought the place proper for their purpose, according to their plan, it is sufficient. Suppose we could prove expressly that they agreed that Frank should be there, and he was there, and you should think it not a well-chosen place for aiding and abetting, must he be acquitted? No! It is not what *I* think or *you* think of the appropriateness of the place; it is what *they* thought *at the time.* If the prisoner was in Brown Street by appointment and agreement with the perpetrator, for the purpose of giving assistance if assistance should be needed, it may be safely be presumed that the place was suited to such assistance as it was supposed by the parties might chance to become requisite.

If in Brown Street, was he there by appointment? was he there to aid, if aid was necessary? was he there for, or against, the murderer? to concur, or to oppose? to favor, or to thwart? Did the perpetrator know he was there, there waiting? If so, then it follows that he was there by appointment. He was at the post half an hour; he was waiting for somebody. This proves appointment, arrangement, previous agreement; then it follows that he was there to aid, to encourage, to embolden the perpetrator; and that is enough. If he were in such a situation as to afford aid, or that he was relied upon for aid, then he was aiding and abetting. It is enough that the conspirator desired to have him there. Besides, it may be well said, that he could afford just as much aid there as if he had been in Essex Street, as if he had been standing even at the gate, or at the window. It was not an act of power against power that was to be done; it was a secret act, to be done by stealth. The aid was to be placed in a position secure from observation. It was important to the security of both that he should be in a lonely place. Now it is obvious that there are many purposes for which he might be in Brown Street:

(1) Richard Crowninshield might have been secreted in the garden, and waiting for a signal;

(2) or he might be in Brown Street to advise him as to the time of making his entry into the house;

(3) or to favor his escape;

(4) or to see if the street was clear when he came out;

(5) or to conceal the weapon or the clothes;

(6) or to be ready for any unforeseen contingency.

Richard Crowninshield lived in Danvers. He would retire by the most secret way. Brown Street is that way. If you find him there, can you doubt why he was there?

If, Gentlemen, the prisoner went into Brown Street, by appointment with the perpetrator, to render aid or encouragement in any of these ways, he was *present,* in legal contemplation, aiding and abetting in this murder. It is not necessary that he should have done anything; it is enough that he was ready to act, and in a place to act. If his being in Brown Street, by appointment, at the time of the murder, emboldened the purpose and encouraged the heart of the murder, by the hope of instant aid, if aid should become necessary, then, without doubt, he was present, aiding and abetting, and was a principal in the murder . . . .

[Peroration]

Gentlemen, I have gone through with the evidence in this case, and have endeavored to state it plainly and fairly before you. I think there are conclusions to be drawn from it, the accuracy of which you cannot doubt. I think you cannot doubt that there was a conspiracy formed for the purpose of committing this murder, and who the conspirators were:

That you cannot doubt that the Crowninshields and the Knapps were parties in this conspiracy:

That you cannot doubt that the prisoner at the bar knew that the murder was to be done on the night of the 6th of April:

That you cannot doubt that the murderers of Captain White were the suspicious persons seen in and about Brown Street on that night:

That you cannot doubt that Richard Crowninshield was the perpetrator of the crime:

That you cannot doubt that the prisoner at the bar was in Brown Street on that night.

If there, then it must be by agreement, to countenance, to aid the perpetrator. And if so, then he is guilty as principal.

Gentlemen, your whole concern should be to do your *duty,* and leave consequences to take care of themselves. You will receive the law from the court. Your verdict, it is true, may endanger the prisoner's life, but then it is to save other lives. If the prisoner's guilt has been shown and proved beyond all reasonable doubt, you will convict him. If such reasonable doubts of guilt still remain, you will acquit him. You are the judges of the whole case. You owe a duty to the public, as well as to the prisoner at the bar. You cannot presume to be wiser than the law. Your duty is a plain, straightforward one. Doubtless we would all judge him in mercy. Towards him, as an individual, the law inculcates no hostility; but towards him, if proved to be a murderer, the law, and the oaths you have taken, and public justice, demand that you do your duty.

With consciences satisfied with the discharge of duty, no consequences can harm you. There is no evil that we cannot either face or fly from, but the consciousness of duty disregarded. A sense of duty pursues us ever. It is omnipresent, like the Deity. If we take to ourselves the wings of the morning, and dwell in the uttermost parts of the sea, duty performed, or duty violated, is still with us, for our happiness or our misery. If we say the darkness shall cover us, in the darkness as in the light our obligations are yet with us. We cannot escape their power, nor fly from their presence. They are with us in this life, will be with us at its close; and in that scene of inconceivable solemnity, which lies yet farther onward, we shall still find ourselves surrounded by the consciousness of duty, to pain us wherever it has been violated, and to console us so far as God may have given us grace to perform it.

Analysis*

In this first model, an effort is made to identify several of the points of theory previously discussed. In some of the subsequent models, more of the burden will be placed on the reader, however, through the use of analytical questions. In other models that follow, a detailed focus on certain techniques will be presented.

*This analysis is from Patrick O. Marsh, *Persuasive Speaking: Theory–Models–Practice.* New York: Harper & Row, Publishers, 1967, pp. 351-352.

For this model, see if you can identify each of the points in the following outline from the text of the speech.

Exordium

ATTENTION. Attention is involuntary and requires no effort on the part of the speaker because this speech is one of the high points of the trial.

ETHOS. Ethos is gained by the expression of the appropriate sense of humility, by the verbal assurance that there will be no attempt to "hurry justice," by disavowing that any prejudice is held against the prisoner as an individual, and that the prosecution is motivated only by a sense of duty to society.

Statement of Position

Because there was no secret regarding the position Webster would take, there was no need to postpone the proposition until the narration had been presented. It is a brief and to-the-point statement that terminates the exordium and introduces the narration.

The style of the speech up to this point has been very plain.

Narration

Notice the point-by-point chronological reconstruction of the crime: (1) The victim went to sleep; (2) the assassin entered through known window; (3) he went upstairs into the victim's room; (4) he stabbed and restabbed the victim; (5) he made certain he was dead; (6) he retreated; and (7) finally, he confessed by his suicide.

As impressive as the orderly telling of the story, is the language used in its telling. Contrast the style of the narration with that of the exordium. Pay particular attention to the diction as exemplified in the following choices: "lion-like temptation springing"; "to glut savage vengeance"; "a cool, calculating, money-making murder"; "a butcherly murder"; "the blood-shot eye emitting livid fires of malice"; "fiend"; "a healthful old man, to whom sleep was sweet"; "beams of the moon, resting on the gray locks of his aged temple"; "he plies the dagger" (a knife would not do); "preyed on by a torment"; and "the fatal secret struggles with still greater violence to burst forth."

This story was so well told, with careful attention given to acceleration, retardation, and climax, that the audience was ready to hear the proofs by the time their imaginations had been thus activated.

Division

Webster clearly sets forth the issues on which this case must turn: (1) Was Captain White murdered in the pursuance of a conspiracy? (2) Was the defendant one of the conspiracy? and (3) Was the defendant's role in the conspiracy such that he could be indicted as a principal?

Confirmation

Captain White, Webster maintains, was murdered in the pursuance of a conspiracy. He supports this contention with an argument from probability (an artistic proof); with witnesses, namely: Palmer, Leighton, and Allen (inartistic proofs); and with a document, namely: Osborn's book (another inartistic proof).

Webster further held that the defendant was one of the conspiracy. Both artistic and inartistic proofs were used for support of this contention: the letters from Palmer (inartistic) and the probable causes for his actions after receiving the letters (artistic).

Up to this point, Webster was concerned primarily with the issue of fact, but he now turns to definition where he supports his interpretation of "aiding and abetting" with inartistic proofs. Then, briefly, he implies that the defendant's actions could not be justified (issue of quality) because they were premeditated. The issue of competence was not a point of controversy in this case and was not, therefore, mentioned by Webster.

How would you characterize the style of the confirmation?

Peroration

Notice the concise way Webster summarizes his case and the amount of time he takes to charge the jury with a sense of duty to public justice.

Appendix C-6

Basic Response-Style Matrix Applications

Case 1.

The Problem. You wish to implement the complexity profile shown in Figure 6.3. The response-style profile indicates that aloofness is low and tension is moderate. What response will a message so designed elicit from your audience, and how do you generate that response?

The Solution. Consult the matrix on Figure 6.1 and discover that the cell described by low aloofness and moderate tension is "contemplative." This is the response you will likely elicit from your message if you design it appropriately. But how do you design it to produce this response? First select *invigorating* music to use during framing and transition periods. Traditional jazz would be a good choice. Then, incorporate purple as the dominant color in graphics, scenery, or costumes. For accent, small amounts of primary colors may be used with the purple if they are off-set by neutrals such as heather, green, or tan. Finally, the storyboard pages should be composed to maximize the prescription from Figure 6.6. Specifically, your shots should be predominantly close-ups, taken at eye-level, and from a subjective point of view. Strive for a slightly imbalanced composition (perhaps achieved by strong lines on the lower-left to upper-right diagonal). If motion is an option, zoom-in or dolly-in, but not the reverse. Cut or fade to another distant shot and repeat the inward motion. Preserve a shallow depth of field and minimize the background.

Case 2.

The Problem. You anticipate that your audience will be in a state of strong *emotion* (pity, joy, fear, etc.) as they begin to receive your message. It will serve your purposes better, however, if they are able to respond *creatively*. How should you profile the earlier and later response-style states, and how can you move smoothly from one to the other?

The Solution. The emotional state in which you find your audience is profiled as *low aloofness* and *high tension.* Your desire is to provide a transition to a *low aloofness* and *low tension* state. You therefore need only to maintain the engagement level, but you must reduce the tension level. Thus, you must avoid creating shock, suspense, or conflict in the script. If it is appropriate to do so, use mood music with voice-over. Begin with romantic selections of moderate passion and segue into compatible, invigorating music with a swing rhythm, then blend into quiet, novel, innovative mixtures of music and sound effects. Sustain the innovative music until the desired response is established. Colors should make a smooth transition from primary to secondary to warm neutrals such as tan. The composition should be close-up shots throughout. Zooming or dollying should always be inward, and the depth of field should be very shallow. The compositional transition should be from high contrast, dark background, low angle, off-balanced, subjective shots to no-shadow "flat" lighting for high-angle shots against a light background. Compositional lines should be mostly horizontal and vertical, object bases should be broad, and the dominant elements should be very shallow. The compositional transition should be from high contrast, dark background, low angle, off-balanced, subjective shots to no-shadow "flat" lighting for high-angle shots against a light background. Compositional lines should be mostly horizontal and vertical, object bases should be broad, and the dominant elements should be balanced.

Case 3.

The Problem. You have good reason to believe your audience is predisposed to be aggressive, yet it serves your purpose to elicit a regimented response-style. If you manifest the *high aloofness/high tension* profile needed to produce the *regimented* behavior, you will probably activate the compulsive *aggressive* behavior instead.

The Solution. The general strategy for a case of this type is: (1) start from the most distant matrix cell from your destination; (2) when that response-style is established, adjust the aloofness and/or tension values to create an intermediate response-style; and (3) make further adjustments in order to return to your destination cell. The underlying assumption for this strategy is that by creating the counterpart conditions in place of the ones which tend to activate the compulsive response, you will avoid that predisposition. Then, by moving in increments toward the desired cell and by keeping the receivers' thoughts occupied in the direction of your choice, you may return to the desired cell without activating the compulsive behavior.

More specifically, given the problem at hand, you should begin at the low aloofness/low tension cell (creative). When, with the aid of appropriate music, colors, composition, and content, you have established the *creative* response-style, modify those elements to produce *calculating* behavior. And, finally, shift from calculating to *regimented* behavior conditions. During this sequence, avoid any suggestion of status difference between source and receiver, since aggressive behavior is usually a function of the aggressor's feeling that inferiors are challenging his or her rightfully superior position.

Appendix C-7

A Sample Contract

Agreement to Design an Instructional Message

This Agreement is made this 30th day of February of 198__, between DESIGN WORKS of Sacramento, California and E-Z LEARNING INSTITUTE of Reno, Nevada.

Whereas, a duly authorized representative of E-Z LEARNING INSTITUTE has sought the services of DESIGN WORKS, and

Whereas, DESIGN WORKS has represented itself as possessing both the competence and experience to produce a design of professional quality;

Now, therefore, in consideration of a sum of $3,500.00 and the mutual promises herein contained, it is agreed that:

1. DESIGN WORKS will conduct an initial interview with the Program Committee in order to ascertain the specific needs and limitations of the instructional message.

2. DESIGN WORKS will consult with the Training Officer upon completion of a tentative purpose statement; again after completion of a storyboard; and again at the completion of a production script.

3. The Training Officer will sign-off at each of the above-mentioned three stages when he or she is satisfied.

4. Any modification required by E-Z LEARNING INSTITUTE after sign-off will be paid for by that party at the cost of $50.00 per person/hour.

5. DESIGN WORKS will provide a maximum of eight hours of consultation during production at no additional cost, but will not accept the responsibility for the technical quality of the production.

6. DESIGN WORKS will submit a final production script within 90 days of this date.

7. E-Z LEARNING INSTITUTE will submit full payment within 30 days of the receipt of the production script.

In Witness Whereof, we have executed this agreement this 30th day of February, 198__.

_____   _____

John Doe, E-Z LEARNING INSTITUTE   Richard Roe, DESIGN WORKS

In the presence of

_____

_____

References

Introduction

McLuhan, Marshall. *Understanding Media: The Extensions of Man.* New York: McGraw-Hill Book Co., 1964.

Miller, George A. "The Magical Number Seven Plus or Minus Two: Some Limits on Our Capacity for Processing Information." *The Psychology of Communication: Seven Essays.* (Miller, G.A., ed.). Baltimore: Penguin Books, Inc., 1967.

Neisser, Ulric. *Cognition and Reality: Principles and Implications of Cognitive Psychology.* San Francisco: W.H. Freeman & Co., 1977.

Schroder, H.M., M.J. Driver, and S. Streufert. *Human Information Processing.* New York: Holt, Rinehart, and Winston, Inc., 1967.

Shannon, Claude and W. Weaver. *The Mathematical Theory of Communication.* Urbana, Ill.: University of Illinois Press, 1949.

Chapter 1

Ausburn, Lynna J. and Floyd B. Ausburn. "Cognitive Styles: Some Information and Implications for Instructional Design." *Educational Communication and Technology Journal,* 26:4, 1978, pp. 337-338.

Black, Henry Campbell. *Black's Law Dictionary.* St. Paul, Minnesota: West Publishing Co., 1968.

Castaneda, Carlos. *Tales of Power.* New York: Simon and Shuster, 1974.

Fleming, M.L. "The Pictures in Your Mind." *A-V Communication Review,* 25:1, 1977, pp. 43-62.

Fleming, Malcolm and W. Howard Levie. *Instructional Message Design: Principles from the Behavioral Sciences.* Englewood Cliffs, N.J.: Educational Technology Publications, 1978, p. 29.

445

Harris, George. *I'm OK–You're OK: A Practical Guide to Transactional Analysis.* New York: Harper & Row, Publishers, 1967.

Kibler, Robert J., Donald J. Cegalia, David T. Miles, and Larry L. Barker. *Objectives for Instructional Evaluation.* Boston: Allyn and Bacon, Inc., 1974.

Koegel, Raymond and Patrick O. Marsh. *Demand Access Instructional Radio: A Report on an Innovative Project for the CSUC System,* 1979.

Mager, Robert F. *Preparing Instructional Objectives* (2nd Ed.). Belmont, CA: Fearon Publishers, 1975.

Marsh, Patrick O. "Pirsig's (undefinable) 'Quality' Defined." An unpublished essay, 1975.

Ornstein, Jack H. *The Mind and the Brain.* The Hague: Nijhoff, 1972.

Pirsig, Robert M. *Zen and the Art of Motorcycle Maintenance.* Toronto/New York/London: Bantam Books, 1974.

Polanyi, Michael. *The Tacit Dimension.* Garden City, N.Y.: Doubleday & Company, Inc., 1966.

Rokeach, Milton. *The Nature of Human Values.* New York: Free Press, 1973.

Sheehy, Gail. *Passages: Predictable Crises of Adult Life.* New York: E.P. Dutton & Co., Inc., 1974.

Sparke, William and Clark McKowen. *Montage: Investigations in Language.* London: The Macmillan Company, 1970, p. 2.

Chapter 2

Blyton, Gifford and Bert E. Bradley, Jr. "Forms of Debate" in James H. McBath (Ed.), *Argumentation and Debate: Principles and Practices.* New York: Holt, Rinehart, and Winston, Inc., 1963, pp. 287-289.

Burke, Kenneth. *The Rhetoric of Motives.* Englewood Cliffs, N.J.: Prentice-Hall, 1950.

Butler, H.E. (Tr.) *The Institutio Oratoria of Quintilian.* Cambridge, Mass.: Harvard University Press, 1921, Book V.

Goffman, Erving. *Frame Analysis: An Essay on the Organization of Experience.* New York: Harper & Row, Publishers. Harper Colophon Books, 1974.

Marsh, Patrick O. *Persuasive Speaking: Theory—Models—Practice.* New York: Harper & Row, Publishers, 1967.

McBath, James A. (Ed.) *Argumentation and Debate: Principles and Practices.* New York: Holt, Rinehart, and Winston, Inc., 1954.

McGuire, W.J. "Inducing Resistance to Persuasion" in L. Berkowitz (Ed.), *Advances in Experimental Social Psychology,* Vol. 1. New York: Academic Press, 1964, pp. 191-229.

Merrill, M. David. "Content Analysis via Concept Elaboration Theory." *Journal of Instructional Development,* 1:1, 1977, pp. 10-13.

Merrill, M. David and Robert D. Tennyson. *Teaching Concepts: An Instructional Design Guide.* Englewood Cliffs, N.J.: Educational Technology Publications, 1977, p. 3.

Neisser, Ulric. *Cognition and Reality: Principles and Implications of Cognitive Psychology.* San Francisco: W.H. Freeman and Company, 1976.

Polanyi, Michael. *The Tacit Dimension.* Garden City, N.Y.: Anchor Books, Doubleday and Company, Inc., 1966, p. 61.

Rogers, Carl R. *Counseling and Psychotherapy: Newer Concepts in Practice.* Boston: Houghton-Mifflin Company, 1942.

Toulmin, Stephen, Richard D. Rieke, and Allan Janik. *An Introduction to Reasoning.* London: Macmillan, 1979.

Watzlawick, Paul. *The Language of Change: Elements of Therapeutic Communication.* New York: Basic Books, Inc., Publishers, 1978, pp. 121-122.

Webster's New World Dictionary of the American Language. Cleveland and New York: The World Publishing Company, 1959, p. 907.

Wellman, Francis. *The Art of Cross-Examination.* Garden City, N.Y.: Doubleday & Company, Inc., 1948.

Chapter 3

Bruner, Jerome S. *Toward a Theory of Instruction.* Cambridge,

Mass.: The Belknap Press of Harvard University Press, 1966, p. 12.

Miller, George A. "The Magical Number Seven Plus or Minus Two: Some Limits on Our Capacity for Processing Information." *Psychological Review,* 63, pp. 81-97 (1956). Reprinted in George A. Miller (Ed.), *The Psychology of Communication. Seven Essays.* Baltimore: Penguin Books, Inc., 1967, p. 36.

Minnick, Wayne C. *Public Speaking.* Boston: Houghton-Mifflin Company, 1979, pp. 97-98.

Zemke, Ron. "What Are High-Achieving Managers Really Like?" *Training,* February, 1979, p. 36.

Chapter 4

Bass, Saul. *Why Man Creates.* A film produced by Kaiser Aluminum, 1968.

Kershner, William K. *The Instrument Flight Manual* (3rd Ed.). Ames, Iowa: Iowa State University Press, 1977, p. 170.

Koegel, Raymond and Patrick O. Marsh. *Demand Access Instructional Radio: A Report on an Innovative Project for the CSUC System,* 1979.

Osgood, C.E., G. Suci, and P. Tannenbaum. *The Measurement of Meaning.* Urbana: University of Illinois Press, 1957.

Travers, Robert M.W. *Man's Information System.* Scranton, Pennsylvania: Chandler Publishing Company, 1970.

Wang, Marilyn D. "The Role of Syntactic Complexity as a Determiner of Comprehensibility." *Journal of Verbal Learning and Verbal Behavior,* 1970, (9), 398-401.

Chapter 5

Bandler, R., J. Grinder, and J. Goleman. "People Who Read People: Neurolinguistic Programming Workshops." *Psychology Today,* 13:66-7, July, 1979.

Berryman, Gregg. *Notes on Graphic Design and Visual Communication.* Los Altos, California: William Kaufmann, Inc., 1979, pp. 8, 9.

Cicero. *De Oratore.* H. Rackham (Tr.) Harvard University Press, 1942, Book III, p. 159.

Demetrius. *On Style.* W. Rhys Roberts (Ed.) Cambridge University Press, 1902.

Dwyer, Francis M. *A Guide for Improving Visualized Instruction.* State College, Pennsylvania: Learning Services, 1972.

Feininger, Andreas. *The Complete Photographer.* Englewood Cliffs, N.J.: Prentice-Hall, 1965.

Flesch, Rudolf. *The Art of Plain Talk.* New York: Harper & Row, Publishers, Inc., 1946.

Flesch, Rudolf. *The Art of Readable Writing.* New York: Collier Books, 1949, pp. 224-230.

Goffman, Erving. *Frame Analysis: An Essay on the Organization of Experience.* New York: Harper & Row, Publishers, Harper Colophon Books, 1974.

Kemp, Jerrold E. *Planning and Producing Audiovisual Materials* (4th Ed.). New York: Harper & Row, Publishers, 1980, pp. 111, 112.

Marsh, Patrick O. *Persuasive Speaking: Theory—Models—Practice.* New York: Harper & Row, Publishers, Inc., 1967, pp. 181-183.

Trabasso, Tom. "Everyone Knows What Attention Is." *Psychology Today,* 2:5, 1968, pp. 30-36.

Travers, Robert M.W. *Man's Information System.* Scranton, Pennsylvania: Chandler Publishing Company, 1970.

Chapter 6

Barnhart, C.L. (Ed.) *The American College Dictionary.* New York: Random House, 1963, p. 326.

Fromm, Erich. *Man for Himself.* New York: Rinehart and Company, Inc., 1947.

Luscher, Max. *The Luscher Color Test.* Ian A. Scott (Tr. and Ed.) New York: Random House, 1969.

McLuhan, Marshall. *Understanding Media: The Extensions of Man.* New York: McGraw-Hill Book Co., 1964.

Wiener, M. and A. Mehrabian. *Language Within Language: Immediacy, a Channel in Verbal Communication.* New York: Appleton-Century-Crofts, 1968.

Chapter 7

Is It Always Right to Be Right? A film produced by Stephen Bosustow Productions, 1970.

Marsh, Patrick O. *Final Report for the U-Curve Plotting Project*, 1973.

Chapter 8

Banghart, F.W. *Educational Systems Analysis.* New York: Macmillan, 1969.

Dunathan, Arni T. "Allocating Resources Between Design and Production." *Audio-Visual Instruction,* March, 1979, p. 17.

Eisenstein, Sergei. *Film Sense.* (Jay Leyda, Tr. and Ed.) New York: Harcourt, Brace, 1947.

Eisenstein, Sergei. *Film Form* (Jay Leyda, Tr.) New York: Harcourt, Brace, 1949.

Garner, Wendell R. *The Processing of Information and Structure.* New York: John Wiley & Sons, 1974.

Hamilton, Harper. *The Guide to Business Contracts.* Boulder, Colorado: Hamilton Press, Inc., 1978, pp. 17, 18.

Hawes, William. *The Performer in Mass Media.* New York: Hastings House, 1978, p. 200.

Hsia, H.J. "The Information Processing Capacity of Modality and Channel Performance." *A-V Communication Review,* 1971, (19), pp. 51-75.

Kemp, Jerrold E. *Planning & Producing Audiovisual Materials* (4th Ed.). New York: Harper & Row, Publishers, 1980.

Koegel, Raymond and Patrick O. Marsh. *Demand Access Instructional Radio: A Report on an Innovative Project for the CSUC System*, 1979.

Linder, Carl. *Filmmaking: A Practical Guide.* Englewood Cliffs, N.J.: Prentice-Hall, Inc., 1976, p. 169.

Mansfield, Edwin. *Principles of Microeconomics* (2nd Ed.). New York: W.W. Norton & Co., Inc., 1977, p. 169.

Minor, Ed and Harvey R. Frye. *Techniques for Producing Visual Instructional Media* (2nd Ed.). New York: McGraw-Hill Book Company, 1977.

Mugnaini, Joseph. *The Hidden Elements of Drawing.* New York: Van Nostrand Reinhold Company, 1974.

Riemer, W. *Handbook of Government Contract Administration.* Englewood Cliffs, N.J.: Prentice-Hall, Inc., 1968.

Shipman, Carl. *How to Select and Use Olympus S.L.R. Cameras.* Tucson, AZ: H.P. Books, 1979, pp. 158, 159.

Young, David R. "How to Make Lettering Big Enough to Read." *Instructional Innovator*, April, 1980, pp. 42, 43.

Chapter 9

There are no references in Chapter 9.

Chapter 10

Bronowski, Jacob. *The Ascent of Man.* Boston/Toronto: Little, Brown and Company, 1973, p. 374.

Watzlawick, Paul, John Weakland, and Richard Fisch. *Change: Principles of Problem Formation and Problem Resolution.* New York: W.W. Norton & Company, Inc., 1974, pp. 82-83.

Appendix A

Ausburn, Lynna J.. and Floyd B. Ausburn. "Cognitive Styles: Some Information and Implications for Instructional Design." *Educational Communication and Technology—A Journal of Theory, Research, and Development*, Winter, 1978, pp. 337-354.

Marsh, Patrick O. *Final Report of the U-Curve Plotting Project,* 1973. (Available from: California State University and Colleges, Office of the Chancellor, Fund for Innovative Instruction, 400 Golden Shore, Long Beach, CA 90802.)

Appendix B

Barnes, Ralph M. *Work Methods Manual.* New York: John Wiley & Sons, Inc., 1944, p. 10.

Bartley, III, William Warren. *Werner Erhard: The Transformation of a Man: The Founding of Est.* New York: Clarkson N. Potter, Inc., Publishers, 1978.

Castaneda, Carlos. *Tales of Power.* New York: Simon and Schuster, 1974.

Coon, Arthur M. "Brainstorming—A Creative Problem-Solving Technique." *Journal of Communication*, 7(3) Autumn, 1957, pp. 111-118.

Dewey, John. *How We Think.* Boston: D.C. Heath & Co., 1933.

Harris, Theodore L. and Wilson E. Schwahn (Eds.). *Selected Readings on the Learning Process.* New York: Oxford University Press, 1961.

Pirsig, Robert M. *Zen and the Art of Motorcycle Maintenance.* Toronto/New York/London: Bantam Books, 1974.

Toulmin, Stephen E. *The Uses of Argument.* Cambridge, England: University Press, 1958.

Toulmin, Stephen E., Richard D. Rieke, and Allan Janik. *An Introduction to Reasoning.* London: The Macmillan Company, 1979.

Watzlawick, Paul, John Weakland, and Richard Fisch. *Change: Principles of Problem Formation and Problem Resolution.* New York: W.W. Norton & Company, Inc., 1974, pp. 82-83.

Appendix C
Marsh, Patrick O. *Persuasive Speaking: Theory—Models—Practice.* New York: Harper & Row, Publishers, 1967, pp. 351-352.

Westbrook, A. and O. Ratti. *Aikido and the Dynamic Sphere.* Rutland, Vermont: Charles E. Tuttle Co., Publishers, 1970.

Index